Robert Louis Stevenson and the Pacific

Robert Louis Stevenson and the Pacific

The Transformation of Global Christianity

L. M. Ratnapalan

EDINBURGH
University Press

To my parents

Edinburgh University Press is one of the leading university presses in the UK. We publish academic books and journals in our selected subject areas across the humanities and social sciences, combining cutting-edge scholarship with high editorial and production values to produce academic works of lasting importance. For more information visit our website: edinburghuniversitypress.com

© L. M. Ratnapalan 2023, 2024

Edinburgh University Press Ltd
13 Infirmary Street
Edinburgh EH1 1LT

First published in hardback by Edinburgh University Press 2023

Typeset in 11/13 Adobe Sabon by
IDSUK (DataConnection) Ltd

A CIP record for this book is available from the British Library

ISBN 978 1 4744 9481 6 (hardback)
ISBN 978 1 4744 9482 3 (paperback)
ISBN 978 1 4744 9483 0 (webready PDF)
ISBN 978 1 4744 9484 7 (epub)

The right of L. M. Ratnapalan to be identified as the author of this work has been asserted in accordance with the Copyright, Designs and Patents Act 1988, and the Copyright and Related Rights Regulations 2003 (SI No. 2498).

Contents

Acknowledgements	vi
Introduction	1
1. Stevenson's Religious Literacy	14
2. Pacific Ethnography and the Anthropology of Christianity	45
3. Rediscovering Religious Community: Samoa, 1890–4	73
4. Inculturation	104
5. The Church in the Mind of Stevenson	131
Conclusion	156
Bibliography	165
Index	183

Acknowledgements

I would like to thank the following for their help with the production of this book: Michelle Houston, Susannah Butler, Fiona Conn, and the team at Edinburgh University Press; the reviewers for Edinburgh University Press; Reverend Latu Latai, Joel Robbins, David Armitage, Stewart J. Brown, Philip Gibbs, S.V.D., Bob Dixon, Reverend Meehyun Chung, Brian Stanley, Brad Bow, Mandel Cabrera, Yannick Fer, Terry Murphy, Peter Paik, Michael Hope, Richard Dury; the staff at the Beinecke Rare Book and Manuscript Library, the Houghton Library, and the National Library of Scotland; the participants at the 2018 Conference of the International Society for Intellectual History at the University of St Andrews, the 2019 Conference of the International Association for the Study of Scottish Literatures at Chaminade University, and the joint session of the Scottish Network for Religion and Literature and the Edinburgh Centre for World Christianity in February 2021.

Chapter 4, 'Inculturation', appeared in an earlier form in *Scottish Literary Review* 12, 1 (2020).

In different but vital ways, three people have helped me throughout this process: Paul Tonks, Robert Beachy, and Robert-Louis Abrahamson. My sincere thanks to all of them. Responsibility for the final work rests, of course, with the author.

Finally, this book would not have been realised were it not for the encouragement of my wife, Francesca.

Introduction

As Scottish studies has sought to engage with themes of global connection and interaction, the Pacific has become an important context for research about one of Scotland's most famous authors, Robert Louis Stevenson (1850–94).¹ It is no coincidence that these developments have taken place simultaneously; it has been aptly argued that the study of Scottish cultural history and the international circulation of Scottish literature are mutually reinforcing pursuits.² The movement of ideas is aided by the movement of materials across borders.³ Stevenson studies has no doubt benefited from the wider re-evaluation of Scottish culture in the wake of debates about Scottish (and British) national identity.⁴ With these political and cultural impetuses, recent decades have seen the publication of a number of strong monographs, all written by scholars

---

¹ *Scotland and the British Empire*, ed. by John M. MacKenzie and T. M. Devine (Oxford: Oxford University Press, 2011); Catriona M. M. Macdonald, 'Imagining the Scottish Diaspora: Emigration and Transnational Literature in the Late Modern Period', *Britain and the World* 5, 1 (2012), 12–42; *Scotland and the 19th-Century World*, ed. by Gerard Carruthers, David Goldie and Alastair Renfrew (Amsterdam: Rodopi, 2012); *The Scottish Diaspora*, ed. by Tanja Bueltmann, Andrew Hinson, and Graeme Morton (Edinburgh: Edinburgh University Press, 2013); Cairns Craig, *The Wealth of the Nation: Scotland, Culture and Independence* (Edinburgh: Edinburgh University Press, 2018); Michael Shaw, *The Fin-de-Siècle Scottish Revival: Romance, Decadence and Celtic Identity* (Edinburgh: Edinburgh University Press, 2020); Carla Sassi, 'Glocalising Scottish Literature: A Call for New Strategies of Reading', *The Bottle Imp – Supplement 1* (March 2014), 1–4.
² Michael Shaw, 'Transculturation and Historicisation: New Directions for the Study of Scottish Literature c. 1840–1914', *Literature Compass* 13, 8 (2016), 501–10 (509).
³ See, in this context, the essays collected in *Robert Louis Stevenson and the Great Affair: Movement, Memory, and Modernity*, ed. by Richard J. Hill (London: Routledge, 2017).
⁴ Sassi, 'Glocalising Scottish Literature', 1.

based outside of Scotland, which have explored Stevenson's Pacific oeuvre from perspectives such as psychology, law, photography, and environmentalism.[5] The aim of the present study is to make a distinctive contribution to this burgeoning field by emphasising the intellectual and cultural significance of religion in his writing. Specifically, the thematic focus of this book is the impact of Pacific Islands Christianity on the mind of Robert Louis Stevenson.

I describe how this takes place by invoking the anthropo-theological term 'inculturation'. Inculturation helps to explain the ways in which Pacific Islands Christians created their own communitarian and supernaturally ordered versions of the European Christianity that Western missionaries brought to the Pacific in the nineteenth century. Although the term 'inculturation' is open to charges of anachronism because it only begins to be used in scholarly literature around the mid-twentieth century, this criticism may be answered by the fact that cognate terms such as 'enculturation' and 'interculturation' have been applied in Scottish literary contexts.[6] I claim that because of his own religious literacy, that is, his experiential knowledge of a religious tradition, Scottish Presbyterianism, Stevenson was particularly well positioned to recognise this Pacific Islands inculturation and the emergence of distinctive Christian communities. I further argue that Stevenson articulated the style and ethos of that emergent Christianity in his later fiction and that he was also moved to rethink his views of European history and ecclesiology.

Christian thought connected the Scottish and Pacific phases of Stevenson's life in significant ways. It provided a sense of continuity from his earliest writings to his last. Scottish Calvinist themes concerning the relationship between literacy and society, nature and the divine, community and authority recur throughout his work. Besides its contribution to understanding Stevenson's thought, the

---

[5] Roslyn Jolly, *Robert Louis Stevenson in the Pacific: Travel, Empire, and the Author's Profession* (Farnham: Ashgate, 2009); Julia Reid, *Robert Louis Stevenson, Science, and the Fin de Siècle* (Basingstoke: Palgrave Macmillan, 2006); Oliver S. Buckton, *Cruising with Robert Louis Stevenson: Travel, Narrative, and the Colonial Body* (Athens, OH: Ohio University Press, 2007); Ann C. Colley, *Robert Louis Stevenson and the Colonial Imagination* (New York: Routledge, 2017 [2004]); Jennifer Fuller, 'The Price of Paradise: Robert Louis Stevenson, Joseph Conrad and British Expansion in the Pacific', in *Dark Paradise: Pacific Islands in the British Nineteenth-Century British Imagination* (Edinburgh: Edinburgh University Press, 2016), 111–53; Carla Manfredi, *Robert Louis Stevenson's Pacific Impressions: Photography and Travel Writing, 1888–1894* (Cham: Palgrave Macmillan, 2018).

[6] See Chapter 4 for further discussion of this subject.

framing of the Pacific period through the lens of religion also provides fresh insight into how his writing developed through these years. In Samoa, for instance, his fiction shifted from an emphasis on individual ethics to the morality and politics of the community, while it also addressed themes of relevance to intercultural or contextual theology. His writing on the subjects of inculturation and the relationship between church and mission make him a valuable non-missionary source on the history of Pacific Christianity who can help to 'triangulate' British missionary records of the period.[7]

The broad argument of this book is, therefore, that the full scope and significance of Stevenson's engagement with Scottish and especially Pacific cultures has been missed because religion has been marginalised in studies of his work. Since it played such a foundational role in his social and intellectual formation, any evaluation of Stevenson's contribution to Pacific culture must take account of his relationship to Scottish Christianity. The need becomes more imperative when it is set against what we know about the Christian character of the hybrid Pacific cultures of the nineteenth century. Stevenson's lifetime, brief as it was, spanned an important globalising moment in world history, which his own writing, when sufficiently contextualised, is uniquely positioned to help us better understand.[8] In this Introduction I will offer a brief overview of Stevenson studies in relation to these subjects and outline the approach of this book.

The primary aim of *Robert Louis Stevenson and the Pacific* is to identify and substantiate the religious contexts of Stevenson's Pacific years, 1888–94, in order to provide a fresh interpretation of his writing. As will be explained in detail in the following chapters, while numerous books and articles have been written about this period of his life, a need for contextual precision remains necessary. We

---

[7] Emma Wild-Wood, 'The Interpretations, Problems and Possibilities of Missionary Sources in the History of Christianity in Africa', in *World Christianity: Methodological Considerations*, ed. by Martha Frederiks and Dorottya Nagy (Leiden and Boston: Brill, 2021), 92–112 (107).

[8] See, for example, Guillaume Daudin, Matthias Morys, and Kevin H. O'Rourke, 'Globalization, 1870–1914', in *The Cambridge Economic History of Modern Europe*, ed. by Stephen Broadberry and Kevin H. O'Rourke (Cambridge: Cambridge University Press, 2019), 5–29; Julia Zinkina, David Christian, Leonid Grinin, Ilya Ilyin, Alexey Andreev, Ivan Aleshkovski, Sergey Shulgin, and Andrey Korotayev, 'The First "Golden Age" of Globalization (1870–1914)', in *A Big History of Globalization: The Emergence of a Global World System* (Cham: Springer, 2019), 195–224.

know that he was often critical of the missionary impact on Pacific cultures, for example, but we do not know very much about the missionaries' backgrounds and the kinds of work that they did.[9] Although wider scholarly attention to the agency of indigenous Pacific Islanders in history has grown, little is understood about the indigenous Christians about whom Stevenson thought and wrote so much.[10] Recognition of the impact of Pacific Islands Christianity on Stevenson's writing remains slight in comparison with accounts of his engagement with the relationship between religion and colonialism.[11] The general picture somewhat resembles the anthropologist Joel Robbins's characterisation of his own discipline: the assumption appears to be that Christianity is no more than a 'veneer' that coats the surface of Pacific culture, beneath which one must look to find the things that are of real substance, such as, presumably, traditional (i.e. pre-Christian) beliefs and practices.[12] Just as with the anthropology of Christianity developed by Robbins and his colleagues, then, the present work can be seen as part of an effort to fully engage religion, in particular Christianity, as an object of the academic study of the past. Religion refers to experiences, beliefs, and practices that reflect our relationship with the cosmos and concern with 'ultimate issues', in the words of David Bebbington.[13] Religion is therefore fundamental, and understanding its impact in historical contexts such as the one presented in this book allows us to make better sense of other knowledge pursuits.

A second aim of the book is to demonstrate the intellectual substance and vitality of Christian thought as a global endeavour in Robert Louis Stevenson's writing. The particular significance of

---

[9] John Coffey and Alister Chapman summarise the 'materialist reductionism' of present-orientated histories of religion in their 'Introduction: Intellectual History and the Return of Religion', in *Seeing Things Their Way: Intellectual History and the Return of Religion*, ed. by Alister Chapman, John Coffey, and Brad S. Gregory (Notre Dame, IN: University of Notre Dame Press, 2009), 11.

[10] A welcome addition is Carla Manfredi's monograph, which considers the agency of Pacific Islanders. See Manfredi, *Stevenson's Pacific Impressions*.

[11] The most serious intellectual and literary exploration of the relationship between religion and Pacific culture in Stevenson's work is John Charlot, 'The Influence of Polynesian Literature and Thought on Robert Louis Stevenson', *The Journal of Intercultural Studies* 14 (1987), 82–106.

[12] Joel Robbins, 'Continuity Thinking and the Problem of Christian Culture: Belief, Time, and the Anthropology of Christianity', *Current Anthropology* 48, 1 (2007), 5–38 (6).

[13] David Bebbington, 'Response: The History of Ideas and the Study of Religion', in Chapman et al., *Seeing Things Their Way*, 240–57 (254).

this point will be highlighted when we consider the impact of the theory of secularisation in traditional accounts of the author's life and work. A summary definition of secularisation theory would hold that the influence of religion declines as societies advance scientifically and technologically.[14] When stated in this way, the theory can offer a ready-made interpretation of one of the defining episodes of Stevenson's life: his break with his parents' religious beliefs in the early 1870s. According to the standard narrative derived from secularisation theory, this event represents Stevenson progressing, with the nineteenth century, out of religion. With industrial modernity and scientific progress comes religious doubt.[15] As I explain in Chapter 1, however, re-evaluations of secularisation theory have led historians of the Victorian period to assess it as one of religious growth and plurality rather than decline. Their conclusions lend weight to an important claim of this book, that the most crucial religious context through which to interpret the young Robert Louis Stevenson's intellectual biography is not secularisation but rather the Disruption of the Church of Scotland in 1843. The impact of this dramatic event on his social environment and on his ideas about the church are respectively explored in the book's first and fifth chapters.

Despite the waning academic influence of secularisation theory, interpretations of Stevenson's life and work continue to be framed by this 'master narrative' of religion in the modern West.[16] Moreover, the larger story of Christianity's expansion in the global South is hardly reflected at all. Research in global religious change has provided abundant evidence to show that, while Christianity may have declined in social and institutional importance in Europe and North America during the course of the nineteenth and twentieth centuries, the more statistically significant phenomenon has been the religion's spectacular growth across sub-Saharan Africa, Latin America, Asia,

---

[14] For modern and postmodern histories of Britain that are relevant to this vast subject, see Hugh McLeod, *Secularisation in Western Europe, 1848–1914* (Basingstoke: Macmillan, 2000); Callum G. Brown, *The Death of Christian Britain: Understanding Secularisation, 1800–2000* (London: Routledge, 2009).

[15] For an interesting discussion of this formula by a renowned religious historian, see Owen Chadwick, *The Secularization of the European Mind in the Nineteenth Century* (Cambridge: Cambridge University Press, 1975), 11–12.

[16] Jeffrey Cox, 'Secularization and Other Master Narratives of Religion in Modern Europe', *Kirchliche Zeitgeschichte* 14, 1 (2001), 24–35. See also Alister Chapman, 'Intellectual History and Religion in Modern Britain', in Chapman et al., *Seeing Things Their Way*, 226–39 (228).

and the Island Pacific during the same period.[17] If we wish to think more concretely about the changes implied in such contested terms as 'secularisation' and 'World Christianity', then studying Stevenson's life and work affords us an unusual opportunity to do so.[18] For this reason, the book positions Stevenson's Pacific years (1889–94) within the context of Christianity's transformation from a principally Western or European religion to one that is truly global.[19]

By no means does this suggest that Stevenson was ready to accept all of the implications of the epochal shift that he was witnessing in places like Samoa. Pacific Islander Christianity came as a shock to him just as it did to his character the white trader Wiltshire in 'The Beach of Falesá'. Philip Jenkins has described the Western experience of Christianity's global transformation as being akin to 'seeing Christianity again for the first time': 'a radically new perspective, which is both startling and, often, uncomfortable'.[20] As awkward and unnerving as it must also have been to Stevenson, he was nevertheless able to grasp that something novel and important was happening to the religion in which he had been raised. We might better appreciate the significance of Stevenson's recognition of this change if we compare him with that of another Scot, the historian Andrew Walls, who experienced something similar over half a century later while he was working in west Africa. As Walls spent time with African Christians, he came to see 'churches in Africa and Scotland as part of a bigger story' and asked himself questions such as, 'How is the faith transmitted and transformed across cultures?' and 'Through what process does the rationalistic faith of Scottish Christians become the visionary, supernaturalised life of Nigerians?'[21] Pacific cultural manifestations of

---

[17] Brian Stanley, *Christianity in the Twentieth Century: A World History* (Princeton, NJ: Princeton University Press, 2018), 4–5.

[18] On the naming and practice of 'World Christianity' as a scholarly endeavour, see Dana L. Robert, 'Locating *Relocating World Christianity: Interdisciplinary Studies in Universal and Local Expressions of the Christian Faith*', *International Bulletin of Missionary Research* 43, 2 (2019), 126–33; Dorottya Nagy, 'Recalling the Term "World Christianity": Excursions into Worldings of Literature, Philosophy, and History', in Frederiks and Nagy, *World Christianity*, 40–64.

[19] On the transformation of global Christianity, see Andrew F. Walls, *The Missionary Movement in Christian History: Studies in the Transmission of Faith* (New York: Orbis, 1996).

[20] Philip Jenkins, *The Next Christendom: The Coming of Global Christianity* (3rd edn, Oxford: Oxford University Press, 2011), 271.

[21] Tim Stafford, 'Andrew Walls: Historian Ahead of His Time', *Christianity Today*, 13 August 2021. In a statement that echoes a similar pronouncement made by Stevenson, Walls wrote that 'Christian proclamation is for the children and grandchildren of the people who hear it'. Walls, *The Missionary Movement in Christian History*, 51.

Christianity stimulated Stevenson's thought in a similar overall manner to the impact of African Christianity on Walls. We will have a better idea of what Stevenson was trying to achieve with his Pacific writing when we are able to grasp the ways in which it was motivated by this dramatic, though mostly unvoiced, experience.

Robert Louis Stevenson and the Pacific is a series of linked thematic essays whose unifying thread is the development of Stevenson's thought on matters concerning religion between the north Atlantic and Pacific periods of his life. The argument of this book therefore rests on presenting new contexts for analysis. A number of under-examined sources are considered, such as Stevenson's unpublished manuscripts on the South Seas, his mother's diaries, and pieces written by missionaries who knew Stevenson. The major task is to establish the soundness and validity of the cultural contexts for Stevenson's Pacific Islands corpus and to use them to analyse the development of his thinking.[22] In making claims about Stevenson's religious thought, I avoid speculating on the matter of his religious beliefs. Much has already been written about this subject and perhaps more could still be said, but my purpose here is to address the ways in which Christianity shaped the author's intellectual life. As I hope to have demonstrated, this can involve looking at his opinions and ideas without positively addressing questions of religious commitment.

Stevenson's Scottish Presbyterian background gave meaning and substance to his thinking about Christianity in the Pacific Islands, while the latter impacted the way in which he thought about subjects such as anthropology, political community, and mission. The thesis is demonstrated through the course of this book in three steps, which I will first briefly summarise before further elaboration in the paragraphs that follow. The first step is to establish that Stevenson was religiously literate. Essentially, this term lays claim to the idea that people who are raised in religious cultures or environments are intellectually distinctive in identifiable ways. They have religious knowledge (of the Bible, for example) and a sense of religion's place in society. They often display an awareness of modes of feeling and temperaments that are associated with religious practices. They

---

[22] Important published collections of Stevenson's Pacific writing on which I have drawn throughout this study are *South Sea Tales*, ed. by Roslyn Jolly (Oxford: Oxford University Press, 1996); *In the South Seas*, ed. by Neil Rennie (London: Penguin, 1998); *Sophia Scarlet and Other Pacific Writings*, ed. by Robert Hoskins (Auckland: AUT Media, 2008).

know how to be religious without necessarily being so themselves – this is precisely what was said about Stevenson by religious-minded observers. Stevenson's religious literacy distinguished him from many other non-missionary travellers to the Pacific. In the second part of the book, I show how this experiential religious knowledge cast as religious literacy enabled Stevenson to meaningfully compare Pacific Christian societies with those with which he was familiar, particularly post-Reformation Scotland. In this section, I adopt another term, 'inculturation', to describe the anthropo-theological reasoning that was stimulated in him by his discovery of Pacific Christianity. From Stevenson's perspective, to reflect on inculturation meant to compare religious belief and practice in historically Christian societies with those places in which Christianity had arrived relatively recently.[23] The third part of the book positions Stevenson's writing on inculturation within his intellectual biography to demonstrate how the Pacific Christian environment influenced his views of mission and church. When we consider that the original context of his intellectual journey was mid-century Scottish debate about established and dissenting churches, then the book comes full circle with its closing chapter on Stevenson's evolving ecclesiology.

Stevenson was able to meaningfully engage with the religious world of the Pacific because he appreciated Christianity's intellectual and cultural influence on his own society. The Disruption of 1843, an event that was of crucial importance to nineteenth-century Scottish Christianity, fundamentally shaped his life and thought and describes the time when the Free Church was born from its separation from the Church of Scotland over issues of establishment and patronage. The further fragmentation of Scottish Presbyterianism in the aftermath of the Disruption and the decline in the authority of the Kirk shaped Stevenson's social and intellectual life since he never found a replacement for the established church after he formally left it in the early 1870s.

Critics have been reluctant to embrace the full significance of Stevenson's Calvinism. In this respect he is not an unusual subject in modern Scottish literature; rather, as Patrick Scott's interpretation suggests, the reduced critical emphasis on Calvinism might be connected to the tendency in twentieth-century Scottish literary studies to '[stigmatise] the Scottish Reformation as an anti-aesthetic

---

[23] For a discussion of other approaches to inculturation, see Stephen B. Bevans, *Models of Contextual Theology* (Maryknoll, NY: Orbis, 2002).

tyranny'.[24] The present study takes similar issue with this line of criticism in order to claim that Stevenson's Presbyterian formation was in fact at the heart of his identity as a writer.[25] Scottish Presbyterianism amounted to a kind of denominational consciousness in him, a basis on which he drew also to engage other religions and beliefs, including other varieties of Christianity. For example, he approached Roman Catholicism not as a neutral or irreligious observer but rather as a Protestant Christian who was raised in the Scottish Presbyterian tradition. What we might characterise as religious realism was responsible for lending his writing a seriousness and subtlety that it is easy to overlook precisely because Stevenson was able to produce it with apparently little effort. As Glenda Norquay and others have convincingly demonstrated, we greatly benefit from taking religion seriously in Stevenson. By doing so we build a more solid foundation on which to appreciate the depth and complexity of his writing, we receive a more accurate impression of the contexts that shaped him, and we raise our chances of arriving at plausible motivations for his literary expression.

In the first chapter, Stevenson is presented as a religiously literate writer and his intellectual and social formation is reviewed through this lens. This opening section explores what he read and reflected on, whom he learned from, and the impact of the religious changes he experienced during his life in Britain. As discussed earlier, although the notion of secularisation is problematic, the term 'religious literacy' can have special conceptual value in the context of a society in which formal or established religion has reduced presence and authority. The philosopher Charles Taylor, whose work I engage in Chapter 1, has shown how articulating religious identity in a secular age is a very complicated task.[26] It requires us to consider, for instance, how many now 'believe without belonging' to any particular church or religious

---

[24] Patrick Scott, 'Introduction: The Ghost at the Feast: Religion in Scottish Literary Criticism', *Studies in Scottish Literature* 45, 2 (2019), 3–6 (4). As Scott further explains, the 'basic argument, that critics have been uncomfortable with Scottish literature's relation to Calvinist beliefs, surely applies to many periods' (4). He also notes in the collection he introduces that 'There's no attempt here to rehabilitate Stevenson as religious writer' (6).

[25] As I discuss in Chapter 1, there are a few exceptions to the prevailing critical pattern, the most important of which is Glenda Norquay, *Robert Louis Stevenson and Theories of Reading: The Reader as Vagabond* (Manchester: Manchester University Press, 2007).

[26] Charles Taylor, *A Secular Age* (Cambridge, MA: Belknap Press, 2007).

organisation.[27] The very notion of religious literacy reinforces a certain understanding of secularity that may be associated with, for example, declining church attendance, reduced religious instruction at school, and the privatisation of forms and symbols of religious expression; these are measures of social change which can impinge on the mental world of believers and unbelievers alike. In similar fashion, the intellectual historical approach taken in this book assumes that religiously literate people do not just 'do' religious things but they think about them as well.[28]

The middle chapters of the book are concerned with the impact of Pacific Islands religion on the mind of Stevenson. The wider scholarly context for these chapters is the field of World Christianity and its impact on a range of academic disciplines. World Christianity, as the term is understood here, refers to social and cultural phenomena that follow from the relatively recent and dramatic growth of Christianity in the global South and include its impact on evangelisation and theology.[29] Chapters 2, 3 and 4 are embedded in the paradigm of Pacific Christianity as a regional context of this larger move of Christianity's demographic centre away from the global North (or West).[30] The historic shift is critical to understanding the development of Stevenson's writing in the Pacific, since it frames his recognition of the fact that Christianity might be becoming more prominent in places such as Samoa than in Scotland.

Western Christianity was not simply being reproduced in the Pacific Islands. Rather, Pacific Christianity was coming to have a reality and forms of its own. Stevenson's religious literacy, his sensitivity towards the relationship between religious belief and a people's social and intellectual expressions, enabled him to sense this development before many others, during what would now be recognised as a relatively early stage in the modern global expansion of Christianity. The lack of a formal missionary obligation also differentiated

---

[27] Grace Davie, *Religion in Britain since 1945: Believing without Belonging* (Oxford: Blackwell, 1994).

[28] Richard Schaefer, 'Intellectual History and the Return of Religion', *Historically Speaking* 12, 2 (2011), 30–1 (31).

[29] For an example of the new scholarship in this field, see Jehu J. Hanciles, *Migration and the Making of Global Christianity* (Grand Rapids, MI: William B. Eerdmans, 2021).

[30] These are by no means simply geographical distinctions, of course, and I am aware that they do not help, for example, to capture the distinctive socioeconomic trajectory of a country such as South Korea in the history of Christianity's recent global expansion.

him from most other kinds of religiously literate Westerners in the Pacific. These themes are explored in the book's middle chapters, which are organised broadly biographically. Chapter 2 is focused on the period of Stevenson's Pacific travel between 1888 and 1890, while Chapters 3 and 4 analyse the writing he produced mainly in Samoa between the years 1889 and 1894. The three chapters try to capture the ambivalence that people from older Christian societies felt when they encountered the faith of new Christians, particularly those that were far from the West.

In Chapter 2, I explore this ambivalence in Stevenson's ethnographic writing, largely composed during his South Seas voyages between the summers of 1888 and 1890. The chapter emphasises the value of interpreting this writing through the perspective of the anthropology of Christianity, whose origins and development are also discussed.[31] Denominational consciousness characterised Stevenson's position as a writer of culture, and I show how this usefully complicates attempts to draw binary distinctions in his ethnography between Pacific Islanders and Westerners. Stevenson's writing also lends itself to a concept of transcendence that is employed by modern anthropologists. I use this idea to explore how he engages themes such as Christian conversion in ways that challenge rationalist and individualist explanations of religious behaviour. The chapter concludes by bringing these insights to bear in a new interpretation of Stevenson's fable 'Something in It', which was composed around the same period. I argue that this story may be understood as an extension of the ethnographic approaches to religion that Stevenson honed in his Pacific travel writing.

The focus of Chapter 3 is the European fiction that Stevenson wrote during the final years of his life in Samoa. In this chapter, the production of these works is situated within the communal religious life of the Samoan society into which Stevenson and his family were gradually incorporated. Because of his own background, discussed above, Stevenson was alert to religious and historical analogies between Scotland and Samoa. He was also involved in the intercultural mission that was centred at Apia, the Samoan capital. In the second half of the chapter, I show how Stevenson's fiction drew on this rich experience to re-examine the history of communal religious life in Europe. In a significant departure from most of his earlier fiction,

---

[31] For an introduction to the subject, see Joel Robbins, 'The Anthropology of Christianity: Unity, Diversity, New Directions', *Current Anthropology* 55, Supplement 10 (2014), S157–71.

I argue, the experience of people in religious and moral communities is much more prominent in late works such as *Heathercat* and *Weir of Hermiston*. The new-found emphasis on communitarian religious experience, as well as a mediated presence of the supernatural, characterised the impact of Samoan Christian culture on his European fiction.[32]

Chapter 4 brings to the fore ideas that have been implicit in what has been discussed so far by looking at the theme of inculturation in Stevenson's Pacific fiction. Inculturation, described earlier as an anthropo-theological concern with the relationship between religion and culture, has a specific historical trajectory in colonial contexts such as the Island Pacific. The chapter explores the relationship between Pacific Islanders' conversion to Christianity and their status as subjects of Western colonialism. I argue that Stevenson's fiction portrays a world in which Christian conversion does not equal colonial subjugation. Rather, what was fundamental to the author's perspective in works such as 'The Beach of Falesá' was his recognition that Christianity's growth in the Pacific was founded on the missionary activity of Islanders, as well as his first-hand knowledge of the ways in which Christianity had been indigenised, that is, adapted and rendered into locally intelligible and transmissible forms. These experiences contributed to the richness of Stevenson's Pacific fiction and they deserve further study by scholars of World Christianity.

In the final part of the book, I connect the Scottish and Pacific periods of Stevenson's writing through the theme of the church in order to demonstrate the value of religious contextualisation in globalising Scottish literary history. As a young man in the 1870s, Stevenson possessed the knowledge and sensitivity to articulate the pressures of being an observant member of the established church while in the middle of a fragmented Scottish religious culture. When he went to the Pacific, this earlier experience helped to make him a compelling witness of the development of the Christian church as a

---

[32] Compare the comment of Philip Jenkins that 'global South Christians retain a strong supernatural orientation and are by and large far more interested in personal salvation than in radical politics'. Jenkins, *Next Christendom*, 11. For a critical commentary, see Werner Ustorf, 'Global Christianity, New Empire, and Old Europe', in *Global Christianity: Contested Claims*, ed. by Frans Wijsen and Robert Schreiter (Amsterdam and New York: Rodopi, 2007), 35–49. Ustorf charges that Jenkins has not 'engage[d] theologically with the Christian experience of the [global] "South"' (47) and has offered instead a highly politicised vision of the global Christian future.

global institution. In the fifth chapter, I excavate Stevenson's writing in relation to ecclesiology from his Edinburgh days through to his view of the role and significance of the Samoan church as it struggled to assert itself under the authority of foreign missionaries. By focusing on the theme of ecclesiology we can assess the impact of changing contextual influences on the mind of Stevenson, from debates about patronage and establishment in the Church of Scotland to the assertion of Pacific Islander agency in conflicts over land preservation. Looking at the development of Stevenson's thought in this way also contributes to our understanding of the missionary direction of ecclesiology in twentieth-century Scottish Presbyterianism.

The book closes with a reflection on the multivalent relationship between religion, Scottish literature, and global intellectual history. At the heart of this study lies an exploration of Stevenson's intellectual, anthropological, social, theological, and institutional engagement with Christianity. In the Conclusion, I connect the Scottishness of his religious-mindedness with recent work on Scottish cultural history. Stevenson's encounter with Christianity in the Pacific Islands can contribute to conversations about Scottish culture's global interactions. By making this connected set of claims about religion and the life of the mind, I also hope to have demonstrated the value of an interdisciplinary approach to studying Stevenson. In order to ask larger questions about his life and his work, we need to be able to enter into conversations about religion and culture that go against what has been described as 'the logic of conventional academic compartmentalization'.[33] I hope that those who labour in the academic fields on which this historian has infringed will regard the book as an acknowledgement of their contribution, and as an attempt to productively engage with what they do.

---

[33] Craig Beveridge and Ronald Turnbull, *Scotland after Enlightenment: Image and Tradition in Modern Scottish Culture* (Edinburgh: Polygon, 1997), 165.

Chapter 1

Stevenson's Religious Literacy

There is a scene in *Kidnapped* in which David Balfour describes the misery of his 'night tramps' with Alan Breck Stewart through the Scottish Highlands as they try to evade capture for the suspected murder of Colin Campbell. To compound matters, David and Alan have fallen out after Alan had gambled and lost all of David's money. 'This was a dreadful time,' remembers David, 'rendered the more dreadful by the gloom of the weather and the country.'[1] At one point during their flight in the dark heather he hears the rain-steeped river in the valley below, 'now booming like thunder, now with an angry cry'.[2] After this the narrative then switches register, as David admits:

> I could well understand the story of the Water Kelpie, that demon of the streams, who is fabled to keep wailing and roaring at the ford until the coming of the doomed traveler. Alan I saw believed it, or half believed it; and when the cry of the river rose more than usually sharp, I was little surprised (though, of course, I would still be shocked) to see him cross himself in the manner of Catholics.[3]

With his characteristic economy Stevenson packs an enormous amount into these two sentences as the passage seamlessly weaves together religious and cultural knowledge.[4] To begin with, he has

---

[1] Robert Louis Stevenson, *Kidnapped* (New York: Charles Scribner's Sons, 1886), 249.
[2] Stevenson, *Kidnapped*, 250.
[3] Stevenson, *Kidnapped*, 250.
[4] Linden Bicket identifies a similar combination of skills on display in Stevenson's short story 'Thrawn Janet', which 'is not only a tale of the Scots folk supernatural' but one in which 'Stevenson skilfully inserts layers of Scottish religious history and scriptural echo'. Linden Bicket, 'Catholic and Protestant Sensibilities in Scottish Literature: Stevenson to Spark', in *The History of Scottish Theology, Volume III: The Long Twentieth Century*, ed. by David Fergusson and Mark W. Elliott (Oxford: Oxford University Press, 2019), 271–87 (274).

David Balfour describe a Scottish folk belief about the Water Kelpie, whose reality David does not accept but in that moment of terror he 'could well understand'. However, Alan at least 'half believed' the story, judging from the observation that 'when the cry of the river rose more than usually sharp' he would 'cross himself in the manner of Catholics'. David, a Presbyterian Lowlander, while educated enough in religious matters to be 'little surprised', is nevertheless 'shocked' at the sight of his Highlander friend adopting what he considered to be a superstitious custom.[5] David therefore learns something about Alan's lived faith while the reader gains an understanding of the differences between neighbouring Christian denominations. All of this takes place in the middle of an excursus on the persistence of Scottish folk beliefs in an enlightened age.[6]

In a novel like *Kidnapped* Stevenson demonstrates the full range of his abilities as a writer, but on matters of religion and belief he is so fluent and subtle that his skill can go unnoticed by modern readers. Even a brilliant critic like Barry Menikoff, in his *Narrating Scotland: The Imagination of Robert Louis Stevenson*, pays little attention to the religious aspects of his subject and instead presents Scotland as an exclusively cultural construct in the mind of Stevenson.[7] The broad

---

[5] *Kidnapped* could be said to occupy the tail end of the mid-nineteenth-century fiction of Catholic revival in Britain. Cf. Andrew Sanders, 'Christianity and Literature in English', in *The Cambridge History of Christianity: Volume 8. World Christianities c. 1815 – c. 1914*, ed. by Sheridan Gilley and Brian Stanley (Cambridge: Cambridge University Press, 2014), 136–41.

[6] On Stevenson, Scottish folklore and the uncanny, see William Gray, *Fantasy, Art and Life: Essays on George MacDonald, Robert Louis Stevenson and Other Fantasy Writers* (Newcastle upon Tyne: Cambridge Scholars Publishing, 2011), 111–39. Ian Campbell has written about the conditions that enable modern Scottish writers 'to depict the psychological pressures of belief in a changing world, and the persistence of half-forgotten beliefs from an earlier Scotland'. Ian Campbell, 'Scottish Literature in a Time of Change', in *The History of Scottish Theology, Volume II: The Early Enlightenment to the Late Victorian Era*, ed. by David Fergusson and Mark W. Elliott (Oxford: Oxford University Press, 2019), 199–212 (212).

[7] Barry Menikoff, *Narrating Scotland: The Imagination of Robert Louis Stevenson* (Columbia: University of South Carolina Press, 2005). While he skilfully recovers and presents the religious texts on which Stevenson drew to compose *Kidnapped* and *Catriona*, Menikoff overlooks the relationship between religion and history in Scottish identity. This close relationship can be traced to Stevenson's own time. For instance, the testimonial writers for Stevenson's application for the Chair of history and Constitutional Law at the University of Edinburgh included a Church of Scotland theologian (John Tulloch) and a minister (James Cameron Lees), and the clergyman Alexander Whyte, a future Moderator of the General Assembly of the Free Church.

loss of Scriptural literacy in Scottish literature since the days of Scott and Hogg has been noted.[8] Yet as historians have recently demonstrated, the portrayal of Scottish identity in literature of the Union era was foremost asserted through debates about religion, specifically 'denominational allegiances, largely within Presbyterianism'.[9] Studies of the impact of industrial modernisation in the later nineteenth century have moreover emphasised the persistence of religion at the centre of Scottish life, albeit in more plural forms than before.[10] To paraphrase another writer, then, why have modern studies of Stevenson 'generally neglected' his 'religious views'?[11]

Framed by this question, the present chapter explores the relationship between the religious and the cultural in Stevenson's writing and argues that, in order to fully grasp Stevenson's richness and complexity as a writer of culture, we need to understand how religion fundamentally shaped his thought.[12] I begin by explaining how the term 'religious literacy' can help to capture what made Stevenson distinctive as a late-nineteenth-century Scottish author.

---

[8] Campbell, 'Scottish Literature in a Time of Change', 209.

[9] Valerie Wallace and Colin Kidd, 'Between Nationhood and Nonconformity: The Scottish Whig-Presbyterian Novel and the Denominational Press', in *Literature and Union: Scottish Texts, British Contexts*, ed. by Gerard Carruthers and Colin Kidd (Oxford: Oxford University Press, 2018), 193–220 (194).

[10] Callum G. Brown, *The People in the Pews: Religion and Society in Scotland since 1780* (Glasgow: Economic and Social History Society of Scotland, 1993); Stewart J. Brown, 'Beliefs and Religions', in *A History of Everyday Life in Scotland*, ed. by T. Griffiths and G. Morton (Edinburgh: Edinburgh University Press, 2010), 116–46 (117).

[11] Robert-Louis Abrahamson, 'Truth Out of Tusitala Spoke: Stevenson's Voice in Post-Darwinian Christianity', in *Persona and Paradox: Issues of Identity for C. S. Lewis, His Friends and Associates*, ed. by Suzanne Bray and William Gray (Newcastle upon Tyne: Cambridge Scholars Publishing, 2012), 237–54 (238). It is instructive to contrast the contemporary critical landscape with the early twentieth century, when religious studies of Stevenson were much more common in the general scholarly conversation about the author. See, for example, John Kelman, *The Faith of Robert Louis Stevenson* (Edinburgh: Oliphant, Anderson and Ferrier, 1903); Edward Beal, 'Stevenson's Ideal Missionary', *International Review of Mission* 7, 3 (1918), 353–62; Gilbert Keith Chesterton, *Robert Louis Stevenson* (London: Hodder and Stoughton, 1927); Doris N. Dalglish, *Presbyterian Pirate: A Portrait of Stevenson* (London: Oxford University Press, 1937); Earl August Weis, 'Stevenson and the Catholic Church; A Background for the Damien Letter' (MA thesis, Loyola University of Chicago, 1948).

[12] Crawford Gribben, 'Afterword: Finding Religion in Scottish Literary History', *Studies in Scottish Literature* 45, 2 (2019), 75–80 (77).

Stevenson's religious literacy consisted of deep lived knowledge of Scottish Presbyterianism combined with imaginative sympathy for neighbouring Christian denominations. I adapt the approaches of other scholars to more precisely define the influence of religion on Stevenson's thought. Then, I offer a reconsideration of his intellectual life to 1888 through the lens of his religious literacy and suggest that the roots of his interest in Pacific Islands inculturation may be found in his experience of the tensions between Christianity and contemporary European culture. 'Secularisation', as we might summarise these tensions, provides a challenging critical context for understanding Stevenson's religious literacy.[13]

Religious Literacy

In March 1889, as Stevenson and his family were visiting the Hawaiian Islands, the American Congregationalist minister Charles McEwan Hyde, later the target of Stevenson's defence of Father Damien of Molokai, observed:

> He [Stevenson] is not a religious man, himself, nor is his wife a pious woman. Very far from it: but his mother is a godly woman, now with him here, the daughter of a Scotch minister. So he knows how religious people view things.[14]

Hyde identified a special characteristic of the author, linked to religion, which he connected to Stevenson's mother. But what precisely does it mean to know 'how religious people view things'? And how might this have influenced Stevenson's writing, his perception of the world and of human affairs? Indeed, what distinguished Stevenson from authors who did not know 'how religious people view things'?

Of the few modern critics that have tried to situate Stevenson's thought within a religious framework, a highly sophisticated approach is taken by Glenda Norquay in her book *Robert Louis Stevenson*

---

[13] An excellent analysis of the debates around the term 'secularisation' is provided by J. C. D. Clark, 'Secularization and Modernization: The Failure of a Grand Narrative', *The Historical Journal* 55, 1 (2012), 161–94.
[14] Hyde to Judson Smith, 25/03/1889, ABCFM Papers, Houghton Library, Harvard University.

and Theories of Reading.¹⁵ Norquay's major claim is that Stevenson's writing was underpinned by

> the aesthetic and philosophic implications of the Calvinist engagement with the Word – in which fiction is simultaneously negated as a falling short of the word of God, but also creatively liberated from the constraints of realism because mimetic reproduction of God's word is impossible.¹⁶

Calvinism distinguished Stevenson 'as writer and theorist' by 'produc[ing] a reluctance to establish himself in the godlike role of authoritative interpreter of our response to the world'.¹⁷ Moreover, Stevenson's 'Calvinist configuration' set him apart from 'the English literary Establishment' and opened creative horizons for him.¹⁸ Norquay's conceptualisation leads her to provide an insightful account of the influence of Calvinist Christianity on Stevenson's literary ethics and its impact on his professional career. Going largely against the scholarly grain, her analysis presents religion as offering the writer a certain kind of aesthetic freedom rather than imposing restrictions upon him that he struggled to overcome.

Norquay's model of a 'Calvinist configuration' could be pressed a little further to explore the overall place of religion in Stevenson's thought. After all, Calvinism denotes a culture (or cultures) through its doctrines, attitudes, and practices.¹⁹ While Norquay's study helps to account for how Stevenson's Scottish Calvinist upbringing distinguished him from English writers, it is less obviously concerned with how Christianity shaped his historical imagination or his sympathetic depiction of religious cultures. In contrast to her use of the term 'Calvinist configuration', I therefore adopt the broader term 'religious literacy' to characterise this distinctive blending of the

---

[15] Glenda Norquay, *Robert Louis Stevenson and Theories of Reading: The Reader as Vagabond* (Manchester: Manchester University Press, 2007). For the model of an insightful theological reading of Stevenson's work, see Alison Jack, 'The Death of the Master: The Gospel of John and R. L. Stevenson's *The Master of Ballantrae*', *Scottish Journal of Theology* 59, 3 (2006), 297–306.
[16] Norquay, *Theories of Reading*, 29.
[17] Norquay, *Theories of Reading*, 45.
[18] Norquay, *Theories of Reading*, 63.
[19] Gijsbert van den Brink and Harro Höpfl, 'Calvin, the Reformed Tradition and Modern Culture', in *Calvinism and the Making of the European Mind*, ed. by Gijsbert van den Brink and Harro Höpfl (Leiden: Brill, 2014), 3–24.

religious with the cultural in Stevenson's writing.[20] I make the distinctive but related claim that Stevenson expressed his Protestant, not just Calvinist, heritage in ways that exercised his feelings as well as his reason. As Charles Hyde noted, Stevenson had a marked ability to see things from the religious point of view.

Today the term 'religious literacy' appears in debates about religious education and is often framed in terms of civic responsibility.[21] Scholars have argued for the importance of religious literacy in teaching within the context of an increasingly secularised Western culture that is no longer able to understand or engage meaningfully with religion.[22] Diane Moore's work takes a cultural studies approach in trying to overcome religious illiteracy in education.[23] By developing and extending her definition of religious literacy it is possible to tease out some of the aspects that are characteristic in Stevenson. Because religious literacy describes a subtle capacity made up of various different components, it may be helpful to approach the matter first in this heuristic way instead of trying to derive it directly from elements of Stevenson's life and work.

In the first place, according to Moore, religious literacy involves being able to understand the 'central texts (where applicable), beliefs, practices and contemporary manifestations' of one or more religious traditions, including different Christian denominations.[24] Along with

---

[20] Charles Taylor's concept of a 'denominational imaginary' can help to characterise a broader Presbyterian affiliation within the context of nineteenth-century Scotland's religious fragmentation and diversity, although for my present purposes this concept is also somewhat limiting. Charles Taylor, *A Secular Age* (Cambridge, MA: Belknap Press, 2007), 450.

[21] Stephen Prothero, *Religious Literacy: What Every American Needs to Know – and Doesn't* (New York: HarperOne, 2007), 11–15; Chris Seiple and Dennis R. Hoover, 'A Case for Cross-Cultural Religious Literacy', *The Review of Faith and International Affairs* 19, 1 (2021), 1–13.

[22] Adam Dinham, 'Public Religion in an Age of Ambivalence: Recovering Religious Literacy after a Century of Secularism', in *Issues in Religion and Education*, ed. by Lori G. Beaman and Leo Van Arragon (Leiden: Brill, 2015), 19–33; Adam Dinham and Matthew Francis, *Religious Literacy in Policy and Practice* (Bristol: Policy Press, 2015). For a critique of the concept and the movement from within the religious studies discipline, see Johannes C. Wolfart, '"Religious Literacy": Some Considerations and Reservations', *Method and Theory in the Study of Religion* (2022), 1–28. Wolfart argues that religious literacy must be better defined and its advocates' claims empirically tested.

[23] Diane L. Moore, 'Overcoming Religious Illiteracy: A Cultural Studies Approach', *World History Connected* 4, 1 (2006).

[24] Moore, 'Overcoming Religious Illiteracy'.

a sound understanding of the Bible derived from both everyday speech and formal religious contexts, other important markers of Stevenson's religious upbringing include knowledge of the Shorter Catechism and works of theology (such as Joseph Butler's *Analogy of Religion*) and regular attendance with his family at the local Church of Scotland parish.[25] These comprised the building blocks of Stevenson's religious literacy and will be discussed further below. Major works written by the author, such as *Treasure Island*, are notably filled with references to Scripture.

Secondly, religious literacy consists of 'a basic understanding of the history' of one or more religious traditions including how 'they arose out of and continue to be shaped by particular social, historical and cultural contexts'.[26] This correlates with Stevenson's many fictional and critical studies inspired by Scottish religious history, which begin with his earliest published work, 'The Pentland Rising' (1866), a narrative that thrills with the language and passion of the seventeenth-century Covenanters. Among his mature writings are essays such as 'John Knox and His Relations to Women' and novels such as *The Master of Ballantrae*, which are the products of a profound engagement with Scottish religious history.[27] These also display the author's facility with primary sources and his ability to enter into his subjects' worldview, for example, by adopting historical manners of speech and narration.[28] Stevenson was not only well versed in Scottish religious history but also fascinated by Christianity in the wider European setting. Examples are plentiful. As a young man, while

---

[25] *The Letters of Robert Louis Stevenson*, ed. by Bradford A. Booth and Ernest Mehew (New Haven, CT: Yale University Press, 1994–5), I, 274. With his Biblical literacy Stevenson could be said to have followed in the tradition of Burns and Scott. G. Ross Roy, 'The Bible in Burns and Scott', in *The Bible in Scottish Life and Literature*, ed. by David F. Wright, Ian Campbell, and John Gibson (Edinburgh: The Saint Andrew Press, 1988), 79–93 (91–2).

[26] Moore, 'Overcoming Religious Illiteracy'.

[27] For an illuminating discussion bringing together these two texts, see Jeremy Lim, 'Calvinism and Forms of Storytelling: Mackellar's Parental Voice in *The Master of Ballantrae*', *Journal of Stevenson Studies* 7 (2010), 83–105.

[28] Douglas Gifford contrasts Stevenson with Scott by claiming that only the latter could be considered a historical novelist in the true sense of the word. Douglas Gifford, 'Stevenson and Victorian Scotland: The Importance of *The Master of Ballantrae*', in *Stevenson and Victorian Scotland*, ed. by Jenni Calder (Edinburgh: Edinburgh University Press, 1981), 11–32. Compare this with Barry Menikoff, who claims Stevenson 'had a scholar's attitude toward history' and emphasises the plausibility of his attempt in 1881 to secure the Chair of History and Constitutional Law at Edinburgh University. Menikoff, *Narrating Scotland*, 10, 22–6.

on a visit to London, out of curiosity he stopped over at a Confessional held at the Roman Catholic Church of Our Lady of Victories in Kensington.[29] An entire section of his youthful *Travels with a Donkey in the Cévennes*, comprising three chapters, is devoted to his encounter with French Trappist monks.[30] One of his last, unfinished works, in which he returns to Jacobitism, a favourite subject, opens with a chapter set in Avignon, 'the city of the Anti-popes'.[31]

Religious literacy also involves 'the ability to discern and explore the religious dimensions of political, social and cultural expressions across time and place'.[32] To think fluently in a religious way means being able to bring together religion's components in language, history, anthropology, and other kinds of knowledge in order to communicate the complexity of human affairs. *Kidnapped*, ostensibly a boys' adventure story about a historical murder, offers a signal instance of the importance that Stevenson placed on religion in understanding Scottish identity through its central pairing of a Presbyterian Lowlander with a Jacobite Highlander. Confessional language and a spiritual tone mark the 'Full Statement' at the conclusion of Stevenson's Gothic scientific horror, *Strange Case of Dr. Jekyll and Mr. Hyde*.[33] Pacific fictions such as 'The Beach of Falesá' are filled with people who perform religious activities (praying, reading the Bible, going to church, interpreting Scripture). These many and varied examples suggest more than material interpretations of the events that take place in the stories.[34]

Stevenson's religious literacy could therefore be described as the product of both *'religious learning* [...] *through a devotional lens'* as well as *'learning about religion* from an academic one'.[35] It could be

---

[29] Stevenson, *Letters* I, 229–30.
[30] Robert Louis Stevenson, *Travels with a Donkey in the Cévennes* (London: Kegan Paul, 1879).
[31] Robert Louis Stevenson, 'The Young Chevalier', in *Lay Morals and Other Papers* (London: Chatto and Windus, 1911), 277.
[32] Moore, 'Overcoming Religious Illiteracy'.
[33] Kevin Mills describes *Jekyll and Hyde* as 'that most Pauline of tales'. Kevin Mills, 'The Stain on the Mirror: Pauline Reflections in *The Strange Case of Dr. Jekyll and Mr. Hyde*', *Christianity and Literature* 53, 3 (2004), 337–48 (338).
[34] L. M. Ratnapalan, 'Missionary Christianity and Culture in Robert Louis Stevenson's "The Beach of Falesá"', *Religion & Literature* 53, 3 (2021), 47–62.
[35] Moore, 'Overcoming Religious Illiteracy'. Note, in this respect, the words of Crawford Gribben: 'Scottish Calvinism was [...] both a credal and a deeply affective religion. It sought to encourage and then to contain religious feeling within boundaries that were eventually outlined in the Westminster Confession of Faith (1647).' Gribben, 'Afterword', 77.

argued that the connection between the two forms of learning gave special form to his thought from an early age. He translated what he absorbed at home and in church, through prayer and other forms of worship, into a way of looking at the world. It produced in him a quality of mind that fed into other aspects of his thought. Critics have sometimes referred to this in terms of a unique ethical or moral commitment. W. W. Robson even wonders whether there was 'ever an author more concerned with moral problems than Stevenson'.[36] Appreciation for religion's place in culture and sympathy with religious lives past and present made Stevenson curious about faith in his day. It also made him a more interesting and attentive writer of culture.

Religion in the Life of the Mind

Such characteristics may seem obvious in the light of Stevenson's Calvinist background, but they are often overlooked in interpretations of his work. One obstacle that has hindered recognition of Stevenson's religious literacy is contemporary religious illiteracy.[37] The reasons for this are complex and contested, and it is beyond the scope of this book to explore them fully, but they are often linked to social attitudes that are dismissive of religious belief for being either unscientific or contrary to contemporary moral beliefs. The commonplace nature of such views has contributed to the devaluation in the appreciation of religion in historical figures such as Robert Louis Stevenson. Accounts of Stevenson's intellectual development seldom touch on the continuing vitality of religious people, ideas, and institutions beyond the late 1860s when he began to absorb modern philosophical and scientific theories. Julia Reid, the author of an excellent and well-researched monograph about the relationship between Stevenson's writing and late-nineteenth-century science claims that Stevenson 'lost his faith in the early 1870s after reading Herbert Spencer's works'.[38] The assumption appears to be that the dissolution of Stevenson's Christian belief was certain once he

---

[36] W. W. Robson, 'On *Kidnapped*', in Calder, *Stevenson and Victorian Scotland*, 97.
[37] The final chapters of Tom Holland's *Dominion: The Making of the Western Mind* (London: Little, Brown, 2019) vividly portray religious illiteracy in modern Western culture.
[38] Julia Reid, *Robert Louis Stevenson, Science, and the Fin de Siècle* (Basingstoke: Palgrave Macmillan, 2006), 60.

was exposed to the strictures of positivism. Reid interestingly situates Stevenson's 'loss of faith' within the 'contradictory intellectual milieu' in which he moved in early 1870s Edinburgh, but to proceed to state that this experience 'precipitated a wholesale realignment of intellectual values and wider loyalties' is too strong: as we shall see in Chapter 5, Stevenson continued to be deeply interested in religious thought and history and he maintained contact with figures associated with the Kirk as well as with other Scottish denominations.[39]

Claims about Stevenson's loss of faith tend to acquiesce in the notion that faith was somehow less compelling to nineteenth-century thinkers than unbelief. This may be a consequence of the dominance of secularisation theory, which Alister Chapman, following the work of Jeffrey Cox, posits as the 'master narrative by which educated people understand religion in European society'.[40] Recent work by religious historians has begun to challenge the credibility of the secularisation narrative in relation to the time in which Stevenson lived. For example, in his study of nineteenth-century British intellectuals, *Crisis of Doubt*, Timothy Larsen demonstrates that 'the Victorian crisis of faith was actually a by-product of the religiosity of the Victorians'.[41] Limited social and intellectual contextualisation has served to uphold a myth concerning the Victorian loss of faith, yet 'Victorians themselves frequently discussed and wrote about the crisis of faith [. . .] because they prized faith so much and therefore feared and cared about its loss.'[42] As the historian Theodore Hoppen remarks, 'Never was Britain more religious than in the Victorian age.'[43] It is becoming clear that the history of religion in the nineteenth century was more interesting, varied, and complex than is suggested by the caricature of the 'crisis of faith'. The age was certainly one of religious conflict, spiritual doubt, and ecclesiastical fragmentation, but

---

[39] Reid, *Stevenson, Science, and the Fin de Siècle*, 113, 114.

[40] Alister Chapman, 'Intellectual History and Religion in Modern Britain', in *Seeing Things Their Way: Intellectual History and the Return of Religion*, ed. by Alister Chapman, John Coffey, and Brad S. Gregory (Notre Dame, IN: University of Notre Dame Press, 2009), 228. For a discussion about the continuing narrative power of 'secularisation', see Jeffrey Cox, 'Master Narratives of Long-Term Religious Change', in *The Decline of Christendom in Western Europe, 1750–2000*, ed. by Hugh McLeod and Werner Ustorf (Cambridge: Cambridge University Press, 2003), 201–17. I discuss secularisation theory further in the Introduction.

[41] Timothy Larsen, *Crisis of Doubt: Honest Faith in Nineteenth-Century England* (Oxford: Oxford University Press, 2006), 10.

[42] Larsen, *Crisis of Doubt*, 10.

[43] K. Theodore Hoppen, *The Mid-Victorian Generation 1846–1886* (Oxford: Oxford University Press, 1998), 427.

these should be seen as signs of religion's liveliness, not its atrophy.[44] Following this more balanced historical appraisal of the period in which Stevenson came to intellectual maturity we may characterise it as one of thought rather than doubt about faith.

The scholarly downplaying of the role of religion in Victorian society helped to distort the picture of Stevenson's intellectual development. Perhaps the most subtle and influential example of this was by Ernest Mehew, whose acclaimed edition of Stevenson's letters helped to lift Stevenson out of academic neglect and established him as a figure deserving of serious critical study.[45] Mehew wrote no explicitly thematic analysis of Stevenson's work except, notably, for a piece summarising the author's religious beliefs.[46] In this essay, Mehew's strategy is to draw a clear line between Stevenson's intellectual development and Christian orthodoxy by presenting evidence that demonstrated his struggles against his Presbyterian upbringing. Mehew's central claim is that the mature Stevenson was 'an agnostic with strongly Christian undertones' rather than a Christian in any traditional sense.[47] Although Stevenson was raised in a Christian household, Mehew argues that the intellectual impact of Darwin and Spencer, along with an inadequate response to his questions about his parents' religious certainties, contributed to his breaking away from the family's traditional faith in his early twenties. Mehew then asserts that

> Stevenson's clearest statement of his mature views on God and religion comes in a long and angry letter he wrote in January 1891 to Adelaide Boodle, a young friend and *protégée* from Bournemouth days, when she told him that on the advice of a friend she had decided that she could not visit him in Samoa because she would be unable to obtain there the consolations of the Anglican Church.[48]

Mehew's use of this letter to demonstrate his point is questionable. His purpose is to show how Stevenson remained consistent in his

---

[44] Mark Knight and Emma Mason, *Nineteenth-Century Religion and Literature: An Introduction* (Oxford: Oxford University Press, 2006), 13–14.

[45] Harold Orel, 'The Letters of Robert Louis Stevenson: A Review Essay', *English Literature in Transition* 40, 1 (1997), 60–8; Roger Swearingen, 'Ernest Mehew in Memoriam', accessed at: http://rogers99.users.sonic.net/ernest_mehew_in_memoriam.pdf on 1 May 2020.

[46] Ernest Mehew, 'God and the Novelists: 12. Robert Louis Stevenson', *Expository Times* 110, 10 (1999), 312–16.

[47] Mehew, 'God and the Novelists', 312.

[48] Mehew, 'God and the Novelists', 314.

agnosticism from the days of his break with his parents' Presbyterianism through to the final years of his life in the Pacific. Stevenson does write in the letter that 'what [God] wants of me, and with what measure he will serve me, I know not, and I do not think it is my business to enquire'[49] – but words about the unknowability of God's purposes do not in themselves denote agnosticism as it is commonly understood.[50] Mehew's interpretation of Stevenson's words is revealing of the scholarly tendency to interpret the author's writing from the perspective of secularisation theory. But placing Stevenson's intellectual life on a course from belief to unbelief (or disbelief, as the Victorians termed it) obscures the substance of the author's thought on a variety of religious subjects about which he continued to show a keen interest.

A second and related problem that is highlighted by Mehew's account of the development of Stevenson's religious thought is that it lacks chronological consistency. Directly after quoting the letter to Adelaide Boodle, which Stevenson had written in 1891 while he was at sea in the Pacific, Mehew tries to support his point with a quotation from an 1886 letter to Edmund Gosse, when Stevenson was living in Bournemouth. Mehew's selective treatment of the subject undercuts the Pacific as a serious intellectual context for understanding Stevenson's writing. His portrayal of Stevenson's mature thought involves minimising his religious encounters in the region.[51] By stopping short of making meaningful connections between these and Stevenson's development as a writer, Mehew implies that Stevenson was not responsive to Christianity in the Pacific. Again, this also has unfortunate consequences for the way in which we perceive the mature Stevenson's relationship to Christian thought considered globally.

Even if we fully embrace Mehew's interpretation of Stevenson's agnosticism, this does not discount Stevenson's religious literacy, which, as the sociologist Grace Davie reminds us, 'must be engaged in context'.[52] To appreciate what made Stevenson distinctive as a religiously fluent writer, we must understand the religious contours of his time and in the parts of the world with which he is associated.

---

[49] Mehew, 'God and the Novelists', 314.
[50] The Bible is full of such sentiments, for example: in the Old Testament, Isaiah 55: 8, 'for my thoughts are not your thoughts and your ways are not my ways, declares Yahweh'; in the New Testament, Romans 11: 34, 'Who has ever known the mind of the Lord?'
[51] Mehew, 'God and the Novelists', 316.
[52] Grace Davie, 'Foreword', in Dinham and Francis, *Religious Literacy*, vii.

One modern myth of the West that I have just explored is that serious thinkers in Stevenson's day were either atheists or undergoing a crisis of faith that was leading them away from religious belief. In a perceptive essay, Alex Thomson has shown how critical representations of Stevenson's work have tended to build on twentieth-century modernist rejections of perceived Victorian values.[53] In response to that movement, Thomson calls for a classical reinterpretation of the writer's art in order 'to do our best to understand Stevenson's work on its own terms'.[54] As a strategy of contextualisation this arguably risks severing our appreciation of Stevenson from the times which helped to form him, but one of Thomson's 'sound guides' to interpreting 'the practice of [Stevenson's] art' offers a compelling framework for his writing.[55]

In 1927, G. K. Chesterton produced a penetrating critical study, titled *Robert Louis Stevenson*, which was the culmination of four decades of the author's engagement with his subject. Chesterton's approach to interpretation grew from his criticism of the overtly adulatory and condemnatory studies of Stevenson in the decades following his death. 'Stevensoniana', as he branded this literature, was characterised by critics' moral inadequacy to fairly apprehend their subject.[56] Chesterton sought to restore a sensible balance against some of the extreme speculations that were made about the author's life. Stevenson was 'in the mature and sane sense a good man', he asserted, but 'that he never did anything he thought wrong is improbable'.[57] Excessive interest in the details of Stevenson's biography had inspired a critical methodology that began with the life and was illustrated by the art, whereas Chesterton deliberately foregrounded his

---

[53] Alex Thomson, 'Stevenson's Afterlives', in *The Edinburgh Companion to Robert Louis Stevenson*, ed. by Penny Fielding (Edinburgh: Edinburgh University Press, 2010), 147–59. Compare David Allan's criticism of a 'Victorian historiography' that obscured the proper study of the roots of the Scottish Enlightenment in Calvinist and humanist culture. David Allan, *Virtue, Learning and the Scottish Enlightenment: Ideas of Scholarship in Early Modern History* (Edinburgh: Edinburgh University Press, 1993), 7. Michael Shaw has also described how, 'in order to vindicate the importance of the [twentieth-century] Scottish Renaissance, the period beforehand had to be portrayed as especially weak'. Michael Shaw, 'Transculturation and Historicisation: New Directions for the Study of Scottish Literature c. 1840–1914', *Literature Compass* 13, 8 (2016), 501–10 (502).
[54] Thomson, 'Stevenson's Afterlives', 152.
[55] Thomson, 'Stevenson's Afterlives', 152.
[56] Chesterton, *Stevenson*, 13.
[57] Chesterton, *Stevenson*, 76.

study with analysis of the art and drew ideas from it to tell 'a certain story'.[58] The story was that of Stevenson's religious life.

Chesterton began by portraying Stevenson's unusual childhood, in which the strictures of his Edinburgh family's 'Puritanism' were somewhat tempered by his poor health and the constantly bedridden state in which it left him. By the end of the nineteenth century, in any case, Chesterton believed that Scottish Calvinism was 'a dead religion'.[59] In spite of the loss or dilution of Calvinist belief, however, as Stevenson aged his 'heart remembered' what it had learned and 'the taste for theology remained'.[60] In Chesterton's view, despair and hopelessness characterised the cultural movements of the early twentieth century and the joy of Stevenson's writing offered a balm for the suffering. Stevenson 'was a Christian theologian without knowing it', for if he 'could bear no witness to the Resurrection', still as a conscientious writer 'he was continually bearing witness to the Fall'.[61] In Chesterton's estimation, Stevenson was the model of a morally serious author who grappled with spiritual questions in a secularising age.

As with Mehew, Chesterton barely engaged Stevenson's intellectual life in the Pacific. He quotes Stevenson approvingly in describing the region as 'a large ocean but a narrow world', and it would be difficult to gain contemporary support for Chesterton's offhand assertion that the Pacific represented a 'simple or semi-savage world'.[62] More significantly, it is plain wrong to suggest, as he does, that Stevenson found insufficient material to interest him in the Pacific. This was far from the case, as attested by Mehew's edition of the *Letters*, which are filled with Stevenson's correspondence about the region and its people. Still, the central ideas of Chesterton's book deserve consideration. Besides growing out of a long relationship with its subject, the book reflected its author's personal knowledge of the likes of Sidney Colvin and Edmund Gosse, both old friends of Stevenson.[63]

---

[58] Chesterton *Stevenson*, 30.

[59] Chesterton, *Stevenson*, 82. Adopting a less oppositional perspective than Chesterton, Linden Bicket highlights the 'mutually enriching' nature of Catholic and Protestant literary imaginaries in modern Scottish literature. Linden Bicket, *George Mackay Brown and the Scottish Catholic Imagination* (Edinburgh: Edinburgh University Press, 2017), 12.

[60] Chesterton, *Stevenson*, 83, 126.

[61] Chesterton, *Stevenson*, 244.

[62] Chesterton, *Stevenson*, 174.

[63] Leo A. Hetzler, 'Chesterton and Robert Louis Stevenson', *The Chesterton Review* 17, 2 (1991), 177–87; Ian Ker, *G. K. Chesterton: A Biography* (Oxford: Oxford University Press, 2011), 109–10.

Its thesis was calculated to raise controversy in the Western culture of the early twentieth century, whose materialistic and psychological gods, Chesterton asserted, were intolerant of the kind of claims to religious truth he himself made as a Christian. The challenge that his study laid down provides us with an opportunity to reflect broadly on Stevenson's oeuvre. In spite of its limitations, Chesterton's book continues to bring Stevenson's life and thought into a larger conversation about the relationship between religion and the modern West.

Stevenson in a Secular Age

We can bring together the ideas discussed above to look at how religious literacy impacted Stevenson's intellectual life in the years leading up to his first Pacific voyage in 1888. The subjects that he thought about were linked to the cultural environment in which it became possible to think them: his view of Scottish Presbyterianism, for example, was shaped by its fragmentation following the Disruption of 1843, perhaps the most important event in nineteenth-century Scottish history.[64] Positioning the development of his religious thought against this dynamic historical backdrop will establish a basis from which to explore the influence of the Pacific world in his later years.

Several points should be made clear at the outset. First, the influence of Stevenson's religious upbringing on his thought was broader and more pervasive than is usually portrayed, and it would do it a disservice to divide it into, for example, 'institutional' (doctrine, ecclesiology) and 'popular' (devotion, history) forms of Scottish Presbyterianism. Rather, such aspects were typically combined. In fact, the blending of these forms made them memorable for Stevenson even when he had stopped practising the faith. From this follows the point that the history of the author's religious life could not just be said to have closed when he came to intellectual maturity in his twenties. Considered from the point of view of his religious activities in the Pacific this would simply be untrue. More than this: while he was living in the West, Stevenson's religious experience took on new dimensions as he began to encounter people and ideas that challenged the beliefs and ideas of his youth. Far from experiencing such encounters as liberating, however, he often found them to be awkward and even

---

[64] Stewart J. Brown, 'The Ten Years' Conflict and the Disruption of 1843', in *Scotland in the Age of the Disruption*, ed. by Stewart J. Brown and Michael Fry (Edinburgh: Edinburgh University Press, 1993), 1–27.

alienating. Such shifts and reversals in Stevenson's intellectual biography require explanation.

In his influential analysis of the idea of secularisation, the philosopher Charles Taylor makes a distinction that can help us to pinpoint the convergence of intellectual and social conditions in which Stevenson grew up. Taylor contrasts the 'porous' self of 'the enchanted world' with the 'buffered' self of modern 'exclusive humanism'.[65] The porous self, he argues, 'is vulnerable, to spirits, demons, cosmic forces. And along with this go certain fears which can grip it in certain circumstances.' Also, 'living in the enchanted, porous world of our ancestors was inherently living socially [. . .] spiritual forces which impinged on me [. . .] often impinged on us as a society, and were defended against by us as a society'. The porous self is characterised by a communal spiritual existence that was attuned to a cosmic sense of reality and penetrable by powers outside of immediate experience. By contrast, 'The buffered self has been taken out of the world of this kind of fear.' In fact, 'the buffered self can form the ambition of disengaging from whatever is beyond the boundary, and of giving its own autonomous order to its life. The absence of fear can be not just ignored, but seen as an opportunity for self-control or self-direction.' The buffered self is the expression of a supreme confidence in human autonomy and the mastery or ordering of the sense of an unbounded reality that presses uninvited into our lives. Taylor describes how with historical modernity comes the gradual replacement of the porous self by the buffered self, although this process is complex, nonlinear, and involves 'cross pressures'. The feeling of religious doubt or scepticism does not pass unencumbered by belief. The narrative that follows in the remainder of this chapter is that of Stevenson's encounter with this modern Western buffered self, which must be seen as simultaneously a social and an intellectual phenomenon. Within this encounter, however, lay the conditions for Stevenson's rediscovery of a porous self, which would mature when he visited the Pacific.

Although he grew up at a time when the demands and ruptures of industrial society were impinging on traditional religious life, Stevenson's sense of self was more precarious than that of others from similar middle-class backgrounds. This was partly due to his poor health and partly because of the way in which he was raised.

---

[65] The quotes in this paragraph are from Taylor, *Secular Age*, 38–42.

Long periods of sickness rendered him bedridden and kept him from experiencing the world like other children. Perhaps as a consequence, the heroes of his stories often endure states of immobility caused by illness and suffering. Chesterton described how scenes in Stevenson's fiction were written so that characters had to come out from themselves, and this drove his narrative forward.[66] It was an act of humility to imagine oneself bound to a reality that was not of one's own making, just as it was an act of faith to accept that freedom lay somewhere outside of oneself.

For all the ambivalence with which Stevenson remembered his childhood inculturation, Christianity provided him with his earliest education in what was right and wrong. In spite of the overenthusiasm of his nurse, Alison Cunningham (1822–1913), to make him 'a religious pattern', still he recounted in an autobiographical piece how as a child he 'believed all things and the good rather than the evil, was very prone to love and inaccessible to hatred, and never failed in gratitude for any benefit I had the wit to understand'.[67] Knowledge of Scripture and religious tradition particularly fed the moral imagination of the young man. Beginning from childhood, he received instruction in the Old and the New Testaments and the Westminster Confession of Faith through that Scottish rite of passage, memorisation of the Shorter Catechism. In later years, he would recall the latter with equal parts respect and reproach, for its eloquence as well as for its 'cobwebs and split hairs'.[68] The Catechism was a classic document of its historical culture, redolent 'of the Long Parliament and the "constitutional party" in religion'.[69] In a pattern of complaint about his spiritual education that he would sound throughout his life, Stevenson wished that the Shorter Catechism had done more to address 'the soul and its strong affections . . . to young minds desiring guidance and requiring trumpet notes of encouragement . . . with a more communicative and engaging ardour'.[70] Nevertheless, he respected its signal contribution to the Scottish religious-philosophical temperament and maintained

---

[66] Chesterton, *Stevenson*, 155.
[67] Robert Louis Stevenson, *The Works of Robert Louis Stevenson, Volume 29: Memories and Portraits; Memoirs of Himself; Selections from His Notebook* (Tusitala Edition, London: William Heinemann, 1924), 157–8.
[68] Stevenson, *Letters* IV, 226.
[69] Stevenson, *Letters* IV, 226.
[70] Stevenson, *Letters* IV, 226. Arguably, his call was reflected in changing nineteenth-century attitudes towards doctrinal statements in Scottish Presbyterianism. Donald Macleod, 'The Significance of the Westminster Confession', in Fergusson and Elliott, *History of Scottish Theology*, Volume II, 1–13.

all his life that its opening question and answer was 'purely sublime':[71] 'Q. What is the chief end of man? A. Man's chief end is to glorify God, and to enjoy Him for ever.'

The Westminster Confession was transmitted to believers through Sunday sermons and the home visits of parish ministers. As a churchgoer in Scotland up to his early twenties, Stevenson was also accustomed to worship on the basis of the 1647 Westminster Directory. At church he would have engaged in established practices like common prayer as well as relatively new ones for the Victorian Church of Scotland, such as the singing of hymns.[72] Stevenson was familiar with the environment and architecture of churches and the organisational hierarchy of the Kirk (elders, ministers, presbyteries, sessions, and the General Assembly).[73] He understood that a church consisted of leaders who commanded obedience and members who were responsible and educated, so that religious commitment spilled out into the wider world in the form of schools, charities, and mission associations.[74] At mid-century, membership of a Scottish church implied that one belonged to a global as well as a national community.[75]

Being a Christian in Edinburgh also meant that one lived in the middle of a fragmented denominational landscape. 'Edinburgh is a city of churches', Stevenson wrote in 1879, 'as though it were a place of pilgrimage'.[76] One reason for this variety was a series of dramatic religious splits, the largest and most recent being the Disruption of 1843, when the Free Church and the Voluntaries voted with their feet against the Church of Scotland. Stevenson ironically alluded to this event in *The Misadventures of John Nicholson* as one of the two causes (along with his family) for which John's severe father

---

[71] Stevenson, *Letters* IV, 226.
[72] A. C. Cheyne, *The Transforming of the Kirk: Victorian Scotland's Religious Revolution* (Edinburgh: The Saint Andrew Press, 1983), 88–109; Bryan D. Spinks, *Scottish Presbyterian Worship: Proposals for Organic Change, 1843 to the Present Day* (Edinburgh: The Saint Andrew Press, 2020), 84–97.
[73] See Chapter 5 for a consideration of Stevenson's relationship with the church.
[74] See his letter 'To the Editor of the Church of Scotland Home and Foreign Missionary Record', in Stevenson, *Letters* I, 212–13.
[75] Esther Breitenbach demonstrates the relationship between Scottish missionary activity and the British empire in the nineteenth century. Esther Breitenbach, 'The Influence of the Missionary Movement in Scotland', in *Roots and Fruits: Retrieving Scotland's Missionary Story*, ed. by Kenneth R. Ross (Padstow: Regnum, 2014), 57–69.
[76] Robert Louis Stevenson, *Edinburgh: Picturesque Notes* (London: Seeley, Jackson and Halliday, 1879), 16.

'entirely lived'.⁷⁷ The later nineteenth century also saw the growth of other denominational groups in Scotland including Episcopalians and Catholics, many of the latter arriving from Ireland in several migratory waves.⁷⁸ The relations between these groups were complex and Scottish Presbyterians often came into conflict with Irish Catholics, whom they regarded as a ghettoised foreign community.⁷⁹ Growing up amid these dense denominational clusters focused one's attention on the connections between religion and ethnicity.

Doctrine, confession, and church multiplied across nineteenth-century Scotland and conveyed a sense of Christianity's cultural expansion. But conditions closer to home anchored religion's pervasiveness in the mind of Stevenson. Knowledge about the various local Christian traditions was enfolded within a culture that was rooted much more securely among the masses than was the Scottish Enlightenment.⁸⁰ Stevenson belonged to the confessional world of the Church of Scotland as a member of a Victorian Evangelical family. This would significantly shape his outlook. According to the historian of religion David Bebbington, 'The tone of Evangelicalism permeated nearly the whole of later Victorian religion outside the Roman Catholic Church' and, despite variations according to time and circumstance, rested on a 'quadrilateral of priorities': '*conversionism*, the belief that lives need to be changed; *activism*, the expression of the gospel in effort; *biblicism*, a particular regard for the Bible; and what may be called *crucicentrism*, a stress on the sacrifice of Christ on the cross'.⁸¹ Several of these elements can be discerned in Stevenson's life and attitudes: the strong emphasis on the authority of Scripture over various forms of modern reasoning as well as over other sources of religious authority, such as the Kirk; the early and lasting admiration for missionary work; the personal and imaginative emphasis on the importance of physical activity; and the overall wariness of 'the priesthood and the sacraments'.⁸²

---

[77] Robert Louis Stevenson, *The Misadventures of John Nicholson*, in *Tales and Fantasies* (London: Chatto and Windus, 1920), 4.

[78] Brown, 'Beliefs and Religions', 133, 134.

[79] Stewart J. Brown, 'Presbyterians and Catholics in Twentieth-Century Scotland', in *Scottish Christianity in the Modern World: In Honour of A. C. Cheyne*, ed. by Stewart J. Brown and George Newlands (Edinburgh: T&T Clark, 2000), 255–82 (258–61).

[80] Brown, *People in the Pews*, 30–2.

[81] David Bebbington, *Evangelicalism in Modern Britain: A History from the 1730s to the 1980s* (London and New York: Routledge, 1993), 2–3.

[82] Bebbington, *Evangelicalism in Modern Britain*, 3.

While homes such as the Stevensons' were typically graced with the Bible and 'dog-eared Puritan and Covenanting devotional works', Robert Louis acquired a personal feel for Presbyterian Christianity because he was the son of devout parents.[83] The Stevenson household observed Sundays strictly as a Sabbath day and regularly set time aside for family prayers. His father Thomas (1818–87), a civil engineer and meteorologist, came from a family of engineers but was also a Latin scholar and wrote Christian apologetics and theology in his leisure, with an Evangelical emphasis on the doctrine of atonement and defence of the supernatural against Humean sceptics.[84] His mother, Margaret Isabella (1829–97), the daughter of Reverend Lewis Balfour of Colinton, came from a faithful Church of Scotland family and was an enthusiastic supporter of missions. Activities such as supporting foreign missions, raising money for church building, and teaching Bible classes were part of the voluntarist Evangelical culture of the urban middle classes in Scotland and, according to the historian Callum Brown, helped to establish their identity against both the older rural church communities and the working classes.[85] The social environment in which the family's religious life was embedded formed Robert Louis Stevenson's peculiarly denominational perspective as much as the works of Scottish Presbyterian history and theology that he read.

The other critical figure in Stevenson's religious education was Alison Cunningham ('Cummy'), who introduced him to adventure stories, Scottish folklore, and the dramatic history of the Covenanters.[86] He dedicated his much-loved *Child's Garden of Verses* to this 'second Mother' and 'first Wife', grateful 'for all the story-books you read'.[87] Fiction conveyed meaning in a way that was different to historical argument, and Cunningham's storytelling influenced how Stevenson would communicate Scottish history. The violent and scary tales that she told the young man also lent a visceral potency to his religious formation. Stevenson inherited a Calvinist conviction in the innate sinfulness of the world but he was also sensitive

---

[83] Brown, 'Beliefs and Religions', 118.
[84] Thomas Stevenson, *Christianity Confirmed by Jewish and Heathen Testimony and the Deductions from Physical Science, etc.* (Edinburgh: David Douglas, 1879).
[85] Callum G. Brown, *Religion and Society in Scotland since 1707* (Edinburgh: Edinburgh University Press, 1997), 101–10.
[86] Lim, 'Calvinism and Forms of Storytelling', 91–5.
[87] Robert Louis Stevenson, *A Child's Garden of Verses* (London: Longmans, Green, and Co., 1885).

'to the presence of ghosts, of spirits out of the past'.[88] There was in addition the sheer thrill of encountering Scottish religious history through stories, which he sought to replicate in his writing. By comparison, Stevenson wrote notably little on key figures of the Scottish Enlightenment such as Adam Smith and David Hume, a subject that a few other Edinburgh Tories of his day did much to recover.[89] Besides literary figures such as Burns and Scott, Stevenson's imagination of Scotland's past was largely made up of people and events that were connected to its religious history, from Alexander Peden and the Pentland Rising to Culloden and Flora MacDonald. Thanks in large part to Cunningham, Stevenson discovered that religion could be an adventure, thrilling and terrifying, and that Scots who were motivated by religious passion were as impressive and worthy of remembrance as the country's celebrated intellectual heroes.

Biographers often identify a key moment in the young Stevenson's life as being his break with his parents' religious beliefs in the early 1870s. Few, however, have followed the progress of his religious views in the years that followed.[90] The remainder of this chapter will explore how, through the process of separating himself intellectually from his parents, Stevenson became sensitive to different ways of being Christian. The experience of alienation after the loss of the shelter provided by family religion contributed to his realisation that one's moral and spiritual life could be powerfully sustained through community, and that the loss of such community was therefore deeply meaningful to the believer.

Historians are beginning to recognise how major intellectual figures of the nineteenth century who were once associated with secularisation, such as Charles Darwin and Karl Marx, were in fact participants in a deeply Christian-influenced debate about the meaning of religion in society and the true ends of human life. Whatever one's formal religious identity, Timothy Larsen asserts that 'No straightforward secularity should be imagined.'[91] Instead, as Frank Turner has shown, what seemed like earnest intellectual disputes

---

[88] Jenni Calder, 'Introduction', in *Stevenson and Victorian Scotland*, 8.

[89] Christopher Harvie, 'The Politics of Stevenson', in Calder, *Stevenson and Victorian Scotland*, 113–14. Stevenson had planned to include Hume in a work to be titled *Four Great Scotchmen* – the other three would have been John Knox, Robert Burns, and Walter Scott. But he admitted there was 'much that I don't yet know as to his work'. Stevenson, *Letters* I, 474–5.

[90] An important exception is Abrahamson, 'Truth Out of Tusitala Spoke'.

[91] Timothy Larsen, *John Stuart Mill: A Secular Life* (Oxford: Oxford University Press, 2018), 8.

between believers and unbelievers were usually complex contests for power, often between different groups of Christians.[92] While the matter of disbelief was taken seriously and felt keenly, in Scotland as well as in other parts of Britain the fundamental religious issue of the second half of the century was the tension between forms of establishment religion and religious dissent.[93] As is now well known, the famous conflict between religion and science was promoted by well-mobilised low church Christians and dissenters, often from less privileged social backgrounds, who were ultimately able to usurp the power of high churchmen from the British scientific establishment.[94] These changes took place over decades, however, and were gradual and uneven. During this period of transition, for example, Scottish university philosophy departments continued to be populated by committed Christians who guided the nation's intellectual reception of German idealism.[95]

Like any intelligent European of the mid-nineteenth century, Stevenson sought to engage with the ideas of modern thinkers, which meant adapting and integrating their work into his own pre-existing worldview. Through his late adolescence into his twenties he read and evaluated many of the important writers of the day. Herbert Spencer (1820–1903), the philosopher of the benign necessity of Progress, was an important influence and Stevenson even wrote some verses about him.[96] Although he barely mentions Spencer in his letters after the early 1880s, in a journal article of 1887, 'Books Which Have Influenced Me', he dedicates a paragraph to this 'persuasive rabbi'.[97] The epideictic vocabulary of this passage is noteworthy. Stevenson praises Spencer for his 'manly and honest' words rather than for 'the vast structure' of his philosophy. He

---

[92] Frank Turner, 'The Victorian Conflict between Science and Religion: A Professional Dimension', in *Contesting Cultural Authority: Essays in Victorian Intellectual Life* (Cambridge: Cambridge University Press, 1993), 171–200.
[93] Hoppen, *Mid-Victorian Generation*, 447.
[94] Turner, 'Victorian Conflict'.
[95] See *Scottish Philosophy in the Nineteenth and Twentieth Centuries*, ed. by Gordon Graham (Oxford: Oxford University Press, 2015), especially chapters 4, 6, and 7, on the reception of Kant and Hegel. The Scottish reception of Hegel influenced Stevenson's religious disagreement with his father. See Stevenson, *Letters* IV, 221 and n.
[96] Stevenson, *Letters* III, 240n. Thomas Stevenson believed that reading Spencer had 'unsettled' his son's faith. Stevenson, *Letters* III, 43.
[97] All quotes from this text are from Robert Louis Stevenson, 'Books Which Have Influenced Me: A Paper Contributed to "The British Weekly", May 13, 1887' (Greenwich, CT: The Literary Collector Press, 1905).

spiritualises the traits of Spencer's writing that he finds laudable: 'a spirit of highly abstract joy', 'a *caput mortuum* of piety', words that are 'wholesome' and 'bracing'. He tries to win Spencer over to his conservative readers by making a moral, even a religious, set of claims about his writing.[98] Rather than conveying the sentiments of a convinced atheist or agnostic, this is an apologetic strategy which was designed to reduce the apparent gap between Christianity and Spencer's view of things.[99]

Stevenson's target throughout 'Books Which Have Influenced Me' is hypocrisy dressed as convention and his constant refrain is that readers are as important as books. In order to make these points he draws on the Western Christian tradition and describes *The Pilgrim's Progress* as 'a book that breathes of every beautiful and valuable emotion'. Terms and distinctions drawn from religion help him to evaluate the excellence of other kinds of writing: Montaigne's *Essays* 'flutter' our 'excited orthodoxies' while Walt Whitman's *Leaves of Grass* 'invigorated his creed'. Between the passages in which these expressions appear there is a pithy paean to the Gospel according to St Matthew, which remained his favourite of the four to the end of his life.[100] Stevenson encourages readers to 'make a certain effort of imagination and read [this Gospel] freshly like a book, not droningly and dully like a portion of the Bible'. The parable of the sower (Matthew 13: 1–23) is the inspiration of the essay's conclusion. In 'the hands of any genuine reader', words 'will be weighed and winnowed, and only that which suits will be assimilated', while words that fall into the hands of one who 'cannot intelligently read' will 'come there quite silent and inarticulate, falling upon deaf ears', and the author's 'secret is kept as if he had not written'. Stevenson's modern gloss on the parable has

---

[98] Jack, 'Death of the Master', 298.

[99] Stevenson pursues a similar critical strategy in his essay about another literary hero, Walt Whitman. Of *Leaves of Grass* he writes, 'There is much that is Christian in these extracts, startlingly Christian.' Robert Louis Stevenson, 'Walt Whitman', in *Familiar Studies of Men and Books* (London: Chatto and Windus, 1882), 127. Stevenson deleted two sentences from his original magazine article and replaced them with this sentence, possibly to please his father. My thanks to Robert-Louis Abrahamson for providing this information.

[100] According to the British missionary in Samoa J. E. Newell, Stevenson found Matthew's Gospel 'most helpful as a portraiture of [Christ's] life and teaching'. J. E. Newell, 'R. L. Stevenson as I Knew Him', *Christchurch Press*, 2 March 1907. National Library of Australia, nla.obj-2739135234. In another list of his favourite books he mentions the Psalms, the Book of Job and Isiah. Harry Ransom Collection, University of Texas at Austin: Robert Louis Stevenson Collection, MS-4035, Miscellaneous, Box 2, Folder 1.

the writer replacing the sower and the word replacing the seed. He blends the image with other Gospel passages concerning judgement (e.g. Matthew 3: 12). Demonstrating Stevenson's facility with New Testament verses and imagery, the effect is playful but also serious about the importance of readers' receptivity.

The tendency to view modern thought with a religious eye was ingrained in him. The philosopher Georg Wilhelm Friedrich Hegel (1770–1831), who 'fascinated a generation of Scotsmen', and of whom Stevenson's opinion appears to have changed over time, was initially the object of Biblical scrutiny in a letter of 1868 to his cousin Bob.[101] Stevenson thought the German 'a most egregious ass' and confirmed his view through Scripture:

> The great old question of the Almighty, which has found an echo in every age and in every heart, ever since it rang to Job upon his dungheap, would seem to apply full well: 'Who is this that darkeneth counsel with words without knowledge?'[102]

The conviction from the Book of Job (38: 2), which expressed the deep unknowability of God, was emblazoned in the young man's mind. The conviction did not discourage thought, either. When he entered Edinburgh University in 1869 he joined the Speculative Society, where in 1872 he gave a talk entitled 'Two Questions on the Relation between Christ's Teaching and Modern Christianity'.[103] In the same month, he proposed a debate on a typical subject of modern Biblical criticism, 'Have we any authority for the inspiration of the New Testament?'[104] These topics prefigured Stevenson's confrontation with the principal source of establishment views of religion: his family.

The episode involving the letter of 2 February 1873 to his friend Charles Baxter, in which Louis relates how 'my father put me one or two questions as to beliefs, which I candidly answered', has sometimes been interpreted as the beginning of a definitive break

---

[101] Paul Guyer, 'The Scottish Reception of Kant', in Graham, *Scottish Philosophy*, 158.
[102] Stevenson, *Letters* I, 143.
[103] Stevenson, *Letters* I, 259n.
[104] Stevenson, *Letters* I, 259. Such themes, redolent of the age, would remain an object of his fascination. 'Robertson Smith is great fun', he wrote to his mother in July 1879. The Free Church theologian was the subject of a famous heresy trial. Stevenson, *Letters* II, 327 and n. On the Scottish excitement over the Robertson Smith trial, see Craig Beveridge and Ronald Turnbull, *Scotland after Enlightenment: Image and Tradition in Modern Scottish Culture* (Edinburgh: Polygon, 1997), 144.

with Christian orthodoxy.[105] Besides being a vivid portrayal of his confused mental state, the letter also portrays a young man's sincere plea to his parents to be allowed to come to his own judgement on matters that all agreed were of ultimate significance. 'I am not (as they call me) a careless infidel' and 'I have not come hastily to my views', he writes. Although Stevenson felt that he had botched the attempt to communicate the news sensitively, he nevertheless thought he was not 'justly to be called a "horrible atheist"'. He wanted only his parents' patience: 'I reserve (as I told them) many points until I acquire fuller information.' In many respects, it was a typical episode in the life of a mid-Victorian Evangelical family: serious, emotional, and filled with allusions to private judgement. Stevenson's resistance demonstrated a thoughtful if youthful stance that would not be driven unreasonably to faith. Rather than representing a break with Christian belief, it better fits the evidence if we view the episode as part of the wider struggle between established religion and dissent. Although the Auld Kirk was usually the last to submit to change, Stevenson grew up in a climate of religious reform in Scotland and was conscious of various innovations and challenges to traditional authority.[106] His characterisation of himself to his parents as a selective adherent of the Westminster Confession would have been quite uncontroversial had his family been members of the Scottish United Presbyterian Church rather than the Church of Scotland, for example.[107]

Nevertheless, this period marked the end of Stevenson's formal participation in religious activity as he had known it since childhood. Referencing another author we might observe that, rather than 'conclusive logical arguments', it was 'the appeal of certain virtues' which pulled him away from Christian orthodoxy and drew him towards positions that reflected 'courage, manliness, and a willingness to confront the world'.[108] And yet at the same time, we should note that it

---

[105] All quotations from this paragraph are taken from Stevenson, *Letters* I, 273. J. C. Furnas, *Voyage to Windward: The Life of Robert Louis Stevenson* (London: Faber and Faber, 1952), 65; Ernest Mehew, 'Robert Louis Stevenson', in *Oxford Dictionary of National Biography* (Oxford: Oxford University Press, 2004), accessed at: https://doi.org/10.1093/ref:odnb/26438 on 5 August 2021; Patrick Parr, 'Robert Louis Stevenson Says No to Religion', *The Humanist* (September/October 2015), 20–2.

[106] Cheyne, *Transforming of the Kirk*.

[107] Brown, 'Beliefs and Religions', 120.

[108] Peter Steinfels, 'Modernity and Belief: Charles Taylor's *A Secular Age*', *Commonweal*, 5 May 2008.

was his initial discovery of the transcendent moral universe of Christianity as revealed through Scriptural sources such as the Book of Job and the Gospel of Matthew that provided him with the basis on which to judge the attitudes and behaviour of conventional society. Not the theological remnant of Calvinism in the modern Church of Scotland but rather its fastidious application of rules, combined with the apparent hypocrisy of bourgeois Edinburgh, provided the tension that enlivens a work such as *The Misadventures of John Nicholson*.

Biblical morality within a Scottish context, rather than modern science and materialist philosophy, would remain the central element in Stevenson's thought. The rhetorical and ethical position of a story such as 'The Body Snatcher' (1884), set in and around Edinburgh in the early nineteenth century, is implicitly and locally Christian. The story's horror centres on the desecration of objects of 'customary piety', and the apparent bravery of Fettes, toasting to 'the memory of Gray' as he expresses his contempt for 'Hell, God, Devil, right, wrong, sin, crime, and all the old gallery of curiosities', becomes gruesomely ironic by the end.[109] As demonstrated through such stories' 'vocabulary, concept and narrative' Stevenson had become an exponent of 'vicarious religion'.[110] He understood and approved of the religious practices of his family although he no longer participated in them. He remained close to the Church of Scotland but he no longer identified as a churchgoing Christian.

The move away from family religion coincided with entry into a different social circle. Stevenson made the first steps in his career as a writer just as he was wrestling with a new religious identity. As we have seen, his Christian formation had consisted of more than assent to the catechetical formulae of the Church of Scotland: it involved his embedding in a community of believers with a distinctive tradition of worship, practices of evangelisation, and religious and social outreach. As he realised his literary ambitions, he broke away from this religious world. During the turbulent mid-1870s, just as the 'full force of doubt came to the social elite', Stevenson became drawn into a predominantly English society of authors, editors, and publishers that appeared to have little time for Christian talk and attitudes.[111] He found that he had to learn to curb his religious instincts and to carve out space to engage the questions of belief that continued to stimulate him.

---

[109] Robert Louis Stevenson, 'The Body Snatcher', in *Tales and Fantasies*, 107–8, 110.
[110] Davie, 'Foreword', ix.
[111] Larsen, *Crisis of Doubt*, 248.

Stevenson enjoyed the literary and artistic freedom of London and the Continent. He could not be so easily a stranger in Edinburgh as he was in the artist's colony at Grez where he met his future wife, the American Frances (Fanny) van de Grift Osbourne (1840–1914), and her children. Although now freely able to fashion a new self-identity, he was often reminded of how much he differed from this set. Religious literacy was proving to be a stumbling block in his interactions. Stevenson was religiously knowledgeable and expressive in a way that many of his peers were not or did not want to be. While he 'continued to use the word "God" without irony', his friends 'had little patience for religious language'.[112] He wrote to Sidney Colvin in half jest that 'my Bible quotations are sadly thrown away on so ignorant an unbeliever as you'.[113] He often had to censor himself in order to maintain social ease. Literary friends who had come from Evangelical backgrounds, such as Leslie Stephen and Edmund Gosse, had effected a much more dramatic separation from their roots than had Stevenson, and they maintained a more antagonistic stance towards Christianity.[114] Although Stevenson had cast aside what he considered to be the joyless strictures of Scottish Calvinism and bourgeois Edinburgh respectability, this was far from a time of liberation among bohemians and freethinkers; instead it was a momentous encounter with the buffered self of modernity. The implicit challenge laid down by his new social and intellectual environment was to teach oneself to be self-possessing and to assume nothing outside of one's self-organised reality. His essays of the 1880s, such as 'Pulvis et Umbra', reflected the sense of courageous striving in the midst of a disordered and unknowable scientific universe: 'Our religions and moralities have been trimmed to flatter us, till they are all emasculate and sentimentalized, and only please and weaken. Truth is of a rougher strain. In the harsh face of life, faith can read a bracing gospel.'[115] The duty of labouring

---

[112] Abrahamson, 'Truth Out of Tusitala Spoke', 242–3.
[113] Stevenson, *Letters* I, 309.
[114] Noel Annan, *Leslie Stephen: The Godless Victorian* (Chicago: University of Chicago Press, 1984); Edmund Gosse, *Father and Son* (Oxford: Oxford University Press, 2004 [1907]). Charles Taylor identifies in Stephen a 'continual need to form and steel the will, to fight off baser desire in the name of duty' which is also present in aspects of the work of other (post-)Evangelical writers, including Stevenson. Taylor, *Secular Age*, 396.
[115] Robert Louis Stevenson, *Across the Plains* (London: Chatto and Windus, 1892), 289–90.

in cause of the unknown, also found in kindred Scottish writers such as George MacDonald (1824–1905), was expressed here in a more austerely materialistic language.[116]

However, less than a decade after the break with his family Stevenson began to show dissatisfaction with the buffered existence and he wrote to his father in a religious vein.[117] He asked Thomas Stevenson to pray for him as he worked on a piece of writing, moved by the death of his friend James Walter Ferrier (1850–83), which was designed to help young men 'who may be, in their youth entire unbelievers'.[118] The social experience of his burgeoning professional career had helped him to better understand his own religious convictions. When 'the creature' is 'judged, as he must be by his creator', Stevenson wrote, he is 'not dissected through a prism of morals, but as the unrefracted ray'.[119] He preached that same holistic outlook on Christianity in 'Lay Morals', the essay he was working on during this period. Christ taught 'not a code of rules, but a ruling spirit; not truths, but a spirit of truth; not views, but a view'.[120] By the following summer Stevenson was writing to ask friends and family for a Bible to read.[121]

Stevenson's other important discovery of the period was the need to nurture one's faith through a sympathetic community, such as a family, which shared the same emotional vocabulary and associations. Characteristically, he best expressed this thought through fiction. Amid the professional successes of the 1880s, Stevenson worked on two historical projects: one on the Anglo-Scottish Union of 1707 and the other on the transformation of the Scottish Highlands in the aftermath of the Jacobite rebellion. These would ultimately bear

---

[116] Martin Dubois, 'Sermon and Story in George Macdonald', *Victorian Literature and Culture* 43, 3 (2015), 577–87 (580).

[117] Abrahamson, 'Truth Out of Tusitala Spoke', 243.

[118] Stevenson, *Letters* IV, 172. The letter is dated 2 October 1883. Thomas Stevenson's reply, on 7 October, expressed his pleasure at his son's request. Stevenson, *Letters* IV, 182n.

[119] Stevenson, *Letters* IV, 183. Cf. Newman's famous words on conscience: 'This law, as apprehended in the minds of individual men, is called "conscience;" and though it may suffer refraction in passing into the intellectual medium of each, it is not therefore so affected as to lose its character of being the Divine Law.' John Henry Cardinal Newman, *Certain Difficulties Felt by Anglicans in Catholic Teaching Considered*, Vol. II (London: Longmans, Green, and Co., 1900 [1874]), 247.

[120] Robert Louis Stevenson, 'Lay Morals', in *The Works of Robert Louis Stevenson; Miscellanies, Volume IV*, ed. by Sidney Colvin (Edinburgh: Longmans, Green, and Co., 1896), 317.

[121] Stevenson, *Letters* IV, 301, 305.

fruit not as works of history but in the form of a historical novel, *Kidnapped*.[122] This profoundly religious work was built on his experiences of buffered modernity and Scottish ecclesiological fragmentation.[123] Stevenson emphasised the character-forming significance of the Highland Jacobite communities and their difference from the less porous civilisation of Lowlanders such as David Balfour. In the enchanted world of the Highlands, organised according to loyalty and obedience, belief is more closely bound to social organisation as communities collectively experienced joy and misery. At one point in the story, the Highlanders Alan Breck and James of the Glens are appalled to hear that David believes only the murderer of Colin Campbell will be punished for the crime.[124] On the contrary, the two men well know that legal responsibility in the Highlands is a corporate affair, whatever the written laws of the state might proclaim, and that the Campbells would be sure to punish Stewarts like themselves for the murder of one of their own on Stewart land. In a similar way, while a man such as Alan Breck might acknowledge faith in rational religion, he would be sure to make the sign of the cross as a protection against evil water spirits. For such communities there was no either/or in these matters: the boundary between the self and the spiritual world was porous. Meanwhile, David Balfour battles with the contradictions of the buffered self, terrified as Alan when he hears the wailing sounds in the river below but struggling nevertheless to discipline his imagination and determine reality through an act of will. Such 'cross pressures', Charles Taylor argues, are characteristic of the secular age.[125]

The year after the publication of *Kidnapped* there arrived that classic novel of Victorian religious crisis, *Robert Elsmere* (1888). The battle of belief was truly in the air.[126] As with his contemporaries,

---

[122] Menikoff, *Narrating Scotland*.

[123] In a fascinating piece, Matthew Grenby offers an overlooked historical context for the writing of *Kidnapped*: the so-called Crofters' War of the 1880s. M. O. Grenby, 'History in Fiction: Contextualization as Interpretation in Robert Louis Stevenson's *Kidnapped*', in *The Oxford Handbook of Children's Literature*, ed. by L. Vallone and J. Mickenberg (Oxford: Oxford University Press, 2011), 275–92. On the relationship between the Highlands, its people, and Christianity in the nineteenth century, see Allan W. MacColl, *Land, Faith and the Crofting Community: Christianity and Social Criticism in the Highlands of Scotland, 1843–1893* (Edinburgh: Edinburgh University Press, 2006).

[124] Stevenson, *Kidnapped*, 193–4.

[125] Taylor, *Secular Age*, chapter 16.

[126] W. E. Gladstone, *'Robert Elsmere' and the Battle of Belief* (New York: Anson D. F. Randolph and Co., [1888]).

questions of faith and doubt were complicated for Stevenson by the variety of positions on offer. Concerning denominational Christianity, he was knowledgeable and cultured as well as imaginative and sympathetic. But Stevenson had resisted many of the demands of conventional Christian life and he was reluctant to accept religious dogma without question. By 1888, he occupied a position that was perhaps more of the church than in the church, although as the letter to Adelaide Boodle demonstrates, he would continue to be passionate about ecclesiology.[127] For the moment, he had come to see how being religiously literate could involve engaging substantially with new ideas and philosophies. He had moved beyond positivist and rationalist theories without entirely casting them aside as he sought to better articulate the modern world. He had also discovered that communities could nurture and sustain a religious humour and sympathy. When his family's religion had proven to be too constricting he sought this community among a new professional group, though to little avail. But, by stages, he returned to the fold, if not quite the prodigal son then at least a wanderer, and continued to seek out his father's spiritual support. Built on a foundation of Scriptural authority that had become problematic, he carried this tangle of discoveries and impulses with him as he set out on his first Pacific voyage in the summer of 1888.

Modern scholarship has overlooked what has been characterised here as Stevenson's religious literacy. The reasons for this are complex and to explore them in depth would require study of the modern conditions of knowledge production and the social basis from which change arises. While that is beyond this book's purview, I have shown how the dearth of attention to religious subjects is not exceptional in the field of Scottish literature or Stevenson studies. The downplaying of religion reflects contemporary secular assessments of its peripheral status. But, as I have tried to demonstrate in this chapter, developing a robust conception of Stevenson's religious literacy is critical because it helps us to form a more accurate and realistic picture of our subject's intellectual trajectory. The simplistic agnosticism of Mehew's Stevenson demonstrates why the claim of Stevenson's religious literacy should be taken seriously, for without it our interpretations of Stevenson's thought are likely to be restricted by the master narrative of secularisation. We will risk missing the richness of Stevenson's encounter with the important ideas of his time.

---

[127] See Chapter 5 for a development of this theme.

Although this portrayal of Stevenson as religiously literate does not depend on analysing his confessional commitment, being more precise about the context and meaning of his writing concerning religious subjects can illumine what constituted belief for him. Religion is not a matter that could easily be compartmentalised in Stevenson. It stimulated his thought, marked his speech, and affected his behaviour. Therefore, the radically different conditions that he encountered in the Pacific particularly inspired him. In contrast to late-nineteenth-century Scotland, and as Rocio Figueroa and Philip Gibbs have argued, 'religiosity is an orthodox and often-taken-for-granted component of Pacific identity' such that 'the differentiation between religious and non-religious experience is foreign to many people of the Pacific'.[128] The basis of the master narrative of Western religious modernity, the line between the secular and the sacred, was hardly relevant at all in places such as Samoa. The impact of this discovery on Stevenson's mind would be considerable. In the next chapter we shall see how it shaped his ethnography.

---

[128] Rocio Figueroa and Philip Gibbs, 'Catholics', in *Christianity in Oceania*, ed. by Kenneth R. Ross, Katalina Tahaafe-Williams, and Todd M. Johnson (Edinburgh: Edinburgh University Press, 2021), 190–204 (191).

Chapter 2

Pacific Ethnography and the Anthropology of Christianity

Between 1888 and 1890 Stevenson and his family travelled widely across the Pacific. During their first period of voyaging, between June 1888 and December 1889, they visited the Marquesas Islands, the Paumotus (Tuamotus), Tahiti, Hawai'i, and the Gilberts (Kiribati). Then, after deciding to settle in Samoa, they went on another journey between February and September 1890, this time visiting Australia, New Zealand, Penrhyn (one of the Cook Islands), the Marshall Islands, and New Caledonia. Stevenson observed carefully while he was on the move and he talked with local leaders, traders, missionaries, and other inhabitants of the islands in order to learn about them. Although he did not remain for longer than a few months in any one place, he was able to visit more of the Pacific than other visitors of his time. He felt confident enough to write to his friend Charles Baxter in September 1888 that he would be able to 'tell you more of the South Seas after very few months than any other writer has done'.[1] In Samoa, from September 1890, he revised the journal of his Pacific travels for serial publication in Britain and the United States.[2] In spite of the fact that he did not complete 'The South Seas', the larger synthetic work that he had planned at the outset of his journey, these published literary South Seas Letters

---

[1] *The Letters of Robert Louis Stevenson*, ed. by Bradford A. Booth and Ernest Mehew (New Haven, CT: Yale University Press, 1994–5), VI, 207.
[2] See Roger Swearingen, 'New Light on the South Seas', *EDRLS* Blog, accessed at: https://edrls.wordpress.com/2014/04/04/new-light-on-the-south-seas/ on 17 September 2021.

contain valuable information about the region and are the focus of the present chapter.³

Scholars of this body of Stevenson's writing have sought to position it within the context of the history of anthropology.⁴ However, rather than seeking to obtain for him a place alongside the discipline's Victorian founders, they have tended to highlight instead Stevenson's problematic relationship to that genealogy. Taking his fiction and non-fiction together, Julia Reid assesses that 'a sustained ambivalence towards anthropology's progressive narrative unites his oeuvre'.⁵ In particular, she notes that Stevenson's posthumously published volume of travel writing, *In the South Seas*, 'draws on Darwinism to challenge the Spencerian *laissez-faire* evolutionism which underlay the new science of anthropology'.⁶ Reid finds that, although Stevenson was highly interested in the work of Victorian anthropologists, he was sceptical of their optimistic claims about human development and resisted theories emphasising cultural progress. Therefore, she concludes, Stevenson's ethnographic writing 'sheds light on the discipline at a pivotal stage in its development, pointing forward intriguingly to the twentieth century's more relativist anthropology and to its developing concern with cultural plurality'.⁷

---

³ For example, a contemporary anthropologist observes that 'historical sources providing information on [the Tuamotu archipelago] in the eighteenth and nineteenth centuries' are 'less abundant' than for other parts of eastern Polynesia. Émilie Nolet, 'Coconuts and Rosaries: Materiality in the Catholic Christianisation of the Tuamotu Archipelago (French Polynesia)', *The Journal of the Polynesian Society* 129, 3 (2020), 275–302 (275). Neil Rennie's introduction to Stevenson's *In the South Seas* provides an account of the breakdown of the author's attempts to write a 'Big Book' about the Pacific. Robert Louis Stevenson, *In the South Seas*, ed. by Neil Rennie (London: Penguin, 1998), viii–xxxv. All bracketed in-text references in this chapter are to this edition of *In the South Seas*.

⁴ See especially Julia Reid, 'Stevenson as Anthropologist: Culture, Folklore, and Language', in *Robert Louis Stevenson, Science, and the Fin de Siècle* (Basingstoke: Palgrave Macmillan, 2006), 107–73; Richard Ambrosini, 'The Four Boundary-Crossings of R. L. Stevenson, Novelist and Anthropologist', in *Robert Louis Stevenson: Writer of Boundaries*, ed. by Richard Ambrosini and Richard Dury (Madison: University of Wisconsin Press, 2006), 23–35; Roslyn Jolly, 'The Travel-Writer as Anthropologist: *In the South Seas*', in *Robert Louis Stevenson in the Pacific: Travel, Empire, and the Author's Profession* (Farnham: Ashgate, 2009), 29–65; Lucio De Capitani, 'World Literature and the Anthropological Imagination: Ethnographic Encounters in European and South Asian Writing, 1885–2016' (PhD thesis, Università Ca' Foscari Venezia, 2019), 69–86.

⁵ Reid, *Stevenson, Science, and the Fin de Siècle*, 139.

⁶ Reid, *Stevenson, Science, and the Fin de Siècle*, 143.

⁷ Reid, *Stevenson, Science, and the Fin de Siècle*, 173.

In her interpretation of Stevenson as anthropologist, Roslyn Jolly establishes significant connections between the author's Pacific ethnography and his intellectual background in Scottish and Roman traditions of comparative law. According to Jolly, Stevenson 'believed that Roman ways of thought had determined the characteristic qualities of the Western mind, with both enabling and disabling effects' and 'Stevenson's anthropological project in the Pacific' was 'to discover "what men might be" who had never been subjected to the influence of the Roman Empire'.[8] The Scottish legal tradition in which Stevenson was educated at the University of Edinburgh trained him 'to make sense of the multiple frames of cultural reference juxtaposed by nineteenth-century imperial expansion: it gave him the habit of comparative thought, which pervades *In the South Seas*'.[9] Jolly tethers Stevenson's comparativist ethnography to the relativist anthropology of the early to mid-twentieth century. His 'investigative project', she claims, 'belongs to a particular strand of Victorian anthropology, which lay outside the mainstream of contemporary anthropological thought, but whose significance would become apparent with the development of social and legal anthropology in the twentieth century'.[10]

Reid and Jolly make important and substantial contributions that cannot be adequately summarised here, which uncover the intellectual roots of Stevenson's Pacific ethnography and demonstrate its significance. But it is my contention that, by paying closer attention to the relationship between religion and anthropology, we can expand the scope of their claims while anchoring them more firmly within appropriate historical contexts. As I outlined in Chapter 1, we benefit from acknowledging the organising function of religion among the various ideas and traditions that characterised Stevenson's intellectual maturity. This is because, by doing so, we gain a sense of the wider stakes of his writing. To give an example related to the present context, as the philosopher Rémi Brague has illuminatingly explained, the Roman Empire and Christianity were complexly related even long after the Empire had fallen. 'In Germany', explains Brague, 'the Reformation resonated especially in areas situated beyond the frontier of the Roman Empire.'[11] So when Stevenson

---

[8] Jolly, *Stevenson in the Pacific*, 35, 36.
[9] Jolly, *Stevenson in the Pacific*, 39.
[10] Jolly, *Stevenson in the Pacific*, 42.
[11] Rémi Brague, *Eccentric Culture: A Theory of Western Civilization*, trans. by Samuel Lester (South Bend, IN: St. Augustine's Press, 2002), 12.

wrote that he was now 'escaped out of the shadow of the Roman Empire' (9) he was, in part, echoing an older Protestant encounter with the fringes of historical Christendom. Stevenson's relationship to 'Romanity' is worth exploring from the perspective of his Protestant heritage.[12] It would offer clues to understanding why he viewed the nineteenth-century Pacific, quite erroneously, as a region that was untouched by the legacy of Rome.

From another perspective, it might also be argued that Scottish comparative cultural analysis of the kind undertaken by Stevenson was not simply a secular endeavour but was significantly a product of the efforts of religious figures such as missionaries.[13] There was a profound relationship between religious learning and the development of the modern 'scientific' disciplines.[14] The more we know about these religious figures, the better we can understand the traditions of comparative analysis that informed Stevenson. Likewise, while both Jolly and Reid rightly emphasise Stevenson's opposition to 'meliorist anthropological narratives',[15] it is important to observe that such a view would have presented little difficulty to, indeed would have been buttressed by, orthodox Scottish Presbyterian ideas of the Fall and the total depravity of humankind. Notions of historical progress and its obverse have discernible origins in Christian anthropology, and the introduction of such religious contexts can deepen and complicate the picture of Stevenson as a modern protoanthropologist. Furthermore, it can help to situate him within traditions that recover the Scottishness of his thought beyond debates centred on older interpretations of the Enlightenment.[16]

One aspect of the development of modern anthropology could also be said to have obscured our appreciation of Stevenson's Pacific ethnography. As anthropologists themselves have begun to observe, through much of its twentieth-century history anthropology either

---

[12] Brague, *Eccentric Culture*, passim.

[13] My thanks to Stewart J. Brown for this point. For a fine study of a British missionary anthropologist whom Stevenson met in the Pacific, see Helen Bethea Gardner, *Gathering for God: George Brown in Oceania* (Dunedin: Otago University Press, 2006).

[14] A classic study is John Hedley Brooke, *Science and Religion: Some Historical Perspectives* (Cambridge: Cambridge University Press, 1991).

[15] Roslyn Jolly, 'Essays on R.L.S.', *English Literature in Transition* 50, 4 (2007), 454–7 (455); Reid, *Stevenson, Science, and the Fin de Siècle*, passim.

[16] An important work on this subject is Craig Beveridge and Ronald Turnbull, *Scotland after Enlightenment: Image and Tradition in Modern Scottish Culture* (Edinburgh: Polygon, 1997).

disregarded or downplayed Christianity as an object of study. Christian traditions were not taken seriously enough in research into the cultures in which they have a presence. Joel Robbins has explained how, in such work, Christianity is portrayed 'as inconsistently or lightly held or as merely a thin veneer overlying deep meaningful traditional beliefs'.[17] When compared with the anthropological study of other world religions, there appears to be a reluctance to engage Christianity as a central element in people's lives, especially in places such as the Island Pacific where its arrival was relatively recent.

The anthropologist Fenella Cannell has produced an insightful analysis of the challenges for her discipline in thinking about Christianity 'as an ethnographic object'. She suggests that the cause of the problem might be the original separation of anthropology from theology:

> Anthropology, as part of social science, defined itself in its origins as what theology was not; since the theology it was repudiating was specifically Christian theology, anthropological theory has always carried within it ideas profoundly shaped by that act of rejection, from which there can therefore never be a complete separation.[18]

Cannell is also critical of some influential anthropologists for subordinating 'the exploration of Christianity' in their subjects of study 'to the narrative of modernization'.[19] Such studies treat Christianity as a 'secondary phenomenon'.[20] Moreover, anthropologists' perspectives on Christianity often take shape against the background

---

[17] Joel Robbins, 'Continuity Thinking and the Problem of Christian Culture: Belief, Time, and the Anthropology of Christianity', *Current Anthropology* 48, 1 (2007), 5–38 (6). For another sophisticated critique of anthropologists' relationship to their subjects' Christianity, see Bronwen Douglas, 'From Invisible Christians to Gothic Theatre: The Romance of the Millennial in Melanesian Anthropology', *Current Anthropology* 42, 5 (2001), 615–50.

[18] Fenella Cannell, 'Introduction: The Anthropology of Christianity', in *The Anthropology of Christianity*, ed. by Fenella Cannell (Durham, NC: Duke University Press, 2006), 1–50 (45). Joel Robbins considers ways of advancing a 'transformative' relationship between anthropology and theology. Joel Robbins, *Theology and the Anthropology of Christian Life* (Oxford: Oxford University Press, 2020), 1–30. See also Joel Robbins, 'Anthropology and Theology: An Awkward Relationship?', *Anthropological Quarterly* 79, 2 (2006), 285–94. Derrick Lemons discusses 'theologically engaged anthropology' as an attempt 'to more adequately account for theology in ethnographic research'. Derrick J. Lemons, 'An Introduction to Theologically Engaged Anthropology', *Ethnos* 86, 3 (2021), 401–7.

[19] Cannell, 'Introduction', 11. See also Robbins, 'Continuity Thinking', 7–9.

[20] Cannell, 'Introduction', 12. See also Robbins, *Theology*, 39–40.

of their knowledge of its past within their area of study. According to Cannell,

> This is particularly and understandably true when Christianity has been forced upon people by the actions of the state or of colonial missionaries. With honorable exceptions, anthropology has tended to come at the problem of the significance of Christianity rather simplistically, and has even tended to view it as a homogeneous thing, often covered by the label 'the church,' whose main distinguishing feature is taken to be its hostility to local patterns of understanding and behavior.[21]

From Cannell's analysis we can draw important connections between Stevenson's Pacific ethnography and the anthropology of Christianity. To the extent that Stevenson also took his Pacific informants' Christianity 'seriously as a cultural fact' and refused 'to marginalize it', his writing and the work of anthropologists of Christianity could be said to share common ground.[22] Stevenson did not marginalise Christianity in the Pacific for the same reason that he did not play down its centrality in shaping the intellectual and cultural traditions of Scotland. To the contrary, he approached Pacific Christian phenomena from the perspective of a Scottish Presbyterian, with the understanding that Presbyterianism could also mean different things in different times and places. This inculturation perspective is a distinctive feature of all his writing about religion in the Pacific.

Stevenson was able to observe how thoroughly the Pacific Islands had been impacted by Christianity.[23] From the close of the eighteenth century, European and American missionaries had conducted evangelisation efforts across the Pacific Ocean.[24] Christianity also soon

---

[21] Cannell, 'Introduction', 12.

[22] Cannell, 'Introduction', 5.

[23] For an overview of the Christian impact on the Pacific, see Manfred Ernst and Anna Anisi, 'The Historical Development of Christianity in Oceania', in *The Wiley Blackwell Companion to World Christianity*, ed. by Lamin Sanneh and Michael J. McClymond (Hoboken, NJ: Wiley Blackwell, 2016), 588–604.

[24] I am referring to the modern period of Pacific evangelisation, which began with Protestant missionaries, although Catholic missionaries had visited parts of the Pacific as early as the 1660s. See the studies of Niel Gunson, *Messengers of Grace: Evangelical Missionaries in the South Seas, 1797–1860* (Melbourne: Oxford University Press, 1978); John Garrett, *To Live among the Stars: Christian Origins in Oceania* (Geneva and Suva: World Council of Churches in association with the Institute of Pacific Studies, 1982); Tony Swain and G. W. Trompf, *The Religions of Oceania* (London: Routledge, 1995), 188–94.

began to spread through the activity of Pacific Islands missionaries and religious leaders.²⁵ By the late 1800s, Christian evangelisation had marked most of the region to varying degrees. For many Pacific Islanders in Stevenson's time, Christianity was not a foreign imposition but part of their everyday life. They thought of themselves as Christians in the same way that many in the West would have considered themselves as such. The critical religious questions in Pacific societies therefore did not concern the acceptance or rejection of Christianity per se but rather the stability and viability of earlier forms of Christianity with respect to the needs and expectations of Islanders' contemporary situation.²⁶

Although matters related to Christianity in the late-nineteenth-century Pacific were not the sole preserve of Western missionaries, the latter did continue to play important roles in evangelisation, pastoral care, and education, which included the study of Pacific societies. Intellectual and institutional boundaries between religious figures and academia were more permeable than they would become in the twentieth century, and missionary contributions to the emerging discipline of anthropology were generally accepted.²⁷ Through his Pacific travels, Stevenson came to know many missionary and religious scholars and their work. In the Marquesas, he met Father Orens Fréchou, a Picpus Father (that is, belonging to The Congregation of the Sacred Hearts of Jesus and Mary), who had composed a vocabulary of the Marquesan island of Ua Pou (92).²⁸ Stevenson's guide on his visit to the 'cannibal high place' in Hatiheu was another Picpus priest, Siméon Delmas, the author of a history

---

[25] Swain and Trompf, *Religions of Oceania*, 194–201.
[26] See Chapters 3 and 4 for further discussion of this subject.
[27] Patrick Harries, 'Anthropology', in *Missions and Empire*, ed. by Norman Etherington (Oxford: Oxford University Press, 2008), 238–60; Allan K. Davidson, 'The Legacy of Robert Henry Codrington', *International Bulletin of Missionary Research* 27, 4 (2003), 171–6 (174). John Hitchen claims that 'the two decades 1889–1909 [. . .] rather than being the beginning of South Pacific anthropology with Haddon as the founding father, could also be understood as the flowering and acceptance in the wider academic world of this long standing heritage of evangelical missionary study of culture.' John M. Hitchen, 'Relations between Missiology and Anthropology Then and Now – Insights from the Contribution to Ethnography and Anthropology by Nineteenth-Century Missionaries in the South Pacific', *Missiology: An International Review* 30, 4 (2002), 455–78 (464).
[28] Nicholas Thomas, 'Further Notes on Marquesan Dictionaries', *Journal of the Polynesian Society* 95, 1 (1986), 127–30.

of the Marquesan mission and of a study of Marquesan religion.[29] In the middle of 1889, Stevenson wrote a lengthy response to a pamphlet about Hawaiian depopulation by the Congregationalist minister, educator, and meteorologist Sereno Edwards Bishop.[30] In his South Seas Letters he also made reference to other Pacific Islands missionary scholars, including the Anglican Robert Henry Codrington, author of *The Melanesian Languages* (28), George Turner, a Scottish clergyman belonging to the London Missionary Society (LMS) (70), who published *Nineteen Years in Polynesia*, and the French Catholic Bishop and Marquesan linguist René Ildefonse Dordillon (23).[31]

Missionary ethnographers constructed bodies of knowledge primarily to promote Christian evangelisation. They gathered and published information in order to tell people who lived far from the missionary's field about that place, although the ideas and assumptions underlying their efforts were not always the same. Despite similarities of intention that crossed theological and cultural boundaries, the missionary scholar's country of origin, denomination, theological training, and the nature of the mission field could all influence their thought.[32] Many of Stevenson's native informants in the Pacific were

---

[29] Stevenson, *In the South Seas*, 262n3; Siméon Delmas, *La Religion ou le paganisme des Marquisiens d'après le missionnaires* (Paris: Braine-le-Comte, 1927); Siméon Delmas, *Histoire de la mission des Marquises* (1904). On the origins of the Picpus Fathers and other Catholic groups in Oceania, see Tracey Rowland, 'Oceania', in *The Blackwell Companion to Catholicism*, ed. by James J. Buckley, Frederick Christian Bauerschmidt, and Trent Pomplun (Malden, MA: Blackwell, 2008), 221–34.

[30] See Laavanyan M. Ratnapalan, 'Sereno Bishop, Robert Louis Stevenson and "Americanism" in Hawai'i', *The Journal of Imperial and Commonwealth History* 40, 3 (2012), 439–57; L. M. Ratnapalan, '"This Greater Issue of Light against Darkness": Sereno Edwards Bishop, Missionary Religion, and the Hawaiian Islands, 1827–1909', *Journal of Religious History* 43, 1 (2019), 3–24.

[31] Robert Henry Codrington, *The Melanesian Languages* (Oxford: Clarendon Press, 1885); Rev. George Turner, *Nineteen Years in Polynesia: Missionary Life, Travels, and Researches in the Islands of the Pacific* (London: John Snow, 1861); and see, for example, Mgr René Ildefonse Dordillon, *Grammaire et dictionnaire de la langue des îles Marquises* (Paris: Institut d'Ethnologie, 1931).

[32] For an overview, see Michael Gladwin, 'Mission and Colonialism', in *The Oxford Handbook of Nineteenth-Century Christian Thought*, ed. by Joel D. S. Rasmussen, Judith Wolfe, and Johannes Zachhuber (Oxford: Oxford University Press, 2017), 282–307. Anthropologists have also begun to recognise the importance of such variations. See Fraser Macdonald and Christiane Falck, 'Positioning Culture within Pacific Christianities', *The Australian Journal of Anthropology* 31, 2 (2020), 123–38 (128, 131).

also Christians. They included the Marquesan Stanislao Moanatini, the half-Tahitian François Donat-Rimarau, the Hawaiian former judge D. H. Nahinu, and the lawyer and writer Joseph Poepoe, 'a clever fellow' who taught Stevenson Hawaiian.[33] Others, such as the Hawaiian King David Kalakaua, were perhaps Christian more in a nominal than an orthodox sense but nevertheless products of a Christian education.[34]

During his years in the Pacific, 1888–94, Stevenson depended on these Christian intellectuals and informants for reliable information. People who were caught up in important cultural changes and who thought deeply about them became his teachers. These unusual historical circumstances form an overlooked context for understanding his Pacific ethnography. Stevenson's religious literacy also enabled him to take the Christianity of Pacific Islanders seriously. He was alert to the difference between true devotion and the performance of worship. He portrayed Pacific Christianity as a contemporary tradition rather than as a superficial layer covering traditional beliefs and to be treated with suspicion. Although he could be sceptical of the piety of some Christians, he did not consider Christianity as a thing separate from other Pacific traditions. As a result, he was able to accept and reflect on the fact that Christianity was a major force in Pacific Islands life.

In this chapter, I build on the framework of Stevenson's religious literacy, which was established in Chapter 1, to identify denominational consciousness as a central theme of his Pacific ethnography. I claim that the author's commitments as an anthropologist are better understood when we pay attention to his distinctively Protestant analytical and rhetorical position. Denominational consciousness, rather than weakening his objectivity, granted ethnographic reflexivity and disrupted the tendency to make bland and uninformed distinctions between Pacific Islanders and Westerners. I also highlight the potential contribution of Stevenson's ethnography to the anthropological concept of transcendence. Stevenson's writing about belief and

---

[33] Stevenson, *Letters* VI, 265; 'Short Biography of the Great Joseph Mokuohai Poepoe, 1912', *Nupepa*, accessed at: https://nupepa-hawaii.com/2016/03/02/short-biography-of-the-great-joseph-mokuohai-poepoe-1912/ on 29 August 2020.

[34] Stevenson names Kalakaua as his source for the story that the first man to kindle the legendary Hawaiian ruler Kamehameha's interest in Christianity 'was an Englishman, and a missionary'. Robert Louis Stevenson, *The Works of Robert Louis Stevenson, Volume 18: In the South Seas*, ed. by Andrew Lang (London: Chatto and Windus, 1912), 210. Hereinafter cited as Stevenson, *In the South Seas* (Swanston Edition).

conversion engages the relationship between this- and other-worldly conceptions of religion. By frequently drawing attention to the connection between the supernatural and the social, he implicitly critiqued an anthropology that was grounded in overly rationalist and individualist accounts of human existence. The chapter concludes with a reflection on Stevenson's fable 'Something in It', which I read in the context of his Pacific ethnography. Scholars have tended to interpret 'Something in It' as an expression of its author's moral relativism, whereas I claim that Stevenson's appropriation of catholicising language to reflect on the relationship between Pacific religion, Western missionaries, and Christian conversion suggests that he was moving into a different intellectual space marked above all by a shift in theological perspective.

Denominational Consciousness

Cannell has emphasised the importance of precision when identifying what is meant by 'Christianity' within a given cultural context, while other anthropologists have noted problems that result when Catholicism is studied through an unexamined Protestant lens.[35] Critical self-awareness and reflexivity is especially necessary when approaching Christians as subjects of anthropological research. To study Christianity as a Western-trained scholar is to approach a subject that has been shaped by historical and institutional assumptions dating from the Reformation and built largely on studies of Protestants. Stevenson could himself be said to have taken on the task of writing about other Christian denominations and non-Christian groups from an Evangelical Presbyterian perspective.[36] He did not try to disguise this fact and in the 'Open Letter' defending the Catholic priest Father Damien of Molokai, he referred to his own Presbyterian 'sect'.[37] But as this example also demonstrates, it was precisely his rootedness in the particular religious culture of Evangelical Presbyterianism that provided Stevenson with the basis from which to write responsibly, with awareness and sensitivity, about people of religious persuasions other than

---

[35] Cannell, 'Introduction', 43; Lemons, 'Theologically Engaged Anthropology', 3.
[36] See Chapter 1 for an account of Stevenson's upbringing in Victorian Scottish Evangelical Presbyterian culture.
[37] Robert Louis Stevenson, *Father Damien: An Open Letter to the Reverend Doctor Hyde of Honolulu* (London: Chatto and Windus, 1890), 7, 8, 10.

his own.[38] In composing his Pacific ethnography, Stevenson was not behaving as a postmodern anthropologist *avant la lettre* but rather exhibiting religious literacy as a Christian from a specific nineteenth-century culture.

By displaying a careful eye for denominational comparison, Stevenson's writing cut across reductive analytical divisions between 'Westerners' and 'Pacific Islanders'. Conscious of his background as a Scottish Presbyterian, he was at pains to present himself as a balanced ethnographer of Roman Catholic culture. Concerning the 'vestment' and 'sacred vessels' of Father Orens Fréchou, of Hiva-oa in the Marquesas Islands, he at first opined that 'there is always something embarrassing in the eagerness with which grown and holy men regard these trifles' (92). But then he added charitably that 'it was touching and pretty to see Orens, his aged eyes shining in his head, display his sacred treasures'. Another time in the Marquesas, he could not help noting that the statue of the Virgin Mary high up on a cliff by the beach in Hatiheu 'looks insignificantly down, like a poor lost doll, forgotten there by a giant child' (46). 'This laborious symbol of the Catholics is always strange to Protestants', he admitted, but 'it was the wise Bishop Dordillon who chose the place, and I know that those who had a hand in the enterprise look back with pride upon its vanquished dangers'. Michel Blanc, the architect of a church in Hatiheu that Stevenson greatly admired, was 'a type of all that is most sound in France', and the missionary brother reminded him of 'an old kind friend of my boyhood [. . .] Dr. Paul, of the West Kirk' (47). These cross-denominational comparisons hint at the effort that Stevenson took to assert his authority as a balanced commentator on Christianity in the Pacific. Rather than trying to demonstrate neutrality in matters of religion, his rhetorical strategy was to emphasise his proximity to received Protestant views of Catholicism, which he then attempted to resolve or soften. In this way, he tried to write from a position of sympathetic awareness.

The religious history of Scotland, particularly in its denominational conflict and fragmentation, provided Stevenson with a ready model for characterising the diversity of Pacific Islands Christianity. Thus, for example, explaining the break-up and reunification of Christian sects in the Paumotus Islands, he compares them with Scottish Cameronians

---

[38] In this sense, Stevenson provides a model of the 'more responsible intellectual existence' that Mark Noll called for from Evangelicals. See Mark A. Noll, *The Scandal of the Evangelical Mind* (Grand Rapids, MI, and Cambridge: William B. Eerdmans, 1994), 27.

and United Presbyterians (131). Given the Paumotuans' highly fractious 'ecclesiastical history' he predicts that the current period of calm they are experiencing will be short-lived as 'these isles bid fair to be the Scotland of the South' (132). Elsewhere, he favourably compares the Hawaiian queen Ka'ahumanu (1768–1832) to Mary I, Queen of Scots (1542–87).[39] Scottish literary history, in the form of Burns's 'Tam o' Shanter', also features in Stevenson's portrayal of the Pacific, when he timidly passes by the church in the Gilbert Island of Butaritari one night as 'service' was taking place, 'and the building glimmered through all its crevices like a dim Kirk Allowa"' (185).

Religious imagination in a broader sense both anchored and gave shape to Stevenson's account of Pacific cultures. He used Scripture to interpret what he experienced and to communicate it through intelligible forms and symbols. In describing unfamiliar parts of the Pacific, he sometimes made Biblical references for a Western audience that he knew possessed sufficient religious literacy to be able to grasp them. Scripture also helped to progress his writing by transforming casual observations into narratives. For instance, because the coconut was a staple of almost every meal in a Pacific atoll, 'the Israelites of the low islands murmur at their manna' (118). Tebureimoa, ruler of the Gilbert Island of Butaritari, was 'the Micronesian Saul wakeful amid his guards', and had his own 'unmelodious David' in the form of the talkative African American barman, Mr Williams (159). A man on the island of Penrhyn was as 'leprous as Naaman'.[40] The name of the native Hawaiian historian David Malo 'should rather have been Nathan' for his prophetic condemnation of the regent Ka'ahumanu's infidelity.[41] References to European religious history also colour the writing from time to time, as when 'throne and church were reconciled' in Butaritari after the king gave up drinking just before the Sunday sermon (188).

Catholicism, in particular, provided the Protestant Stevenson with a vocabulary with which to communicate the alterity of non-Christian Pacific religion to his mainly Protestant audience.[42] Before

---

[39] Stevenson, *In the South Seas* (Swanston Edition), 214.
[40] Robert Louis Stevenson, 'A Pearl Island: Penrhyn' and 'Leprosy at Penrhyn', *The Sun* (New York), 24 May 1891, 23–30.
[41] Stevenson, *In the South Seas* (Swanston Edition), 213.
[42] For a stimulating discussion of Stevenson's short story 'Ollala' and its Gothic 'fascination with the dark allure of Catholic rite, ritual and iconography' (273), see Linden Bicket, 'Catholic and Protestant Sensibilities in Scottish Literature: Stevenson to Spark', in *The History of Scottish Theology, Volume III: The Long Twentieth Century*, ed. by David Fergusson and Mark W. Elliott (Oxford: Oxford University Press, 2019), 271–87.

exploring this further in Stevenson's Pacific ethnography, it will be useful to compare his use of religious language with that of the most celebrated Victorian anthropologist, Edward Burnett Tylor (1832–1917). Timothy Larsen has explained how, although Tylor was a Quaker who formally left his faith in 1864, his 'anthropological thought as a religious sceptic was littered with survivals (to adapt his parlance) from his Quaker past'.[43] Thus, in *Anahuac* (1861), his travel narrative about Mexico and its culture, Tylor offered 'a Quaker critique of Catholicism', with a 'polemical pay-off' in 'the assertion that Catholicism was little better than the pagan religion of the Aztecs'.[44] Larsen connects Tylor's loss of faith to his inability 'to find a way to think anthropologically and as a Christian at the same time'.[45] The teleological case against religion appeared to have been too compelling for him. Over time, as the Quaker Tylor's anti-Catholicism developed into the atheist Tylor's anti-Christian polemic, he began to argue that Christianity 'is fundamentally pagan' and showed this 'by describing savage religion with words familiar from Christian contexts [. . .] and by insisting that Christian beliefs were no different from savage ones'.[46]

Although Stevenson's ethnographic language resembles Tylor's, his rhetorical strategy was markedly different to the anthropologist's, which suggests that the two men had distinctive attitudes towards religion and in particular Catholicism. Unlike Tylor, Stevenson did not wish to denigrate Catholicism – quite the opposite, in fact, as he took great care to write respectfully about it. What he lacked, however, was a descriptive vocabulary with which to articulate the 'pagan' Pacific. Terms associated with Catholicism therefore provided him, as it would have Tylor, with a convenient expressive vehicle. Yet, in marked contrast to Tylor, Stevenson's engagement with the Christianity of his ethnographic subjects was active and sympathetic. Through his writing he sought clarity and understanding rather than a means with which to highlight superstition and error.

---

[43] Timothy Larsen, *The Slain God: Anthropologists and the Christian Faith* (Oxford: Oxford University Press, 2014), 33. On the genealogy of Tylor's concept of the survival, see Laavanyan Ratnapalan, 'E. B. Tylor and the Problem of Primitive Culture', *History and Anthropology* 19, 2 (2008), 131–42. On Stevenson's application of Tylor's concept, see Laavanyan Ratnapalan, 'Stevenson and Cultural Survivals in the South Seas', *Journal of Stevenson Studies* 3 (2006), 69–85.
[44] Larsen *Slain God*, 17.
[45] Larsen, *Slain God*, 20.
[46] Larsen, *Slain God*, 30–1.

Catholic terminology formed a significant component of Stevenson's ethnography. To describe the historic importance of cannibalism in Marquesan society, for example, he adopted the use of terms such as 'sacrament' and 'feast' that was informed by his awareness of medieval European history: 'The Marquesans intertwined man-eating with the whole texture of their lives; long-pig was in a sense their currency and sacrament; it formed the hire of the artist, illustrated public events, and was the occasion and attraction of a feast' (71).[47] A sacramental anthropological language, which renders invisible power visible, cloaks his description of Equator Town, the taboo-protected residence that King Tembinok' of Apemama prepared for the Stevenson family. Stevenson contrasts the 'outward and visible sign' of the 'mystic rampart' that ringed the complex, made of 'a few ragged coco-leaf garlands round the stems of the outlying palms', with its real meaning, which 'reposed on the tremendous sanction of the *tapu* and the guns of Tembinok' (220).[48] When Stevenson compares Hawaiian and Western attitudes towards the sacred, he describes how 'the Hawaiian remembers the repository of the bones of old, and is still jealous of the safety of ancestral relics', while 'the white man comes and goes upon the hunt for curiosities'.[49] The ruined Hawaiian City of Refuge contained a temple that was the 'House of Keawe, or reliquary of his royal bones'.[50] Although the remnants of 'many monarchs of Hawaii' were kept there, it had been named for Keawe as he 'was the reigning and the hallowing saint'. The wryly catholicising language continues: 'And Keawe can produce at least one claim to figure on the canon, for since his death he has wrought miracles.' Hawaiian cities of refuge offered absolution to a certain class of people that had been marked as sacrificial offerings, and, while European churches offered 'a sanctuary for the time', the 'immunities' of the sacrificial victim in places such as Tahiti and Hawai'i 'exceed those of the medieval priest and jester rolled in one'.[51]

---

[47] Carla Manfredi claims that Stevenson misunderstood 'the complex situation' in the Marquesas, where cannibalism formed a repertoire of violent acts 'to frighten or impress European visitors'. Carla Manfredi, *Robert Louis Stevenson's Pacific Impressions: Photography and Travel Writing, 1888–1894* (Cham: Palgrave Macmillan, 2018), 41.

[48] Mark Knight and Emma Mason describe sacramentalism as when 'the whole of the created order is seen as a sign of the presence of God'. Mark Knight and Emma Mason, *Nineteenth-Century Religion and Literature: An Introduction* (Oxford: Oxford University Press, 2006), 199.

[49] Stevenson, *In the South Seas* (Swanston Edition), 202.

[50] Stevenson, *In the South Seas* (Swanston Edition), 205.

[51] Stevenson, *In the South Seas* (Swanston Edition), 206–7.

Stevenson made one of his most insightful observations about Pacific religion within the context of a discussion about a relatively recent 'post-Christian' story that was told in Tahiti:

> A princess of the reigning house died; was transported to the neighbouring isle of Raiatea; fell there under the empire of a spirit who condemned her to climb coco-palms all day and bring him the nuts; was found after some time in this miserable servitude by a second spirit, one of her own house; and by him, upon her lamentations, reconveyed to Tahiti, where she found her body still waked, but already swollen with the approaches of corruption. It is a lively point in the tale that, on the sight of this dishonoured tabernacle, the princess prayed she might continue to be numbered with the dead. (150–1)

He concludes by asking his readers to note 'The seemingly purgatorial labours, the helpful kindred spirit, and the horror of the princess at the sight of her tainted body.' Not only do these comments reveal his sensitivity to the cultural impact of Christianity in Tahiti, such as the difference between the pre-Christian belief in the materiality of spirits and 'the horror of this princess at the sight of her tainted body', but they also demonstrate his interest and skill in identifying the influence of Catholic beliefs and practices within the Tahitian story: the state of purgatory, in which one suffers in reparation for one's earthly sins, and the intercessory aid of a friendly and 'kindred' spirit.

Stevenson's use of catholicising expressions to communicate the otherness of Pacific Islands religious beliefs and practices supports the established historical claim that Protestantism continued to be an important marker of British identity well into the nineteenth century.[52] Both the author and much of his audience would have thought of Catholicism as the familiar other, so that with comparatively little effort, Stevenson would be able to translate and domesticate what seemed strange and different in Pacific societies. But he did not apply

---

[52] Hugh McLeod, 'Protestantism and British National Identity, 1815–1945', in *Nation and Religion: Perspectives on Europe and Asia*, ed. by Peter Van der Veer and Hartmut Lehmann (Princeton, NJ: Princeton University Press, 1999), 44–70 (44–5); John Wolffe, 'Anglicanism, Presbyterianism and the Religious Identities of the United Kingdom', in *The Cambridge History of Christianity: Volume 8. World Christianities c. 1815 – c. 1914*, ed. by Sheridan Gilley and Brian Stanley (Cambridge: Cambridge University Press, 2014), 301–22 (312–13).

his religious literacy merely to ease the burden of cultural analysis: he also pursued ethnographic reflexivity through denominational identification. He connected with his own sense of the religious in order to better understand and communicate religious phenomena. This effort of self-reflection can be traced to his Presbyterian intellectual formation.[53] The anthropologist Webb Keane has situated the effort to be an honest and sincere witness to what one thinks and feels within distinctively Protestant ways of understanding the relationship between self and world.[54] For Stevenson, to try to understand a culture meant to honestly strive to achieve a balance of perspectives rather than to aim for an impossible impartiality. Sincerity also necessitated a constant effort not to fall into conventional forms of communication, which were perceived as inauthentic. Joel Robbins has explained how

> For people in many societies, and in Western Europe prior to the Reformation, the goal of a speaker was not to convey sincerely his or her thoughts or feelings, but rather to show deference to his or her interlocutor by employing appropriate forms of politeness.[55]

On this basis, we might say that the language of Stevenson's Pacific ethnography does not fit easily into either the pre- or post-Reformation schemata. The mixture of the sincere and the ironic in his portrayal of Pacific Islands religious life rather suggests that he faced peculiar challenges as a descriptive writer. The need to faithfully communicate the otherness of the culture to a Western audience seemed to have come up against the surprise of encountering familiar religious phenomena and dynamics.

---

[53] Catriona Macdonald claims that Stevenson's 'ironic yet self-reflective perspective' was already developed before 'his later engagement with the world as a Scot in Samoa', in works such as *Edinburgh: Picturesque Notes*, which was written in France. This makes even more sense when seen in the light of the religious basis of Stevenson's irony. Catriona M. M. Macdonald, 'Imagining the Scottish Diaspora: Emigration and Transnational Literature in the Late Modern Period', *Britain and the World* 5, 1 (2012), 12–42 (41).

[54] Webb Keane, 'Sincerity, "Modernity", and the Protestants', *Cultural Anthropology* 17, 1 (2002), 65–92.

[55] Joel Robbins, 'Transcendence and the Anthropology of Christianity: Language, Change, and Individualism', *Suomen Antropologi: Journal of the Finnish Anthropological Society* 37, 2 (2012), 5–23 (16).

The Anthropology of Transcendence

Anthropologists of Christianity work with a notion of the transcendent, typically understood as a realm beyond the mundane (or immanent) world that is given to the senses, in order to articulate situations that they commonly find across Christian cultures. Robbins develops the idea of Christianity as 'a tradition in which the relationship between the mundane and the transcendent is caught between this- and other-worldly tendencies and is therefore fundamentally unstable'.[56] Differences in the relationship between the transcendent and the mundane 'can do much to account for the range of this variation', he claims, 'in Christian approaches to change, language, and individualism'.[57] Cannell describes Christianity as 'a religion of radical discontinuity'.[58] In its conceptions of conversion and of a hierarchy between this world and 'the "world beyond"', she explains, there is a 'link between Christian ideas of time and event and Christian ideas of transcendence'.[59] Of course, as many scholars have also noted, Christianity is not a purely other-worldly religion and, throughout history, Christians have intervened to shape and transform the affairs of this world.[60] But the idea of transcendence has helped anthropologists of Christianity to situate this religious tradition according to the ideas and practices in which it exists. Transcendence serves as a kind of umbrella concept under which anthropologists study cultural phenomena such as belief, language, and time.

Stevenson also affirmed the idea of religious transcendence as a cross-cultural category. He thought of it as an other-worldly reality that

---

[56] Robbins, 'Transcendence', 10. With an implicit nod to Reformed theology, Gijsbert van den Brink and Harro Höpfl describe how 'Both the Christian and the Platonist mystical traditions – to say nothing of other traditions – have always recognized that the highest form of communion with God is not the product of any human activity – "raising" – but on the contrary of divine "condescension", and that all human endeavours and exertions in this context are merely preparatory, a kind of ground-clearing.' Gijsbert van den Brink and Harro Höpfl, 'Introduction', in *Calvinism and the Making of the European Mind*, ed. by Gijsbert van den Brink and Harro Höpfl (Leiden: Brill, 2014), 3–24 (13).

[57] Robbins, 'Transcendence', 20.

[58] Cannell, 'Introduction', 8.

[59] Cannell, 'Introduction', 38.

[60] Robbins, 'Transcendence', 10. From a historical perspective, see the contrast between atonement and immanence that is set up by Boyd Hilton in *The Age of Atonement: The Influence of Evangelicalism on Social and Economic Thought, 1785–1865* (Oxford: Clarendon Press, 1988).

was beyond material or sensory reach. Importantly too, he regarded the transcendent realm as a social phenomenon that was not restricted to the private sphere. The importance of the transcendent social is well expressed in his reflection about how the conditions of religious belief in the Pacific were more open than in Europe and North America. It was 'scarce possible to exaggerate the extent and empire of [the Pacific Islander's] superstitions', he insists; 'they mould his life, they colour his thinking; and when he does not speak to me of ghosts, and gods, and devils, he is playing the dissembler and talking only with his lips' (140). Ordinary people lived and moved in this supernatural world of 'ghosts', 'gods', and 'devils'. Christianity was flourishing in these conditions, but this was not the rational religion that was to be found in post-Enlightenment Europe. Rather, it seemed to Stevenson as it did to other foreign observers that Pacific Islands Christians maintained a bracing openness to the transcendent. In the words of the historian John Garrett, for Pacific Islanders 'the union of natural and supernatural, as their ancestors knew it under pre-Christian religions, persists within the church'.[61]

Stevenson used examples featuring Pacific Christians in order to demonstrate this more expansive spiritual credulity. He related how, one day, his Samoan workman Lafaele (Rafael) returned in fright after a solitary daytime trip to a banana patch on their estate because he was 'afraid of "spilits in the bush"' (140). Stevenson contrasted such an attitude with modern Western scientific rationalism. 'To the native mind', he reflected, 'our medical opinions seem unfounded. We smile to hear of ghosts and gods; they, when they are told to keep warm in fevers or to avoid contagion.'[62] He identified a pattern of values linking the transcendent with the social.[63] Islander resistance to laws prohibiting contact with lepers was an outgrowth of 'the family bond', an 'undignified fervour of attachment' rather than an individualistic commitment to liberty. One did not believe in private but as a member of a community giving collective witness to the supernatural.

Stevenson's engagement with transcendence as an anthropological category can be seen in his discussions about denominational fragmentation and conversion. Instead of addressing these subjects

---

[61] Garrett, *To Live among the Stars*, 311.
[62] Stevenson, *In the South Seas* (Swanston Edition), 216.
[63] On individualism and relationalism as variant impacts of Christianity, see Nofit Itzhak, 'A Sacred Social: Christian Relationalism and the Re-enchantment of the World', *Journal of the Royal Anthropological Institute* 27, 2 (2021), 265–84.

from a purely materialist point of view, the examples he presents frequently and deliberately test the boundaries of scientific credibility. Take the case of the Whistlers, according to Stevenson apparently a Mormon sect in the Paumotus, who claimed that an invisible spirit joined them during their prayers and by means of 'an aerial whistling' communicated messages to the congregation (133–4). The sociologist Yannick Fer has explained that the modern-day 'Charismatic culture' of Christianity in the Polynesian islands was 'inspired by English evangelical "revivals"', knowledge of which London Missionary Society (LMS) missionaries brought into the Pacific.[64] In the midst of these dramatic new ideas, the appearance of unorthodox religious mixtures would have been common. Stevenson was greatly interested in the new 'Traits and Sects', as he titled one of his South Seas Letters: prophetic modes of Christianity that went beyond established institutional forms. The anthropologist John Barker has described how these 'sometimes stabiliz[ed] into independent churches with distinctly Oceanic conceptions of Christianity'.[65]

In the religious lives of Pacific Islanders Stevenson discovered idiosyncrasy as well as heterodoxy. An often noted example is that of the Tahitian woman, 'very religious, a great church-goer', who 'privately worshipped a shark' (141). Apart from its amusing juxtaposition, the case reflected the fact that converts were neither mere followers nor resisters of the missionaries' message. Rather, they interpreted Christianity according to their own understanding and prevailing beliefs.[66] Stevenson also described the story of the Paumotuan man who, walking alone on the beach one day, recognised that a corpse was coming to kill him. So he immediately prayed because 'Prayer was the weapon of the Christian in the Valley of the Shadow' (143). To underline the point, Stevenson explained that 'it is to prayer' that the Paumotuan man 'attributes his escape. No merely human expedition had availed' (143). In the crowded Pacific spiritual world,

---

[64] Yannick Fer, 'Politics of Tradition: Charismatic Globalization, Morality, and Culture in Polynesian Protestantism', in *The Anthropology of Global Pentecostalism and Evangelicalism*, ed. by Simon Coleman and Rosalind I. J. Hackett (New York: New York University Press, 2015), 228–42 (228–9).

[65] John Barker, 'Comments to Part 1: Christian Transcendence and the Politics of Renewal', in *Christianity, Conflict, and Renewal in Australia and the Pacific*, ed. by Fiona Magowan and Carolyn Schwarz (Boston: Brill, 2016), 23–33 (24).

[66] Brian Stanley, 'Editorial: Appropriations of Christianity', *Studies in World Christianity* 23, 1 (2017), 1–3 (1).

Christianity had become a part of the native armoury, a force to be reckoned with.

The spirit world was being manipulated against converts in a battle that was being played out beyond Polynesia and across the wider region. Neophytes such as the 'half-Christian folk' at Abaiang in the Gilbert Islands were likely to be 'shocked', just as the 'half-heathen' in them would be 'alarmed', as they witnessed the incantation of a local witch (244). The gathered crowd let out a 'laugh of terror' at the spectacle. Why should they not be nervous and scared, Stevenson wondered: these were times when knotted palms, the sign of 'Devil-work', could be found placed in the roof of the island's little Christian chapel. 'Half blood and whole, pious and debauched, intelligent and dull, all men believe in ghosts, all men combine with their recent Christianity fear of and a lingering faith in the old island deities' (142). Sensitivity to the relationship between Christian and pre-Christian religion framed his view of the convulsions that Pacific Islands societies were undergoing. But was he describing continuity between the old culture and the new or a rupture caused by the advent of the Christian religion and its unambiguous rejection of local deities? The question is pertinent to anthropologists who debate how best to understand phenomena of Christian conversion. John Barker puts it pithily: 'At what point do Melanesians cease to be converts and begin to be Christians?'[67]

Stevenson appeared to have grasped that Christian conversion was a Pacific-wide phenomenon, in which seemingly isolated islands and cases must be seen as part of a broader regional circulation of ideas and knowledge. In the same way, he acknowledged the persistence of in-between cultures in which Christians performed 'ontological preservation' by accepting the presence of occult forces such as spirits and witches.[68] The activity of the dead animates Stevenson's writing about societies such as the Marquesas, where he suggests that the Christian event had not caused a rupture in the precise sense meant by modern theorists of transcendence. Instead, and combining the thrill of the novelist with a reporter's certitude, he tells us that certain 'presences, called *vehinhae*', 'frequent and make terrible the nocturnal roadside' (28). In the Paumotuan atoll of Fakarava, as in other low islands, 'the beach of the ocean is a place accursed and

---

[67] John Barker, 'Converts, Christians and Anthropologists: A Critique of Mark Mosko's Partible Penitent Thesis', *The Australian Journal of Anthropology* 30, 3 (2019), 277–93 (277).

[68] MacDonald and Falck, 'Positioning Culture', 124.

deserted, the fit scene only for wizardry and shipwreck, and in the native belief a haunting ground of murderous spectres' (113).[69] The beach of another atoll, Apemama in the Gilbert Islands, was the site of the king's 'pray place' and the 'devil-work' of his wizards. Like beaches, graveyards were also liminal zones in which communication between this world and another took place. Directly after the funeral of a Paumotuan man, a young woman called on the island's governing resident to take her place as food for the deceased's ghost, a terrifying 'new spirit' (139). As ever, Stevenson owed a large share of his understanding of these cases to knowledge of his homeland, where 'to-day, the theological Highlander sneaks from under the eye of the Free Church divine to lay an offering by a sacred well' (142).

Stevenson's categorical interest in the transcendent did not mean that he reduced Pacific Islanders to a group that is 'homogenous, depersonalized, ahistorical'.[70] On the contrary, he wrote about Islander beliefs with a sympathy and self-awareness that was derived from personal experience, such as the stories told him by his nurse Alison Cunningham, as well as from wide travel and reading about the Pacific's diverse cultures and their histories. But because he wrote for a Western audience that was coming to see the self and social communities as naturally separated from the religiously transcendent, Stevenson's Pacific ethnography has an apologetic quality as he strives to convince readers of the truth of things they associated with people that were less intelligent and civilised than themselves.[71] The extent to which his adoption of Pacific Islands spellings and usages was smoothed over or exoticised by the producers of the published text provides a sense of the intellectual distance between Stevenson and his Western readership.[72] The editorial hyphenation of terms, which the literary scholar Barry Menikoff claims 'represented a conservative

---

[69] One imagines that such places inspired Stevenson's magical short story 'The Isle of Voices'.

[70] Bronwen Douglas identifies this trope within a certain kind of scholarly writing about '*the* Pacific world'. Bronwen Douglas, *Science, Voyages, and Encounters in Oceania, 1511–1815* (New York: Palgrave Macmillan, 2014), 31.

[71] In this connection, see the suggestion of John MacKenzie and Tom Devine that there is 'a Scottish tradition of studying indigenous peoples' in imperial settings that links East India Company Orientalists with Sir James Frazer's *The Golden Bough*. John M. MacKenzie and T. M. Devine, 'Introduction', in *Scotland and the British Empire*, ed. by John M. MacKenzie and T. M. Devine (Oxford: Oxford University Press, 2011), 15.

[72] Laavanyan Ratnapalan, 'Robert Louis Stevenson's South Seas Writing: Its Production and Context within the Victorian Study of Culture' (PhD thesis, University of London, 2007), 127–9.

printing stance', created a deliberately exotic result out of such words as 'cocoa palm', altered in the published version to 'cocoa-palm'.[73] Stevenson's attention to the native pronunciation of words such as the hibiscus 'burao' was softened by others to 'purao'. Forthright claims made by the author, such as 'rightly speaking, to eat a man's flesh after he is dead is far less hateful than to oppress him whilst he lives', are altered, probably by his editor, in this case from 'eat' to 'cut'.

Stevenson's realistic depiction of Pacific societies was edited to make it read more like the tropical romance that his audience expected from him. He knew how ethnographic reports about ghosts and eldritch phenomena would sound to readers in London and New York. According to the account of someone whom he describes as 'Tasmanian born, educated, a man who has made money – certainly no fool', when two young Paumotuan men began to play on the sleeping-mats of a powerful woman, following local lore 'their bellies began to swell; pains took hold on them', and their sufferings came to an end only when a ritual involving a coconut, herbs, and spells was conducted by the 'man of the house' (134–5). The account closes with a rebuke of the modern sceptic:

> The reader may stare. I can assure him, if he moved much among old residents of the archipelago, he would be driven to admit one thing of two – either that there is something in the swollen bellies or nothing in the evidence of man.

In his South Seas Letters, Stevenson strove to maintain an authorial stance that tested the limits of the encroachment of the modern self by the supernatural. In one of his most enigmatic Pacific tales, he turned to confront disbelief head on.

'Something in It'

The anthropology of Christianity highlights the continuing significance of Stevenson's Pacific ethnography. I have analysed his writing from the perspective of religious literacy to show how denominational consciousness grounded his views of Pacific culture and to highlight the parallels between his work and modern anthropological theories. As is often the case with Stevenson, however, his views

---

[73] Ratnapalan, 'Robert Louis Stevenson's South Seas Writing', 127.

of the relationship between Pacific culture, religion, and the borders of the modern self are most fully fleshed out in his fiction. In particular, the fable 'Something in It' vividly communicates the results of his ethnographic encounter with Pacific religion. The story affirms transcendent religious experience in a way that is given ballast by the author's denominational perspective on mission, conversion, church, and sacrament.

'Something in It' originally appeared in book form in the collection *Fables*, which was published posthumously in 1896.[74] In the introduction to the volume, Stevenson's editor Sidney Colvin describes how most of the fables were composed before the author's South Seas voyages but that there were 'one or two' later additions. Along with Pacific Islands names for figures and objects that appear in the story, such as 'Miru' and 'kava', 'Something in It' shares many of the concerns of Stevenson's South Seas Letters and it is very likely that it was composed during the same period. The strong theme of respecting one's taboos, for example, also appears in the Letter on 'Chiefs and Tapus' (42). Stevenson's observations about the Marquesan practice of 'man-eating' (71) offers a clue to the fable's inspiration.[75] Elsewhere in the Letters, he describes a 'lurid Mangaian legend, in which infernal deities hocus and destroy the souls of all' (150), a statement that both in concept and expression strongly resembles the writing in 'Something in It'. The story almost certainly emerged from the writing process that produced the Pacific ethnography.

'Something in It' is about a missionary who does not believe the 'stories' told him by Pacific Islands natives until, one day, he is magically transported to a watery netherworld to meet the supernatural beings of which the natives had spoken. There, in spite of the pull of his own desire, the missionary resists the spirits' tempting offers of food and drink and thereby keeps his vow to his religious vocation. He is finally sent back to the world of the living, where he is forced to admit that there may be something in the natives' stories after all. As with many of Stevenson's fables, 'Something in It' focuses on moral themes and has often been interpreted as a relativist critique of Christian dogmatic certainty. For John Charlot, 'Something in It' portrays 'religious relativism', while Ann Colley suggests that

---

[74] Robert Louis Stevenson, *Fables* (New York: Charles Scribner's Sons, 1896).

[75] On the ritualistic aspects of cannibalism in the Pacific in connection with Stevenson's writing, see Sylvie Largeaud-Ortega, 'A Scotsman's Pacific: Shifting Identities in R. L. Stevenson's Postcolonial Fiction', *International Journal of Scottish Literature* 9 (2013), 85–98 (91).

the fable emerged from 'Stevenson's impatience with the missionaries' unwillingness to acknowledge the validity of indigenous beliefs and superstitions'.[76] Roslyn Jolly notes that 'The missionary's point of view' in the story 'is irrational and bigoted' although 'it redeems him', adding that 'The ambiguous ending grants parity to the missionary's and the islanders' world-views', with neither group's beliefs 'able to command universal authority'.[77] These modern interpretations adopt either a relativistic or secular viewpoint to analyse the fable. Although Stevenson undoubtedly wished his readers to understand that the missionary had undergone a chastening experience, his commentators tend to smooth out the story's details in order to frame it as a moral lesson about respecting cultural differences. I would like to suggest that this richly symbolic tale contains more than that. In fact, when it is returned to its original context, the Pacific ethnography, 'Something in It' develops into a meditation on the major religious themes of the South Seas Letters: transcendence, denominational consciousness, and the relationship between church and mission.[78]

In the first place, the story affirms the reality of transcendent religious experience in the Pacific. Rather than attempting to rationalise the transcendent or to reduce it to a material cultural phenomenon, it upholds the integrity of believers by gradually unveiling the veracity of indigenous Pacific belief in a world that is beyond the senses. 'Something in It' opens by relating how 'the natives' warned the missionary about a taboo against touching a house that was situated within a bay, which would make the transgressor subject to the supernatural figures Akaänga and Miru.[79] We also learn such supernatural details as how 'the flaming of Akaänga's torch drew near in the night', how 'misshapen hands groped in the meshes of the net' that captures the missionary when he bathes in the tabooed bay, of Miru 'ruddy in the glow of the ovens', and of her four daughters making 'the kava of the dead'. The appearance of these figures and the transcendent world that they inhabit transforms the natives' warnings to the missionary

---

[76] John Charlot, 'The Influence of Polynesian Literature and Thought on Robert Louis Stevenson', *The Journal of Intercultural Studies* 14 (1987), 82–106 (84); Ann C. Colley, *Robert Louis Stevenson and the Colonial Imagination* (New York: Routledge, 2017 [2004]), 40.

[77] Jolly, *Stevenson in the Pacific*, 56.

[78] For the development of Stevenson's thought on the church and mission, see Chapter 5.

[79] Robert Louis Stevenson, 'Something in It', in *South Sea Tales*, ed. by Roslyn Jolly (Oxford: Oxford University Press, 1996), 255–7 and 289n. All quotes from 'Something in It' are from this source.

from unsubstantiated 'stories' into facts. The implication is that natives' beliefs should be taken seriously, not because they are another culture's opinions, but because they are true. This makes them worthy of the missionary's contemplation no matter how much his religion has usurped their social power. There appears to be a gesture towards this transition in the story itself. The song of the daughters of Miru was 'in the old manner of singing', perhaps indicating that its origins were prior to the missionaries and their taboos. The words of the song describe a lost natural world and the awakening into a hellish reality: 'for life is a deceit, and the bandage is taken from your eyes'.

The supernatural figures are personal beings rather than abstractions. When the missionary refuses to drink the kava of the dead, Akaänga 'reasoned with the missionary' like the God of Israel in the Old Testament.[80] Such Biblical allusions pepper the tale and lend it a strange familiarity. The place of the ovens of Miru is reported as being 'a dread place to reach for any of the sons of men'.[81] When he is brought to the ovens the missionary lusts for the kava he is offered there like 'a bridegroom for his bride', as in the Song of Songs.[82] While Scriptural knowledge forms the core of Stevenson's religious literacy, he deftly weaves in religious history to enflesh a Protestant theological imagination. The missionary is 'a blue-ribbon man', that is, an evangelical advocate of temperance. This is the reason why he refuses to drink the kava in spite of its potency, which is redolent of communion wine (and has been experimented with as such in the Pacific).[83] The kava was known to 'hocus' its drinkers: the term emerged in post-Reformation decades out of a culture of Protestant ridicule of the Catholic 'Hoc est enim corpus meum' ('For this is my body'), spoken by the priest during the liturgy of the Eucharist, during the transubstantiation of bread and wine into Christ's body and blood.[84] The expression 'hocus pocus', which has come to be

---

[80] Isaiah 1: 18.
[81] The expression 'sons of men' is frequently found in the Book of Psalms.
[82] Song of Songs 4: 1–15.
[83] Matt Tomlinson, *God is Samoan: Dialogues between Culture and Theology in the Pacific* (Honolulu: University of Hawai'i Press, 2020), 66, 74, 75. Stevenson's mother describes communion at a 'native' church she visited in Tahiti as consisting of 'bread fruit cut in very small pieces' along with wine. Margaret Isabella Stevenson, 'Diaries [1874–1889 {1888}]', GEN MSS 664, Box 54, Folder 1177, Beinecke Library, Yale University.
[84] For a cross-confessional study of the Eucharist, see Lee Palmer Wandel, *The Eucharist in the Reformation: Incarnation and Liturgy* (Cambridge: Cambridge University Press, 2006).

associated with magic and conjuring, may also represent Protestant rejection of what was believed to be a superstitious Catholic practice. As in his South Seas Letters, also in this story Stevenson connects the otherness of indigenous Pacific religion with Roman Catholicism.[85] There is a suggestive comparison between bodies being 'baked in the ovens and eaten' like the Eucharistic host and Stevenson's observation of the 'currency and sacrament' of man-eating in Marquesan society. The communal eating of the bodies in this supernatural tale echoes modern theological dialogue about the importance of place in eucharistic inculturation.[86] The setting of Miru's ovens, with its 'comers out of the islands of the living, dripping and lamenting', raises visions of a purgatorial space between bodily death and annihilation.

Akaänga's exasperation with the attitude of the missionary, who clings to his pledge of sobriety, leads to the accusation that the missionary is a 'sea-lawyer', that is, one who protests rather than assents.[87] Akaänga expels the missionary, fearing 'worse will come of it' if things are left as they are. It seems that the missionary's conviction of faith over all else has the power to transform even this deathly world. When he is returned to the island 'he rang the bell for service'. While he was probably not announcing the start of mass, the presence of a ritual bell suggests that he was not ministering to a low church congregation either. There are other ecclesiastical images in the story, such as the place of Miru's ovens with its communion of the dead, and while swimming in the bay the missionary discovers a house made 'of yellow reeds tied with black sinnet', with calabashes tied all around. As soon as he touches one of the calabashes – gourd-shaped plants connected with communal eating in the Hawaiian Islands – he is transported from earthly reality into a supernatural realm.

The fable also explores the relationship between missionaries and converts. Beside the missionary at Miru's ovens is one of his own converts, who taunts him, 'And how about your story?' The missionary produces the tearful reply, 'It seems . . . that there was nothing

---

[85] A related way to interpret this is through the lens of phenomenology and literary modernism. See Richard Kearney, 'Sacramental Imagination: Eucharists of the Ordinary Universe in the Works of Joyce, Proust, and Woolf', in *Through a Glass Darkly: Suffering, the Sacred, and the Sublime in Literature and Theory*, ed. by Holly Faith Nelson, Jens Zimmerman, and Lynn Szabo (Waterloo, ON: Wilfrid Laurier University Press, 2010), 183–222.

[86] Thomas O'Loughlin, 'Inculturation: The Eucharistic Dimension', *Japan Mission Journal* 74, 3 (2020), 146–53.

[87] Stevenson, *South Sea Tales*, 289n.

in them.' The convert seems unsurprised about where he has ended up but he is amazed that the missionary clings to his 'taboo' against drinking the kava of the dead despite all of his other taboos having been 'proved wrong'. The missionary, although resigned, sees no reason to break his pledge of temperance. Yet out of all who were transported to Miru's ovens, 'the missionary was most concerned', because his contempt for indigenous beliefs had left him utterly unprepared for this ordeal. The experience shatters his previous understanding and, in spite of his eventual release from the clutches of Akaänga, the narrator tells us that 'Much matter of thought was in that missionary's mind.' The convert has played a significant part in the reconfiguration of the missionary's thinking. The steps of the missionary's ordeal are indicated throughout the story by the change in the way he utters the central refrain, beginning with 'There is nothing in it', and 'there can be nothing in it', to 'A body can think there was something in this', and, by the end, 'Perhaps there is not much in it, as I supposed; but there is something in it after all.' This experience is sure to mark his future evangelical endeavours.

It is in the story form that we can best discover Stevenson's religious thought. He was at his most assured and expressive as a writer of fiction, where there was less need to offer reasons or explanations. The sheer descriptive power of 'Something in It' carries its message with sufficient force. Moreover, religious thought in Stevenson need not be thought of in conflictual terms between, for example, 'Protestant' and 'Catholic' sensibilities but rather, as Linden Bicket has suggested in another context, as 'mutually enriching, artistically inspiring sites of interaction and exchange'.[88] 'Something in It' can be seen as a Protestant writer's attempt to describe a sacramental reality, in which divinity unveils its redeeming presence in the world. It is unusual to find Stevenson, so often the reliable proclaimer of the world's fallenness, here upholding the notion of divine restoration, albeit within a supernatural reality. The story also indigenises and symbolically reinterprets the traditional Reformed Protestant sacraments of baptism (in the missionary's bathing in the tabooed bay) and communion (in the heavenly kava and baked bodies of the dead). In the teeth of his mortal trial, the missionary not only survives but also undergoes a conversion experience. This is because, as the closing moral teaches, he has held to 'one pin-point of the truth'. Describing Stevenson's writing,

---

[88] Linden Bicket, *George Mackay Brown and the Scottish Catholic Imagination* (Edinburgh: Edinburgh University Press, 2017), 12; Cannell, 'Introduction', 25.

Robert-Louis Abrahamson explains that 'Conviction comes from an assent deep within us, a confirmation that we have (for the moment at least) perceived something true and right.'[89] With 'Something in It', Stevenson has produced a Pacific fable that explores the redeeming and transforming power of that assent.

In the next chapter, we move from the period of Stevenson's Pacific travels to look at how his writing in Samoa, particularly his later historical fiction, embodied a collective commitment to a religious way of life.

---

[89] Robert-Louis Abrahamson, 'Truth Out of Tusitala Spoke: Stevenson's Voice in Post-Darwinian Christianity', in *Persona and Paradox: Issues of Identity for C. S. Lewis, His Friends and Associates*, ed. by Suzanne Bray and William Gray (Newcastle upon Tyne: Cambridge Scholars Publishing, 2012), 237–54 (249).

Chapter 3

Rediscovering Religious Community: Samoa, 1890–4

Scholars of Stevenson's Samoan period have tended to focus on the author's fascination with the imperial wrangling of the three great powers, Britain, Germany, and the United States, and their disastrous involvement in local politics.[1] The critical consensus is that there was a notable shift in the forms as well as the tone of Stevenson's writing of this period which was dictated by these circumstances.[2] Stevenson

---

[1] For the historical context, see Paul M. Kennedy, *The Samoan Tangle: A Study in Anglo-German–American Relations, 1878–1900* (St Lucia: University of Queensland Press, 1974); Peter J. Hempenstall, *Pacific Islanders under German Rule: A Study in the Meaning of Colonial Resistance* (Acton: ANU Eview, 2016 [1978]), 25–50; W. David McIntyre, *Winding Up the British Empire in the Pacific Islands* (Oxford: Oxford University Press, 2014), 12–13. For a perspective that blends colonial with cultural history, see Benjamin Sacks, *Cricket, Kirikiti and Imperialism in Samoa, 1879–1939* (Cham: Palgrave Macmillan, 2019). For a political history of Samoa during this period, see R. P. Gilson, *Samoa 1830–1900: The Politics of a Multicultural Community* (Melbourne: Oxford University Press, 1970).

[2] See especially Roslyn Jolly, *Robert Louis Stevenson in the Pacific: Travel, Empire, and the Author's Profession* (Farnham: Ashgate, 2009) in which she mainly focuses 'on the Pacific non-fiction – *In the South Seas*, *A Footnote to History*, and the letters to the Times – because', among other reasons, 'these works best represent Stevenson's new sense of writing as action in the world' (27). Along similar lines, Graham Tulloch would like to treat *Footnote* 'as a political tract (of a very sophisticated kind) which deploys not only history but also literature, geography and psychology as a means of achieving a political purpose'. Graham Tulloch, '*A Footnote to History*: Stevenson, the Past and the Samoan Present', in *Robert Louis Stevenson and the Great Affair: Movement, Memory, and Modernity*, ed. by Richard J. Hill (London: Routledge, 2017), 148–61 (148). Stevenson is portrayed as an anticolonial writer in Joseph Farrell's *Robert Louis Stevenson in Samoa* (London: Quercus, 2017). For an archival study of Stevenson's political activities in Samoa, see Kenneth Starr Mackenzie, 'Robert Louis Stevenson and Samoa 1889–1894' (PhD thesis, Dalhousie University, 1974).

wrote about the political life of the Islands in letters to *The Times* and to his metropolitan correspondents. Perhaps not since his account of his first Atlantic sea journey had he written in such an unromantic and documentary vein.³ By the end of the nineteenth century, Western colonialism had become a major force across the Pacific, and Stevenson expressed his views about this in his fiction as well as his non-fiction. Yet, for all that they enlighten, studies of Stevenson's later work whose sole contextual focus is politics arguably do not go far enough in addressing the impact of Samoa on his writing, because they overlook what was foundational to Samoan life: religion.⁴ As Ronald Crawford emphatically asserts in his account of the nineteenth-century Samoan church, 'In practically every aspect [of Samoan society], religious conceptions and practices form an important, and perhaps indispensable part.'⁵ By not acknowledging the specifically religious character of Samoan society, we miss many of the subjects and themes that animated Stevenson's work of this period, since, as we have already seen, he was himself highly conscious of the importance of religion in the Islands.

One way in which to confirm this is by turning to perhaps the most explicitly political work that Stevenson ever wrote, *A Footnote to History: Eight Years of Trouble in Samoa* (1892). In this long pamphlet, he vividly portrays a period in which the Samoan political system was upturned by the interference of Britain, Germany, and the United States. By 1892, when it was published, the two rival claimants to the Samoan throne, Malietoa Laupepa and Mataʻafa Iosefo, were backed or opposed by different colonial factions. Stevenson made no bones about his preference for Mataʻafa: 'I have visited and dwelt in almost every seat of the Polynesian race, and have met but one man who gave me a stronger impression of character and parts.'⁶

---

³ This account has recently been published in the form originally intended by Stevenson: Robert Louis Stevenson, *The Amateur Emigrant*, ed. by Julia Reid (Edinburgh: University of Edinburgh Press, 2018).
⁴ The emphasis on politics at the expense of religion appears to be a problem in the Samoan historiography too, according to Featunaʻi Ben Liuaʻana. See his 'Samoa Tulaʻi: Ecclesiastical and Political Face of Samoa's Independence, 1900–1962' (PhD thesis, Australian National University, 2001), 287.
⁵ Ronald James Crawford, 'The Lotu and the Faʻasāmoa: Church and Society in Samoa, 1830–1880' (PhD thesis, University of Otago, 1977), 54.
⁶ Robert Louis Stevenson, *A Footnote to History: Eight Years of Trouble in Samoa* (London: Cassell and Co., 1892), 313. All references to *Footnote to History* are to this edition. The Samoan historian Malama Meleisea finds Stevenson's 'understanding of Samoan political organization' 'fairly superficial' but 'his rich powers

Yet he could see no winner between Laupepa and Mata'afa. 'They may be said to hold the great name of Malietoa [or paramount ruler] in commission; each has borne the style, each exercised the authority, of a Samoan king', he observed, and explained that

> one is secure of the small but compact and fervent following of the Catholics, the other has the sympathies of a large part of the Protestant majority, and upon any sign of Catholic aggression would have more. With men so nearly balanced, it may be asked whether a prolonged exercise of power be possible for either.[7]

Stevenson's assessment of Samoan politics was set within his grasp of the society's religious organisation. In fact, *A Footnote to History* begins with an extended description of 'native actors' that included 'Christians, church-goers, singers of hymns at family worship':

> The religious sentiment of the people is indeed for peace at any price; no pastor can bear arms; and even the layman who does so is denied the sacraments [. . .] But if the church looks askance on war, the warrior in no extremity of need or passion forgets his consideration for the church. The houses and gardens of her ministers stand safe in the midst of armies; a way is reserved for themselves along the beach, where they may be seen in their white kilts and jackets openly passing the lines, while not a hundred yards behind the skirmishers will be exchanging the useless volleys of barbaric warfare.[8]

In Samoa, politics – even modern, violent, colonial politics – bowed to religion. And according to Stevenson's portrayal of the conflict, religiosity appeared to be concentrated in its central political figures. Laupepa had been 'educated for the ministry' and 'still bears some marks of it in character and appearance', while Mata'afa is 'a devout Catholic', 'with an air of a Catholic prelate'.[9]

---

of description are extremely useful in understanding this extraordinary period in Samoan history'. Malama Meleisea, 'Introduction', in Robert Louis Stevenson, *A Footnote to History: Eight Years of Trouble in Samoa* (Honolulu: University of Hawai'i Press, 1996), vii–xvi (viii).

[7] Stevenson, *Footnote to History*, 319.
[8] Stevenson, *Footnote to History*, 8–9.
[9] Stevenson, *Footnote to History*, 48, 157–8, 312. According to a Samoan historian, Laupepa attended the LMS seminary at Malua 'and was considered a faithful Christian and an asset for the LMS'. Liua'ana, 'Samoa Tula'i', 21.

The critical oversight concerning Samoan religion has led to some incomprehension. The author of an account of Stevenson's Samoan years finds it 'striking' that Stevenson spoke 'from inside a Christian framework', 'as though he were a staunch believer and not the sceptic whose disbelief had so outraged his father'.[10] Understanding the local context helps us to make sense of this apparently sudden shift in Stevenson's perspective. Once we come to see, as Stevenson did, that religion mattered above all else in Samoan life, then we can better appreciate this period of exhausting productivity for the author. Between September 1890, when he settled into his Vailima estate on the Samoan island of Upolu, and his death in December 1894, in addition to the publication of his South Seas Letters, Stevenson completed three novels (*The Wrecker*, *Catriona*, *The Ebb-Tide*), a collection of stories (*Island Nights' Entertainments*), a book of poetry (*Ballads*), and *A Footnote to History*. Among his unfinished works were several other novels that remained at various stages of incompletion at the time of his death: *St. Ives*, *Heathercat*, *The Young Chevalier*, and *Weir of Hermiston*. In spite of their European subject matter, these last works were deeply influenced by the religious culture of Samoa.

Above all, these fictions reflect the idea of religion as a communal phenomenon. Samoan pre-Christian or 'traditional' religion could be described as a community religion, which means that it is 'particular to a single society' and 'practiced by all the members of the society and no one outside it'.[11] Christianity's global reach contrasts with such traditional religions, 'often described as localized, kinship orientated, and organized according to systems of lineage, with a primary focus on ancestors'.[12] In conditions of globalisation, some writers have theorised that Christian universalism provides traditional religions 'with a world view that enlarges or magnifies their original localized perspectives and thus enables them to engage positively with powerful international threats to their habitual way of life'.[13]

---

[10] Farrell, *Stevenson in Samoa*, 165. In his earlier historical study, Mackenzie says something similar, based on similar reasoning: 'There was also a new element in Stevenson's sphere of activities in Samoa – the religious. Having received an overdose of Christianity as a child, RLS had shunned religion.' Mackenzie, 'Robert Louis Stevenson and Samoa', 160.

[11] J. Platvoet, quoted in James L. Cox, 'Traditional Religions and Christianity', in *The Cambridge Dictionary of Christian Theology*, ed. by Ian McFarland, David A. S. Fergusson, Karen Kilby, and Iain R. Torrance (Cambridge: Cambridge University Press, 2011), 513–14.

[12] Cox, 'Traditional Religions and Christianity'.

[13] Cox, 'Traditional Religions and Christianity'.

On this basis, it is possible to suggest that during the nineteenth century, Samoan religion adjusted to the pressures of globalising forces such as Western colonisation by becoming Christianised.

Witnessing and participating in this process then prompted Stevenson to consider the Christian inheritance of his homeland. Through this complex cultural transfer, his depictions of Scottish religious community may also be distinguished from those of his contemporaries, the 'kailyard' writers. While the latter are criticised for providing an 'exaggerated and often roseate picture [. . .] of a late nineteenth-century Scotland where the Church was still central', their sources were 'country parishes far from the cities and their problems'.[14] Stevenson's communitarian images were taken from the Scottish past but they were inspired by his immediate and direct experience of Samoan religiosity. Such a global context for Stevenson's explorations of Scottish community can add to the more British-centred interpretations of the 'myth' of Scottish egalitarianism and its roots in the loss of independent statehood after 1707.[15] It provides another reason why diasporic experience should be factored into assessments of the modern Scottish national imaginary.

In this chapter, then, I interpret Stevenson's later historical fiction as a reflection of his experience of Samoa as a religious community . I begin by drawing on nineteenth-century Samoan history to describe the growth of Christianity as a local – that is, Samoan and Pacific – phenomenon. Samoans absorbed and indigenised Christianity into familiar forms and this religious process of change generated new 'frameworks of meaning' transforming previous social ideas and relationships.[16] In the transition to a Christian Samoan culture, Stevenson perceived elements of the historical experience of Scotland, whose society and institutions the Protestant Reformation had

---

[14] Ian Campbell, 'Scottish Literature in a Time of Change', in *The History of Scottish Theology, Volume II: The Early Enlightenment to the Late Victorian Era*, ed. by David Fergusson and Mark W. Elliott (Oxford: Oxford University Press, 2019), 199–212 (201).

[15] Scott Lyall, '"Tenshillingland": Community and Commerce, Myth and Madness in the Modern Scottish Novel', in *Community in Modern Scottish Literature*, ed. by Scott Lyall (Leiden and Boston: Brill, 2016), 1–24 (4).

[16] David Bebbington, 'Response: The History of Ideas and the Study of Religion', in *Seeing Things Their Way: Intellectual History and the Return of Religion*, ed. by Alister Chapman, John Coffey, and Brad S. Gregory (Notre Dame, IN: University of Notre Dame Press, 2009), 240–57 (253–4).

similarly transformed.¹⁷ Samoan Christianity fascinated Stevenson, who revelled in the apparent commonalities between Scottish and Samoan culture. It inspired him to reimagine the history of Scotland as well as wider European history. In historical fiction such as *Heathercat*, he drew on his Samoan experience to intensify the depiction of communal religiosity in the European past. Such works may be characterised as products of the 'diasporic experience', which in some senses 'escape the obligations of history and rigid periodization' in their emphasis on mood and theme.¹⁸ Again and again in these late stories, Stevenson stresses the community rather than the individual as the basis of culture. In contrast to conditions in the modern West, he portrays religion and culture as unseparated. In continuity with his earlier stories, we also find a mediated presence of the supernatural as compared with the rational religion that issued from the eighteenth century. On the whole, in his last years, Stevenson appeared to be moving away from the pattern of his earlier work, in which the primary agents were individuals who experienced moral or spiritual struggles. Here in Samoa, the central theme of his major work was the experience of the religious or moral community and its influence on the individual.

The Growth of Samoan Christianity

During the nineteenth century, Christianity became the religion of Samoa. However, as Stevenson discovered, this was not the rational and individualistic religion of the post-Enlightenment West but a communal religion with a much stronger emphasis on the presence of the supernatural in everyday life. As the historian John Garrett observed

---

¹⁷ The Reformation continued to impact Scottish society and intellectual life down to Stevenson's day. For example, William Robertson Smith argued that the orthodoxy of his method of Biblical criticism rested on its inspiration in the Protestant Reformers. William Robertson Smith, 'What History Teaches Us to Seek in the Bible', in *Lectures and Essays of William Robertson Smith* (London: A. & C. Black, 1912). From another point of view, Scottish society in the nineteenth century became increasingly marked by anti-Catholicism. Stewart J. Brown, 'Presbyterians and Catholics in Twentieth-Century Scotland', in *Scottish Christianity in the Modern World: In Honour of A. C. Cheyne*, ed. by Stewart J. Brown and George Newlands (Edinburgh: T&T Clark, 2000), 255–82 (258–61).

¹⁸ Catriona M. M. Macdonald, 'Imagining the Scottish Diaspora: Emigration and Transnational Literature in the Late Modern Period', *Britain and the World* 5, 1 (2012), 12–42 (27).

of the Pacific as a whole, 'the community values of the pre-Christian period, never surrendered, have been reaffirmed'.[19] In Samoa, community values were reaffirmed through incorporation and adaptation in a process that sometimes dismayed Western missionaries and which conflicted with the colonial authorities who assumed power over the region.[20]

Like most Pacific Islanders, Samoans today are an overwhelmingly Christian people. A 2006 census found that over 97 per cent of the Samoan population belonged to one of the country's Christian denominations, and another author conservatively estimates that over 80 per cent of the population attends church on a weekly basis.[21] Another recent account of Christianity in the region reports that the Samoan population in 2020 was 98.8 per cent Christian.[22] In the same study the claim is made that

> Christianity is an integral part of the *fa'asāmoa* [Samoan way or culture] and has influenced Sāmoan society and traditional structures in such a profound way that it is difficult to imagine a Sāmoa without its presence. The physical presence of Christianity throughout Sāmoa is such that one cannot help but notice its centrality in the lives of Sāmoans. Large church structures and places of worship beautify the countryside, prayers are offered at every function of either a secular or a religious nature, church bells ring in the early hours of the morning throughout the week to signify worship, and families gather in the evenings for dedicated family vespers. On Sundays it is normal

---

[19] John Garrett, *To Live among the Stars: Christian Origins in Oceania* (Geneva and Suva: World Council of Churches in Association with the Institute of Pacific Studies, 1982), 308. See also John Barker, 'Comments to Part 1: Christian Transcendence and the Politics of Renewal', in *Christianity, Conflict, and Renewal in Australia and the Pacific*, ed. by Fiona Magowan and Carolyn Schwarz (Boston: Brill, 2016), 23–33; Stuart Piggin and Allan Davidson, 'Christianity in Australasia and the Pacific', in *The Cambridge History of Christianity: Volume 8. World Christianities c. 1815 – c. 1914*, ed. by Sheridan Gilley and Brian Stanley (Cambridge: Cambridge University Press, 2014), 542–59 (552).

[20] For a study looking at the relationship between Samoan independence and the Samoan LMS Church, see Liua'ana, 'Samoa Tula'i'.

[21] *Samoa: Population and Housing Census Report 2006* (Apia: Samoa Bureau of Statistics, 2008), 14; Rex Tauati Ahdar, 'Samoa and the Christian State Ideal', *International Journal for the Study of the Christian Church* 13, 1 (2013), 59–72 (67).

[22] 'Christianity by Country', in *Christianity in Oceania*, ed. by Kenneth R. Ross, Katalina Tahaafe-Williams, and Todd M. Johnson (Edinburgh: Edinburgh University Press, 2021), 377–83.

practice that congregants bring gifts of food and money for clergy and their families.[23]

Even a scholar who is sceptical about the theological claims that are sometimes made about the nation's religious identity acknowledges the wide observance of Christian ritual in Samoan society and that Samoan law is intended to be based to a significant degree on Christian principles and teachings.[24] The Samoan embrace of Christianity is reflected in its present Constitution, which was updated in 2017 to make it explicit that it was the national religion. The preamble states that 'the Leaders of Samoa have declared that Samoa should be an Independent State based on Christian principles and Samoan custom and tradition'.[25] By specifically enshrining Christianity and not just the supremacy of God over its Constitution, the Samoan government went a step further than its postcolonial neighbours in formalising a regional phenomenon.[26]

The core of Samoa's Christian culture is to be found within its churches. The oldest and largest established church in the country is the one established from 1830 by the London Missionary Society (LMS) and known today as the Congregational Christian Church of Samoa (CCCS). The 2006 Census found that a third of all Samoans were members of the CCCS, with the next highest denomination being the Roman Catholic Church at just under a fifth of the total population.[27] The reasons for the pre-eminence of the Congregational Church and the ubiquity of Christian denominations in Samoa date to the early nineteenth century. The establishment of the LMS in Samoa resulted from prior Christian evangelisation in other parts of the Pacific. Samoans gave the name 'Lotu Ta'iti' to the Congregationalist Church because of the LMS's regional foundations in Tahiti and the Society Islands at the end of the eighteenth century.[28] In 1834, LMS missionaries brought

---

[23] Fetaomi Tapu-Qiliho, 'Samoa and American Samoa', in Ross et al., *Christianity in Oceania*, 50–7 (56).

[24] Ahdar, 'Samoa and the Christian State Ideal', 64, 67. See also Angelica Saada, 'Samoa: A Truly Religious Place? Views toward Religion in Samoa' (SIT Samoa, 2008).

[25] Constitution of the Independent State of Samoa (2017).

[26] See Bal Kama, 'Christianising Samoa's Constitution and Religious Freedom in the Pacific', Devpolicy Blog (2017), accessed at: https://devpolicy.org/christianising-samoas-constitution-religious-freedom-pacific-20170427 on 10 December 2020.

[27] The Methodists (14 per cent) and the Mormon Church (13 per cent) make up the leading four denominations, according to the 2006 Census.

[28] Malama Meleisea and Penelope Schoeffel Meleisea, *Lagaga: A Short History of Western Samoa* (Suva: University of the South Pacific, 1987), 55.

the first Samoan books into the Islands – hymnals, catechisms, and educational materials – which were printed in the Society Islands before a printing press was established in Samoa in 1839.[29] Christian educational institutions and printed Bibles began to appear by mid-century with the first Samoan newspaper (1839), Malua school and theological college (1842), and the Samoan New Testament (1848) and Old Testament (1855). As early as 1839, the first Samoan missionaries had left for Vanuatu (the New Hebrides).[30] Many more Samoan missionaries would head for other parts of the Pacific in the following decades.[31]

Across the Pacific, the growth of local forms of Christianity involved both conflict and accommodation. As with the Marquesas and Hawai'i, nineteenth-century Samoa also became a place of denominational rivalry.[32] To some extent this was a consequence of Christianity's origins in the Islands. Traditional accounts emphasise tensions between groups of Western missionaries and their supporters but this is to overlook the evangelical work of Pacific Islanders.[33] The birth of Samoan Christianity followed from the activity of its Island neighbours. When the Samoan leader Malietoa

---

[29] Meleisea and Meleisea, *Lagaga*, 58.

[30] Meleisea and Meleisea, *Lagaga*, 59. On the historiography, see Doug Munro and Andrew Thornley, 'Pacific Islander Pastors and Missionaries: Some Historiographical and Analytical Issues', *Pacific Studies* 23, 3–4 (2000), 1–31 (14–17).

[31] A pioneering collection of essays on Pacific Islands missionaries is *The Covenant Makers: Islander Missionaries in the Pacific*, ed. by Doug Munro and Andrew Thornley (Suva: Pacific Theological College and the Institute of Pacific Studies at the University of the South Pacific, 1996).

[32] Sharon W. Tiffany, 'The Politics of Denominational Organization in Samoa', in *Mission, Church, and Sect in Oceania*, ed. by James A. Boutilier, Daniel T. Hughes, and Sharon W. Tiffany (Ann Arbor: University of Michigan Press, 1978), 423–56. In the Marquesas Islands, Stevenson observed at close hand the contest for political authority between groups that allied with Catholic or Protestant missionaries. Robert Louis Stevenson, *In the South Seas*, ed. by Neil Rennie (London: Penguin, 1998), 55. The complex political conflict that engulfed the Hawaiian Islands at the end of the nineteenth century cannot be explained solely by denominational competition but there was nevertheless a significant religious dimension since the business and commercial interest group that seized power from King David Kalakaua in 1887 and paved the way for US annexation in 1898 was nicknamed the 'Missionary' party on account of the Presbyterian religious background of many of its members. See Laavanyan M. Ratnapalan, 'Sereno Bishop, Robert Louis Stevenson and "Americanism" in Hawai'i', *The Journal of Imperial and Commonwealth History* 40, 3 (2012), 439–57.

[33] Peggy Brock emphasises this point with respect to the wider literature on missions and cultural change. Peggy Brock, 'Introduction', in *Indigenous Peoples and Religious Change*, ed. by Peggy Brock (Leiden: Brill, 2005), 1–11 (2–3).

Vainu'upo enthusiastically welcomed the LMS's John Williams and his Samoan crew members in 1830, close contacts between Samoans and Tongans also led to the arrival of Methodism through Tongan Wesleyans.[34] Because of the Tongan connection, the Methodists in Samoa were known as 'Lotu Toga'. By advocating Protestant interdenominational cooperation Williams was able to formally exclude Methodist missionaries from Samoa, but in 1848 Tongan Methodists responded by sending a native pastor, Benjamin Latuselu, to serve the Methodist community in Samoa.[35] After repeated requests by the Tongan monarchy, in 1857 the Methodists decided to send European missionaries to Samoa. A Wesleyan theological college was also eventually established on the Samoan island of Upolu.

The story of the arrival of 'Lote Pope' to Samoa displays a similar pattern, with French Marist priests from Wallis Island arriving in 1845 as part of a group that included two Samoan men.[36] Stevenson's mother described the well-tended Catholic mission at Mount Vaea, 'with a chapel and several houses built in stone'.[37] When the Church of Jesus Christ of Latter-Day Saints ('Lotu Mamona') emerged at the end of the nineteenth century amid the challenging conditions of the Samoan civil wars, indigenous Pacific Islanders – the Hawaiian missionaries Elder Manoa and Elder Belio – again played a crucial early role in its establishment.[38] These four denominations, Congregationalist, Roman Catholic, Methodist, and Mormon, would grow to become dominant in twentieth-century Samoa's kaleidoscopically Christian society. As Crawford has pointed out, it is important

---

[34] Meleisea suggests that Malietoa Vainu'upo's enthusiasm for Christianity in Samoa might have been owing to a prophecy from the goddess Nafanua. Meleisea, 'Introduction', x. For an account that seeks to 'complicate' the traditional history of Christianity's origins, see Andrew E. Robson, 'Malietoa, Williams and Samoa's Embrace of Christianity', *Journal of Pacific History* 44, 1 (2009), 21–39.

[35] Meleisea and Meleisea, *Lagaga*, 61–2. According to the LMS's Samuel Whitmee, a not impartial source, Stevenson 'deprecated the presence of the Methodist Mission in Samoa', whose history he knew, because he felt it 'a waste of workers and of money and also a hindrance to Christian harmony'. Samuel James Whitmee, Extracts from 'My two years in Samoa with Robert Louis Stevenson', 1. Series. South Seas Personal, 1818–1939. Records of the London Missionary Society (as filmed by AJCP), National Library of Australia.

[36] Meleisea and Meleisea, *Lagaga*, 62–4; Andrew Hamilton, 'Nineteenth-Century French Missionaries and Fa'a Samoa', *Journal of Pacific History* 33, 2 (1998), 163–77 (167).

[37] Margaret Isabella Stevenson, *Letters from Samoa 1891–1895*, ed. by Marie Clothilde Balfour (London: Methuen, 1906), 308–9.

[38] Meleisea and Meleisea, *Lagaga*, 65–6.

to recognise that this flourishing denominational competition was also an extension of pre-existing Samoan rivalries.[39] Christianity, regardless of denomination, was interpreted as a means of access to supernatural power (*mana*), and in this respect its ready acceptance represented continuity within Samoan culture.

Stevenson, Scotland, and Samoa

In Samoa, Stevenson became a more active participant in a religious society than he had been since the early 1870s in Edinburgh. The comparison is not coincidental. Stevenson thought that there were important historical and cultural parallels between Scotland and Samoa as national communities organised on a religious basis.[40] Furthermore, the social conditions of his life in Samoa, in which he was dependent on missionaries and converts to mediate his experience, contributed to his appreciation of the religious basis of culture. These factors helped to establish the significance of communities of religious belief.

Covenant Parallels

Along with the growth and diversification of denominational Christianity, which Scotland experienced in the centuries after the Reformation, it shared with Samoa theological claims and emphasised the election of a covenanted community of believers. In fact, both nineteenth-century Samoa and post-Reformation Scotland displayed

---

[39] Crawford, 'The Lotu and the Fa'asāmoa', 391.

[40] It is also important to note the differences in the two Christian cultures. Samoa lacked any kind of priesthood prior to the arrival of Christianity, so that there was none of the conflict between church and state which animated Scottish Protestant history. On the growth in confidence of the Samoan pastorate, see Steve Mullins and David Wetherell, 'LMS Teachers and Colonialism in Torres Strait and New Guinea, 1871–1915', in Munro and Thornley, *Covenant Makers*, 203–4. Unlike their Reformed Scottish counterparts, Samoan laity would not be encouraged to challenge their pastors about the way in which they lived and for the doctrines that they preached. And while Reformed Scots enthusiastically 'extirpated the "idolatry" of decoration and ceremonial from buildings and services', in Samoa the building of churches and their adornment grew apace with Christianity's earliest beginnings. Paul Tonks, 'Shaping Scotland's Identity: The Historical Impact of Covenanting Presbyterianism', *Korean Journal of British Studies* 18, 12 (2007), 321–40 (329); Garrett, *To Live among the Stars*, 278.

kinship or feudal ties which extended socially through a covenantal relationship. The idea of the religious covenant dates back to the Hebrew word *b'rith*, which means 'bond' or 'fetter that carries a sense of obligation'; according to traditional accounts, such a 'normative' and 'communal' conception originated in Biblical Israel.[41] The classic formulations are in the Books of Genesis, with God's promise to Abraham, and Exodus, with the divine promulgation of the Mosaic Law. Ever since the advent of Christ, Christian theologians have tried to reconcile the 'old' Jewish and 'new' Christian covenants under a single dispensation.[42] The idea of a special covenant with God as legislating human relationships within a community has proven remarkably influential, particularly in polities associated with Reformed ecclesiology. From Calvin's Geneva to the English Separatists in Plymouth, an important strand of modern Western political thought can be traced to a Biblical/covenantal rather than a secular/contractual understanding of the basis of political community.[43] Calvinist Scotland offers one of the most potent early modern manifestations of this 'theo-political' phenomenon.[44]

Many distinctive aspects of nineteenth-century Scottish identity resulted from the intellectual and political battles that its national covenant bearers had fought in earlier centuries. 'Covenanting', according to a historian of early modern Scotland, 'was a very important feature of the Scottish Reformation' from which the Scottish Church 'was seen as being governed in the closest way by the Word of God'.[45] The Calvinist reformer John Knox (1514–72) helped to establish belief in the purity of the Reformed Church of Scotland. In his essay on Knox, Stevenson described him as the man who 'recreated Scotland' and observed that in Knox, 'we see foreshadowed the whole Puritan Revolution and the scaffold of Charles I'.[46] Scottish

---

[41] James W. Skillen, 'Covenant', in McFarland et al., *The Cambridge Dictionary of Christian Theology*, 119–20.

[42] See, for example, Joseph Cardinal Ratzinger, *Many Religions, One Covenant: Israel, the Church, and the World* (San Francisco: Ignatius Press, 1999).

[43] Daniel J. Elazar, *Covenant and Polity in Biblical Israel: Biblical Foundations and Jewish Expressions. The Covenant Tradition in Politics, Volume I* (Abingdon: Routledge, 2017 [1995]), 19–34.

[44] The expression is Elazar's, in *Covenant and Polity*, 1. On Scottish society's transition through the Reformation, see Jenny Wormald, *Court, Kirk, and Community: Scotland 1470–1625* (Edinburgh: Edinburgh University Press, 1991).

[45] Tonks, 'Shaping Scotland's Identity', 331, 332.

[46] Robert Louis Stevenson, *Familiar Studies of Men and Books* (New York: Charles Scribner's Sons, 1891), 7, 320–1.

people in the century after Knox believed that they had received the inheritance of Biblical Israel and were bound within a new Christian covenant. In the British religious and political conflicts of the seventeenth century, many Scots from all social groups signed or observed the National Covenant (1638) and the Solemn League and Covenant (1643) to preserve Scottish unity as a nation of the elect. After the restoration of the British monarchy under the Stuarts in 1660, there was a further period of violence as Scottish Protestants who were dissatisfied with the new religious settlement were punished for their beliefs and rebelled. These Covenanters often paid the ultimate price and were remembered as martyrs.[47] Stevenson made his own moving contribution to Covenanter memorialisation with a dedicatory poem, which was written in Samoa:

> Blows the wind to-day, and the sun and the rain are flying,
> Blows the wind on the moors to-day and now,
> Where about the graves of the martyrs the whaups are crying,
> My heart remembers how!
>
> Grey recumbent tombs of the dead in desert places,
> Standing Stones on the vacant wine-red moor,
> Hills of sheep, and the howes of the silent vanished races,
> And winds, austere and pure!
>
> Be it granted me to behold you again in dying,
> Hills of home! and to hear again the call;
> Hear about the graves of the martyrs the peewees crying;
> And hear no more at all.[48]

While the 'Killing Time' of the later 1600s has been often recalled through verse and story, the succeeding period of political union with England and Wales has been remembered more prosaically. The 1706–7 Acts of Union delivered Scottish political sovereignty into English hands, but the agreement was grounded in an Anglo-Scottish understanding that the two peoples constituted a single Protestant nation, while Scottish control of the Kirk importantly

---

[47] On Scottish commemoration of the Covenanters, see James J. Coleman, *Remembering the Past in Nineteenth-Century Scotland: Commemoration, Nationality and Memory* (Cambridge: Cambridge University Press, 2014), chapter 5.

[48] Robert Louis Stevenson, 'To S. R. Crockett', in *Songs of Travel and Other Verses* (London: Chatto and Windus, 1896), 84.

secured continuity with the Reformed tradition.[49] Through the following two centuries, however, elements of Scottish popular religion, Seceders from the Church, and even many within the established church continued to draw inspiration and legitimacy for protest from the Covenanters, while the sense that Scotland was a nation of the elect would persevere.[50]

Stevenson described himself as 'a child of the Covenanters' and memorably named the ship on which David Balfour was kidnapped the *Covenant*.[51] He was naturally attentive to Samoan interpretations of covenant and accounts of religious community. On one side of his tombstone on Mount Vaea, built by Samoans and 'out-islanders', is marked in Samoan the covenantal lines from the Book of Ruth (1: 16–17):

> Wherever you go, I shall go,
> wherever you live, I shall live.
> Your people will be my people,
> and your God will be my God.
> Where you die, I shall die
> and there I shall be buried.[52]

The word 'covenant' also features in the third edition of a dictionary of the Samoan language owned by Stevenson. The dictionary's compiler, the English LMS missionary George Pratt (1817–94), offered two definitions for the Samoan term *feagaiga*. The first

---

[49] See Linda Colley's classic account of the importance of the Union in the forging of a Protestant British identity in *Britons: Forging the Nation 1707–1837* (New Haven, CT: Yale University Press, 1992). Karin Bowie provides an account of Union within Scottish religious contexts in 'Popular Resistance, Religion and the Union of 1707', in *Scotland and the Union, 1707–2007*, ed. by T. M. Devine (Edinburgh: Edinburgh University Press, 2008), 39–53.

[50] Tonks, 'Shaping Scotland's Identity', 337–8; Stewart J. Brown, *Thomas Chalmers and the Godly Commonwealth in Scotland* (Oxford: Oxford University Press, 1982), xvi–xviii.

[51] *The Letters of Robert Louis Stevenson*, ed. by Bradford A. Booth and Ernest Mehew (New Haven, CT: Yale University Press, 1994–5), VII, 111.

[52] This is a modern translation. Teuila [Isobel Osbourne], 'The Tomb of Robert Louis Stevenson on Mount Vaea' (1897), National Library of Scotland. The land on which his grave rests has been set aside as the Stevenson Memorial Reserve. According to a local ordinance, it 'shall be maintained in perpetuity by the Government of Samoa in memory of Robert Louis Stevenson and his love for the people of Samoa'. 'Stevenson Memorial Reserve and Mount Vaea Scenic Reserve Ordinance 1958', Pacific Islands Legal Information Institute, accessed at: http://www.paclii.org/ws/legis/consol_act/smramvsro1958612/ on 31 March 2021.

is 'an established relationship between different parties', such as between chiefs and their village, and the second is 'An agreement, a covenant.'[53] The word for 'Testament' in the 1872 edition of the Samoan Bible, to which Pratt contributed, is *feagaiga*.[54] The Samoan church historian Latu Latai explains that the word also 'has a sacred element' that comes from 'feagai', which, according to Pratt's *Dictionary*, means 'to be opposite to each other' but also 'To correspond' and 'To dwell together cordially, to be on good terms.'[55] Thus Latai claims that *feagaiga* 'does not denote a state of agonistic conflict but rather of persons being in a reciprocal or mutual status and valuation'.[56] He explains that '*Feagai* is a crucial aspect of Samoan life, which dictates how people relate to each other and is deeply connected to values such as *tapu* (taboo), *faaaloalo* (mutual respect) and va tapuia (sacred and relational space).' The Samoan idea of relationships built on reciprocity establishes hierarchy and orders cultural life even down to details such as the seating arrangements at social gatherings. The anthropologist Serge Tcherkézoff claims that such ordering should not be understood according to modern Western notions of equality but rather 'in terms of those at the top encompassing others'.[57] Stevenson found the Scottish clan system reflected in this Samoan ideal of embracing authority. As we shall see, playfully yet also problematically, he attempted to reproduce the clan system in Samoan conditions.

---

[53] George Pratt, *A Grammar and Dictionary of the Samoan Language* (The Religious Tract Society, 1893), 153. Pratt spent forty years (1839–79) in Samoa as a representative of the London Missionary Society. Stevenson admired Pratt's Samoan translations in his *Fables from Many Lands* (1890). See Stevenson, *Letters* VII, 77 and n. Raeburn Lange suggests that the LMS missionaries may also have invested the Samoan *feagaiga* concept with 'Puritan theology and ecclesiology'. Raeburn Lange, *Island Ministers: Indigenous Leadership in Nineteenth Century Pacific Islands Christianity* (Christchurch: Macmillan Brown Centre for Pacific Studies, University of Canterbury, and Canberra: Pandanus Books, Research School of Pacific and Asian Studies, the Australian National University, 2005), 98.

[54] London: British and Foreign Bible Society, 1872.

[55] Pratt, *Grammar and Dictionary*, 152–3. The discussion in this paragraph draws from Latai's doctoral thesis: Latu Latai, 'Covenant Keepers: A History of Samoan (LMS) Missionary Wives in the Western Pacific from 1839 to 1979' (PhD thesis, Australian National University, 2016), 43–6.

[56] Crawford, quoting another writer, observes that while *feagaiga* 'involves co-operation and complementarity (in external relations)' it also involves 'rivalry and competition (in internal relations)'. Crawford, 'The Lotu and the Fa'asāmoa', 42.

[57] Serge Tcherkézoff, quoted in Latai, 'Covenant Keepers', 43.

Missionary Mediation

Stevenson was a critical friend of missionaries and his own evangelical activities are overshadowed by his sometimes stern evaluations of the work of the LMS and other religious organisations.[58] Among the visitors at his Vailima residence, Stevenson's cousin Graham Balfour remembers 'the Independent and Wesleyan missionaries; the French Bishop; the priests and sisters'.[59] Stevenson's decision to spend a significant portion of his time in Samoa among foreign missionaries, those 'best and most useful whites in the Pacific', rested on his admission that it was the missionary's 'business to make changes'.[60] To the LMS's Samuel James Whitmee he confided, 'I regard the presence of you missionaries in these Islands as the one redeeming feature of the presence of white men in Samoa.'[61] While he did not offer much overt support to them, this is not to say that he was insignificant to or uninterested in missionaries' work. He was always respectful and engaged, and his mother Margaret, who joined the family in Samoa in March 1891, was undoubtedly an influence on him as she maintained her long-standing interest in missions.[62] The two regularly attended the Sunday evening English church service in the nearby town of Apia, where Stevenson was 'reverent in attitude' and, according to the LMS's William Clarke (1854–1922), 'usually spent the week-end at the mission house' afterwards.[63] However we interpret his view of missionaries, we must recognise that Stevenson lived with them as a participant rather than looking on their work as a disinterested observer.

Even before Margaret Stevenson's arrival in Samoa, her son had taken on an important mediating role on behalf of the foreign Christian presence in Apia. Robert Louis Stevenson was involved in the affairs of the mission at several levels. Although Clarke remembers

---

[58] For an informative account that focuses on Stevenson's relationship with the LMS missionaries in Samoa, see Ann C. Colley, *Robert Louis Stevenson and the Colonial Imagination* (New York: Routledge, 2017 [2004]), chapter 1.

[59] Graham Balfour, *The Life of Robert Louis Stevenson* (London: Methuen, 1920), 247. Margaret Stevenson wrote of a visit to the Stevenson household from Mormon missionaries. Stevenson, *Letters from Samoa*, 129–31.

[60] Stevenson, *In the South Seas*, 34, 64.

[61] Whitmee, Extracts, 1.

[62] Lesley Graham, 'From Scotland to Sāmoa: Margaret Isabella Balfour Stevenson in Polynesia', *Studies in Travel Writing* 24, 1 (2020), 1–15 (10).

[63] W. E. Clarke, 'Personal Recollections of Robert Louis Stevenson', *Chronicle of the London Missionary Society* (April 1908), 66–71 (68); W. E. Clarke, 'Robert Louis Stevenson in Samoa', *Yale Review* 10 (1921), 275–96 (283–4).

only two occasions on which he contributed towards the 'English church', he 'never refused his personal service when it was asked'.[64] And according to Whitmee, he always made an annual contribution to the native Samoan mission.[65] At the behest of another LMS missionary, James Newell, Stevenson addressed seminary students at the Malua theological college at an afternoon service.[66] He also taught a class of mixed-race children at the European Church's Sunday school.[67] Margaret Stevenson, who attended the talk, recalls how her son 'took the parable of the talents as a foundation':

> he told them that there were three talents at least that they all possessed, and must try to make a good use of: *tongues* that they must use to cheer and make happy all around them; *faces* that they must keep bright as new shillings, so that they might shine like lamps in their homes; and *hands* that must be kept employed in useful work cheerfully done, and if they spent their lives in doing these things for the good of others, they might be told at the last, *Inasmuch as ye did it to the least of these, ye did it unto Me.*[68]

The fact that the careful and scrupulous LMS missionaries should have given him this delicate task illustrates the trust and confidence they reposed in him. Stevenson also took on a diplomatic role between the missionaries and the 'beach', the European community at Apia, who sometimes did not see eye to eye over issues of propriety, and he interviewed and reported to Clarke on the views of European traders about the work of the missionaries and of LMS-trained native pastors. 'In this way', Clarke acknowledges, 'I learnt many useful facts about native life, and the lives of the solitary white "Beachcombers", which otherwise would have been a sealed book to me.'[69] Without Stevenson's knowledge of issues that were pertinent to missionary activity, the LMS would have found less use for him and his own efforts would have been ineffective. If, on the one hand, Stevenson seems to have been drawn into a role that was created for him by the missionary context, then on the other, his engaged presence helped to

---

[64] Clarke, 'Stevenson in Samoa', 285.
[65] Whitmee, Extracts, 1.
[66] J. E. Newell, 'R. L. Stevenson as I Knew Him', *Christchurch Press*, 2 March 1907. National Library of Australia, nla.obj-2739135234.
[67] Clarke, 'Stevenson in Samoa', 285.
[68] Stevenson, *Letters from Samoa*, 233–4.
[69] Clarke, 'Personal Recollections', 72.

engender a sense of what the LMS representatives, the white population of the beach, and Samoan Christians had in common.

Stevenson enjoyed good relationships with several of the LMS missionaries in Samoa. He was especially close to William Clarke, whom he respected as a missionary pastor that was considerate of Samoan culture and sought to reach sensible compromises where possible.[70] Stevenson pointed out to Clarke that the character of the missionary 'Tarleton' in his novella 'The Beach of Falesá' was modelled on him.[71] Theology may also have brought Clarke and other products of English 'dissenting academies' closer to Stevenson, who was more familiar with the Reformed tradition in which they had been trained than he was with the ritualist Anglicanism of the later nineteenth century.[72] Clarke had attended the theologically orthodox Western College, which was founded in the previous century as an Independent/nonconformist institution and had trained many ministers for service, including thirty-eight LMS missionaries.[73]

Stevenson also wrote a short story, 'The Bottle Imp', for the LMS's Samoan missionary journal *O le Sulu Samoa*. He worked on the story's translation with the Reverend Arthur Claxton, spending 'an evening over each chapter'.[74] Claxton was the journal's editor and noted that Stevenson 'was rapidly picking up Samoan' and enjoying 'the balancing of rival expressions in the Samoan idiom of the idea to be rendered'. The story's local popularity caused a 'great increase' in the magazine's circulation. William Clarke observed that the Stevensons had wanted to run their Samoan home like a 'missionary household'.[75] It required

---

[70] See, for instance, the dialogue between the two men over the episode of the Samoan *Siva* or 'national dance' in Clarke, 'Personal Recollections', 86–7.

[71] The name 'Tarleton' was adapted from the Samoanised form of Clarke, 'Talati'. Clarke, 'Personal Recollections', 68.

[72] David A. S. Fergusson, 'Reformed Theology in the British Isles', in *The Cambridge Companion to Reformed Theology*, ed. by Paul T. Nimmo and David A. S. Fergusson (Cambridge: Cambridge University Press, 2016), 248–68 (248).

[73] James Sibree, 'Clarke, William Edward', in *A Register of Missionaries, Deputations, etc. from 1796 to 1923* (London: London Missionary Society, 1923), 110; J. Charteris Johnstone, 'The Story of the Western College', *Transactions of the Congregational History Society* 7, 2 (1916–18), 98–109 (98, 109).

[74] A. E. Claxton, 'Stevenson as I Knew Him', *Chronicle of the London Missionary Society* (May 1908), 89–90.

[75] Clarke, 'Stevenson in Samoa', 278. Mackenzie describes Stevenson's operation of his estate as having been 'very much in the manner of a Scottish laird – and thus very close to the way in which a Samoan village was run'. Kenneth Starr Mackenzie, 'The Last Opportunity: Robert Louis Stevenson and Samoa, 1889–1894', in *More Pacific Islands Portraits*, ed. by Deryck Scarr (Canberra: Australian National University

Clarke's assistance as well as concerned Samoan parents' understanding that Stevenson was friends with 'misi' to allow him to adopt a family of Samoan Christian boys. Clarke describes how the Stevenson household became responsible for these Samoans' attendance at mission school, their education in 'some of the amenities of civilization', and for providing 'a daily object lesson in the life of a Christian home'.[76] In time, Stevenson's domestic retinue changed and expanded to take in Islanders from other parts of the Pacific. He enjoyed playing the role of clan chief or paterfamilias and he expressed great satisfaction when he noticed that his domestic servants were beginning to attach themselves to him.[77]

Margaret Stevenson explained how, during a birthday celebration thrown for a friend, her son had 'the servants dressed for the first time in the "Vailima livery", Royal Stewart tartan – *lava-lavas* and white shirts, the girls wearing the same *lava-lavas* with their chemises, and all with flowers in their hair'.[78] Such behaviour is open to criticism from postcolonial scholars for whom Stevenson could be seen as enacting a doubly exoticised Highland fantasy.[79] It is worth observing that from a Samoan point of view, the *aiga*, or domestic household, was the source of one's identity. From this relationship one 'receives security and the necessities of life' and 'to it he offers service' out of love.[80] For Stevenson too, such a relationship was meaningful, especially in the light of the breakdown of a sense of community across modern Scotland. The fact that many of his domestic retinue were Christians also reaffirmed the idea, which would have been familiar to him from Scottish theology, that faith was best 'nurtured through personal experience in an organic community'.[81]

Both the mission community at Apia as well as ordinary Samoans thought of Stevenson as a 'Christian man' and he was expected to give a good example to others by behaving according to established

---

Press, 1978), 155–72 (159). On the intercultural development of the 'Samoan parsonage family', see Sadat Muaiava, 'The Samoan Parsonage Family: The Concepts of Feagaiga and Tagata'ese', *Journal of New Zealand & Pacific Studies* 3, 1 (2015), 73–83.

[76] Clarke, 'Stevenson in Samoa', 278.
[77] Stevenson, *Letters* VIII, 186.
[78] Stevenson, *Letters from Samoa*, 231.
[79] Alessia Polatti, 'The "Myth of Tusitala" in Samoa: R. L. Stevenson's Presence in Albert Wendt's Fiction', *Loxias* 48 (2016), accessed at: http://revel.unice.fr/loxias/index.html?id=8233 on 2 November 2021.
[80] Crawford, 'The Lotu and the Fa'asāmoa', 19, 32.
[81] Brown, *Thomas Chalmers*, 7–8.

missionary codes.[82] Naturally, this caused some awkwardness in a man who had gone to some length earlier in life to establish his independence from religious norms. But when Stevenson was involved in a game that broke the LMS's Sunday rules, Clarke was impressed by his 'moral courage' and witness in openly expressing his contrition for the 'misspent Sabbath'.[83] Such injunctions had been achieved and maintained with difficulty and it is remarkable to observe Stevenson grappling with obligations of communal religious life in Samoa that he had rejected in his youth in Scotland.[84] While Roslyn Jolly has demonstrated Stevenson's interest in ideas of taboo in the Pacific, it is important to recognise that his first experience of public religious sanctions would have been in the form of the Scottish Sabbath.[85] The latter was also something that he wrote about in the Pacific, as we shall see below. The loss of the wider context of beliefs and obligations in which taboos such as the Sabbath resided was something that fascinated him as a theorist of culture.[86]

The watchful presence of Christian Pacific Islanders encouraged Stevenson's efforts to conform to local norms. We might say, adopting the language of Charles Taylor, that a distinctively Samoan 'social imaginary' ('the ways we are able to think or imagine the whole of society') was drawing Stevenson out of the buffered self of Western secular modernity.[87] He was becoming part of the moral community that was forged by the Samoan experiment with Christianity. The Sunday evening English-language service at the Apia Foreign Church consisted of a 'curiously mixed congregation of Europeans of various nationalities' but it also contained a 'good choir of half-castes'.[88] Stevenson supported this 'poor relation of the Protestant churches in Samoa', according to one historian, 'with his presence, money, and

---

[82] Clarke, Personal Recollections', 71. Stevenson is remembered fondly by Samoans, not just in terms of written history but also through their oral history. He could see what Christianity meant to Samoans and Samoans related to him because he was a Christian as well as a foreigner. Latu Latai, personal communication, 2021; Bob Dixon, personal communication, 2021.

[83] Clarke does not provide a date for this incident in his 'Personal Recollections', 71.

[84] On Stevenson's reflections on the missionary impact on Islander society, see L. M. Ratnapalan, 'Missionary Christianity and Culture in Robert Louis Stevenson's "The Beach of Falesá"', *Religion & Literature* 53, 3 (2021), 47–62.

[85] Jolly, *Stevenson in the Pacific*, 49–52.

[86] Cf. Alasdair MacIntyre's discussion of the breakdown of the Polynesian taboo system in *After Virtue: A Study in Moral Theory* (Notre Dame, IN: University of Notre Dame Press, 2007), 111–12.

[87] Charles Taylor, *A Secular Age* (Cambridge, MA: Belknap Press, 2007), 156.

[88] Clarke, 'Personal Recollections', 68.

efforts'.[89] The regular evening prayers conducted in the Stevenson household, as they still are in most Samoan homes, was an intercultural affair with prayers written by Stevenson and interspersed with Samoan hymns.[90] To his friend Elizabeth Fairchild he wrote in March 1892:

> I was called down to eight o'clock prayers, and have just worked through a chapter of Joshua and five verses, with five treble choruses of a Samoan hymn, but the music was good, our boys and precentress ('tis always a woman that leads) did better than I ever heard them and to my great pleasure I understood it all except one verse.[91]

A Christmas card he sent to Clarke adopted the Samoan terms for greetings ('Manuia!') and Sunday ('Aso Sa') as well as the Samoan name of his daughter-in-law Belle Strong ('Teuila'), who designed the card.[92] He closed his message to Clarke with a traditional religious greeting: 'I pray God bless and further you throughout the year.'

Lloyd Osbourne described Stevenson as 'wholly an unbeliever' who preferred 'denominational religion' to 'materialism' for its 'least spark of sincerity', thought the 'multitude [. . .] needed supernaturalism, ritual and sensuous impression to stir the little ideality that it possessed', and 'had an illogical sort of inherited love for religious forms and ceremonies' and 'the beautiful and touchingly patriarchal aspect of family devotions'.[93] In contrast to his stepson, who seemed unable to accept the religious roots of the moral, ethical, and aesthetic impulses that he inherited, Stevenson strove to exercise Christian behaviour in Samoan society. That this was how Samoans saw him is shown by the events which followed his death. His funeral was an intercultural and interdenominational event in which the community rose up in grief and mourning for the loss of a cherished friend and leader.[94] Along with one of the prayers that

---

[89] Mackenzie, 'Last Opportunity', 162.
[90] Robert Louis Stevenson, *Prayers Written at Vailima, with an Introduction by Mrs. Stevenson* (New York: Charles Scribner's Sons, 1904). The prayers also display the extent to which Scottish Presbyterianism had absorbed Anglican styles by this time. I am grateful to Robert-Louis Abrahamson and to Stewart J. Brown for these insights.
[91] Stevenson, *Letters* VII, 254.
[92] Clarke, 'Personal Recollections', 69–70.
[93] Lloyd Osbourne, quoted in Alanna Knight, *The Robert Louis Stevenson Treasury* (London: Shepheard-Walwyn, 1985), 34.
[94] A thorough account is provided by Mehew in Stevenson, *Letters* VIII, 401–10.

was written by Stevenson himself, the funeral ceremony included an Anglican service conducted by Clarke and a brief address in Samoan that was delivered by Newell.[95] These missionaries tolerated Samoan customs of vigils for the dead ('a relic of the old heathen days', according to Clarke) that included the placing of traditional mats beside the deceased, as well as Catholic prayers in Latin and rites performed by some of Stevenson's young Pacific Islander servants.[96]

Religious Community in the Later Historical Fiction

The better Stevenson grew to know Samoa, the more difficult he found it to communicate his absorption in it to friends and colleagues in Europe and North America. As he stammered to an uncomprehending Sidney Colvin in October 1894, 'Mataafa and Tui and Po'e are of my surroundings and flow naturally into what I write.'[97] He translated the thrill of Samoan military conflict into activist journalism, but participation in a religious community re-enlivened his historical imagination. The Samoan present helped to refashion the European, and especially the Scottish, past. The immediacy of communal religious life, the public piety of Islander worship, and collective belief in the supernatural combined to create a strong impression which inevitably found its way into his fiction. Coming from the Europe of Darwin and Nietzsche, Stevenson's lens was decidedly modern, yet he implicitly understood that in Samoa, as in the rest of the Pacific, religious piety rested on pre-Enlightenment assumptions about the supernatural.[98] He wrote to Colvin about how one of his household servants, a Wallis Islander named Paatalise, had to be restrained in bed by other members of his retinue after experiencing a vision of deceased family members calling to him from outside the house. He remarked on how his other domestic servants

> *believed P's ravings*, they *knew* that his dead family, thirty strong, crowded the front verandah and called on him to come to the other

---

[95] Clarke, 'Stevenson in Samoa', 296; 'Obituary', *Samoa Weekly Herald* 2, 106, 8 December 1894, p. 2.
[96] Clarke, 'Stevenson in Samoa', 294; Balfour, *Life*, 265.
[97] Stevenson, *Letters* VIII, 370.
[98] Crawford, 'The Lotu and the Fa'asāmoa', 54–5.

world. They *knew* that his dead brother had met him that afternoon in the bush, and struck him on both temples.[99]

In later stories such as *Heathercat* and *Weir of Hermiston*, we find a similar presence of the supernatural embodied in the beliefs and assumptions of the community.

Of course, the sense of the supernatural always provided a conduit for Stevenson's creativity, as can be seen in such earlier tales as 'Thrawn Janet' (1881/1887) and 'The Body Snatcher' (1884). But Pacific Islanders' open and collective expression of belief in the supernatural was novel for him. He inscribed the Samoan experience into his European fiction in a thematically distinctive way by establishing religious belief as the basis of community. This is at least implicit in all of the later works and constitutes a major theme in most of them.[100] Unlike Stevenson's prior explorations of the individual grappling with religious morality, in the Pacific he focuses on how shared belief gives motivation and vitality to groups. As a transcendent organising principle, religion is depicted as the driver of society, capable of producing unity but also division. As a reflection of denominational competition across the Pacific, Stevenson's European fiction depicts historical settings in which Christian traditions are in conflict. The buffered self is less visible in this portrayal of societies existing in an open cosmos, as characters struggle between rival sources of belief rather than between belief and unbelief.

Catriona (or *David Balfour*), originally published in 1893, is the first in the cycle of historical fictions completed in Samoa. 'Why did I take up *David Balfour*?' Stevenson asked himself in a letter of March 1892: 'I don't know. A sudden passion.'[101] In a certain sense, however, the novel was in planning ever since he finished writing the last

---

[99] Stevenson, *Letters* VII, 310. Carla Manfredi 'highlight[s] Stevenson's Gothic vision of Samoa in which colonial violence gave rise to new forms of *aitu* [spirits or ghosts]'. Carla Manfredi, *Robert Louis Stevenson's Pacific Impressions: Photography and Travel Writing, 1888–1894* (Cham: Palgrave Macmillan, 2018), 191.

[100] The idea is also present in his other writing, such as his October 1894 address to the Samoan supporters of Mata'afa. Robert Louis Stevenson, *Sophia Scarlet and Other Pacific Writings*, ed. by Robert Hoskins (Auckland: AUT Media, 2008), 121–5.

[101] Stevenson, *Letters* VII, 243.

words of *Kidnapped*.[102] In its hero's frequent turn to conscience and to the resources of prayer and sacrament, but without the overtly religious settings of later works like *Heathercat* and *Weir of Hermiston*, *Catriona* could be said to represent an intermediate stage in its author's journey towards the theme of believing communities.[103] As Stevenson noted, it was also the last of his major works to be written in the first person and even this followed the need to continue its hero's narrative in *Kidnapped*.[104]

The dramatic and highly charged events of *Catriona* take place in Scotland, the Netherlands, and northern France. The first half sees David Balfour attempt to save James Stewart from the gallows for the murder of Colin Campbell. 'I was acting for the sake of justice', decides David to himself in one of his introspective moments, in a way that makes '*the death of any innocent man a wound upon the whole community*'.[105] But David soon experiences the machinations of political expediency that cloud the face of the justice he seeks. His first encounter with Lord Advocate Prestongrange sets up the conflict: '"You are head of justice in this country," I cried, "and you propose to me a crime!" "I am a man nursing with both hands the interests of this country," he replied, "and I press on you a political necessity!"'[106] David ultimately fails to save James Stewart, who is hanged by a legal authority that consists of the Stewarts' political enemies.

As a means of resolving the inner conflict between law and politics, David frequently resorts to the voice of conscience in private prayer. After all, 'A good conscience is eight parts of courage.'[107] This David Balfour is more given to interior self-examination than the impulsive young man of *Kidnapped*. He responds to internal crises by turning to Scripture and theology, such as during a moment of

---

[102] Roslyn Jolly distances herself from Barry Menikoff's continuity claim based on the similarity of inspiration between *Kidnapped* and *Catriona* by arguing that *Catriona* is filled 'with ideas and emotions that stemmed from Stevenson's exposure to Pacific life and colonialist politics in the period 1888–92', although she acknowledges that her analysis of the 'legal plot' is only relevant to the first half of the novel. Jolly, *Stevenson in the Pacific*, 120, 119.

[103] Jolly discusses the issue of conscience, in the first half of *Catriona*, within a legalistic presentation of Stevenson's literary imagination. Jolly, *Stevenson in the Pacific*, 113–56.

[104] Stevenson, *Letters* VII, 251.

[105] Robert Louis Stevenson, *David Balfour* (New York: Charles Scribner's Sons, 1905), 28; my italics.

[106] Stevenson, *David Balfour*, 49.

[107] Stevenson, *David Balfour*, 130.

emotional confusion when he remembers 'the common, old, public, disconsidered sin of self-indulgence'. Immediately recalling the words *'How can Satan cast out Satan?'* (Matthew 12: 26), he resolves that 'the hurt that had been caused by self-indulgence must be cured by self-denial; the flesh I had pampered must be crucified'.[108] These battling words signify the careless young man discovering sanctuary in his Covenanting roots.

Also to a far more significant degree than in *Kidnapped*, religious worship and devotion form the sustaining interior reality of the main characters in *Catriona*. This can be seen in the unusual behaviour exhibited by a familiar figure such as Alan Breck. At the beginning of chapter 12, early one morning, Alan tells David that while the young man was sleeping, 'I have done a thing that maybe I do over seldom.' When asked what that was, he answers, 'Oh, just said my prayers.'[109] At Gillane Sands, after seeing Alan off, David observes men appearing to capture him. So 'I shut my eyes and prayed.'[110] In Leyden, while they are living together, David and Catriona 'made some kind of shift to hold worship privately in our own chamber'. David confesses that 'there was scarce anything that more affected me, than thus to kneel down alone with her before God like man and wife'.[111] In chapter 8, relieved after an aborted duel, David walks away to the tune of 'a very good air, that is as ancient as the Bible', the original words being from the first book of Samuel: '"*Surely the bitterness of death is passed*"' (15: 32). Following this distressing encounter, David is thirsty. He drinks at the holy St Margaret's well 'and the sweetness of that water passed belief'.[112]

As described earlier, while travelling in the Pacific Stevenson became attuned to the presence of the supernatural in the everyday as well as to a more public mode of addressing religion.[113] In *Catriona*, we find a new freedom in the way he describes religious ideas. After David is kidnapped but left at liberty to roam the Bass Rock, he reflects on the island's 'chapel' or 'hermit's cell' and the prison: 'There were times when I thought I could have heard the pious sound of psalms out of the martyrs' dungeons.'[114] The place is described in a manner reminiscent of the Hawaiian cities of

---

[108] Stevenson, *David Balfour*, 131–2.
[109] Stevenson, *David Balfour*, 139.
[110] Stevenson, *David Balfour*, 160.
[111] Stevenson, *David Balfour*, 320.
[112] Stevenson, *David Balfour*, 99.
[113] See Chapter 2.
[114] Stevenson, *David Balfour*, 170.

refuge and activates a kind of religious memory. The prison 'was a place full of history, both human and divine'.[115] David believes that the three Highlanders who are guarding him carry a 'superstitious fear' of the Bass Rock, like the Pacific Islanders who were afraid of the secluded parts of a beach. The Bass Rock was an 'isolated place' caught up 'among endless strange sounds of the sea and the sea-birds'.[116]

The influence of the Pacific, quite submerged in *Catriona*, is more palpable in Stevenson's other European fiction. These are the works of a novelist who carries a vivid impression of societies that organise themselves around a transcendent principle. To borrow Craig Beveridge and Ronald Turnbull's felicitous expression, the stories descended from a 'moral-religious milieu'.[117] The neglected adventure *St. Ives* looks back at Scottish religious community with a sort of wistful, half-amused reverence.[118] 'There are few religious ceremonies more imposing', observes the eponymous hero, a French Catholic aristocrat, than the *sawbath*, 'that weekly trance to which the city of Edinburgh is subjected'.[119] Much of the chapter is written in the ethnographic vein of Stevenson's Pacific travel writing, while early nineteenth-century Scottish denominationalism provides the butt of the humour. When his Scottish landlady unexpectedly asks St. Ives (whose real identity she does not know) about the 'denoamination' of his beloved Flora, the Frenchman replies,

> 'Upon my word, ma'am, I have never inquired,' cried I; 'I only know that she is a heartfelt Christian, and that is enough.'
> 'Ay!' she sighed, 'if she has the root of the maitter! There's a remnant practically in most of the denoaminations. There's some in the McGlashanites, and some in the Glassites, and mony in the McMillanites, and there's a leeven even in the Estayblishment.'
> 'I have known some very good Papists even, if you go to that,' said I.

---

[115] Stevenson, *David Balfour*, 170.
[116] Stevenson, *David Balfour*, 176.
[117] Craig Beveridge and Ronald Turnbull, *The Eclipse of Scottish Culture* (Edinburgh: Polygon, 1989), 111.
[118] For an account that situates the production of *St. Ives* and *Weir of Hermiston* within wider networks of literary publishing, see Glenda Norquay, *Robert Louis Stevenson, Literary Networks and Transatlantic Publishing in the 1890s: The Author Incorporated* (London: Anthem Press, 2020).
[119] Robert Louis Stevenson, *St. Ives: Being the Adventures of a French Prisoner in England* (New York: Charles Scribner's Sons, 1905), 286.

'Mr. Ducie, think shame to yoursel'!' she cried.
'Why, my dear madam! I only—' I began.
'You shouldnae jest in sairious maitters,' she interrupted.[120]

There is also a Sabbath scene in the fifth chapter of *Catriona* that is entertained more briefly than *St. Ives*.[121] Stevenson tells us that David Balfour is 'less impressed by the reasoning of the divines than by the spectacle of the thronged congregation in the churches', of which he visits several and finds them busy and full, 'like what I imagined of a theatre'.[122] Again there is an echo of the Pacific ethnography, in which Stevenson describes full churches and religious congregations.

The settings and themes of Stevenson's later fictions are primarily religious, from the Calvinist severity of the 'hanging judge' Adam Weir in *Weir of Hermiston* to the Covenanter pastoral *Heathercat*, with its vivid description of the Killing Time, to *The Young Chevalier* with its memorable opening 'in the city of the Anti-popes'.[123] The subject closest to the author's heart was the seventeenth-century Covenanters. As progenitors of modern Scotland, they and their religious predecessors, such as John Knox, fascinated Stevenson in a way that the leading figures of the Scottish Enlightenment never could. As Callum Brown has demonstrated, this fact should not surprise us about a writer from a Victorian social class for whom national religious traditions remained definitive.[124]

The major religious fault line in western Europe, between episcopalian (that is, Roman Catholic and Anglican) and dissenting traditions, forms the backdrop to *Heathercat*. 'The Traquairs were always strong for the Covenant; for the king also, but the Covenant first; and it began to be ill days for Montroymont when the Bishops came in and the dragoons at the heels of them.'[125] The theme of the story

---

[120] Stevenson, *St. Ives*, 292.
[121] Stevenson, *David Balfour*, 54.
[122] Stevenson, *David Balfour*, 54.
[123] Robert Louis Stevenson, 'The Young Chevalier', in *Weir of Hermiston; Some Unfinished Stories* (London: William Heinemann, 1924), 171. Julia Reid has identified a 'community's cultural evolution' in the linked settings of *Heathercat*, 'Thrawn Janet', and *Weir of Hermiston*. Reid, *Robert Louis Stevenson, Science, and the Fin de Siècle* (Basingstoke: Palgrave Macmillan, 2006), 166. Andrew Lang provided the original inspiration for *The Young Chevalier*. Stevenson, *Letters* VII, 220n.
[124] Callum G. Brown, *The People in the Pews: Religion and Society in Scotland since 1780* (Glasgow: Economic and Social History Society of Scotland, 1993), 30.
[125] Stevenson, *Weir of Hermiston*, 144.

is religious communities in conflict; communities that overlapped regionally and even within families. The Lady Montroymont cannot abide her husband's tolerance of the system imposed across the country by the new government of Charles II. '"Oh hellish compliance"', she complains to her barely comprehending son, '"I would not suffer a complier to break bread with Christian folk. Of all the sins of this day there is not one so God-defying, so Christ-humiliating, as damnable compliance."'[126]

Another key to these texts is the importance of interdenominational conflict over the pre-Christian past. The latter is dead and gone. The battle now was for the identity of the Christian soul, not that of the 'pagan' convert. This also described the state of affairs in Samoa and much of the Pacific in the later nineteenth century, where the missionary struggle was to preserve religious orthodoxy rather than to induce conversion. In a vivid and bracing scene in *Heathercat*, Stevenson portrays a conventicle – an outlawed religious gathering – in bare and rainswept country. The meeting takes place among ancient standing stones, 'the very threshold of the devils of yore'.[127] In an image that is reminiscent of his description of Gilbertese Christians gathered together in Abaiang, he writes of how the assembly 'sat [. . .] partly among the idolatrous monoliths and on the turfy soil of the Ring itself'.[128] Huddled together against the world amid this heathen memorial is the Covenanting community:

> They were the last of the faithful; God, who had averted His face from all other countries of the world, still leaned from Heaven to observe, with swelling sympathy, the doings of His moorland remnant; Christ was by them with His eternal wounds, with dropping tears; the Holy Ghost (never perfectly realised nor firmly adopted by Protestant imaginations) was dimly supposed to be in the heart of each and on the lips of the minister. And over against them was the army of the hierarchies, from the men Charles and James Stuart, on to King Lewie and the Emperor; and the scarlet Pope, and the muckle black devil himself, peering out the red mouth of hell in an ecstasy of hate and hope. 'One pull more!' he seemed to cry; 'one pull more, and it's done. There's only Clydesdale and the Stewartry, and the three Bailieries of Ayr, left for God.' And with such an august assistance of powers and principalities looking on at the last conflict of good and evil, it was scarce possible to spare a thought to those

---

[126] Stevenson, *Weir of Hermiston*, 153.
[127] Stevenson, *Weir of Hermiston*, 160–1.
[128] Stevenson, *In the South Seas*, 244.

old, infirm, debile *ab agendo* devils whose holy place they were now violating.[129]

In *Weir of Hermiston*, his last unfinished work, Stevenson draws the major tension from out of the historical conflict between Enlightenment liberalism and Calvinist conservatism, which he combines with a highly personal study of the encounter between justice and mercy. In the grimly impartial judgments of the 'hanging judge' Adam Weir we are shown what makes people fear God, while in his late wife there seemed to be much of God's tenderness. The revolutionary French are the enemy in the shadows, ready backers of 'radical' elements among the Scots and against whom the General Assembly of the Church of Scotland promised to be on careful watch.[130] Weir's young son, Archie, is sensitive and highly impressionable. Revulsion at his father's lack of mercy in condemning an obviously guilty man to death leads to a rebellious desire 'to overthrow the usurping devil that sat, horned and hoofed, on her throne'.[131] But Archie quickly comes to regret his actions and is firmly put in his place by the judge, who warns him that 'there's no room for splairgers under the fower quarters of John Calvin'.[132] This sets up the young man's exile to the family estate at Hermiston where the rest of the surviving narrative is played out. Unlike earlier stories such as *Jekyll and Hyde*, *Weir* explores not Calvinist theology per se but rather what is described in the novel as 'superstition'. Stevenson wrote to Colvin from Samoa in November 1890 about his former 'insensibility to superstition' and wondered whether he was 'beginning to be sucked in' in this new religious climate.[133] In *Weir of Hermiston*, with remarkable technical and imaginative power, he sustains the tension between 'superstition' and 'incredulity'.[134]

The centrality of religious belief upholds elements in the novel such as character. Jean Hermiston, Archie's mother, 'was a true enthusiast,

---

[129] Stevenson, *Weir of Hermiston*, 161.
[130] 'Acts: 1793' ['The General Assembly's dutiful address to His Majesty on the subject of the present War'], in *Acts of the General Assembly of the Church of Scotland 1638–1842*, ed. by Church Law Society (Edinburgh: Edinburgh Printing & Publishing Co., 1843), 840–2. *British History Online*, accessed at: http://www.british-history.ac.uk/church-scotland-records/acts/1638-1842/pp840-842 on 10 April 2021.
[131] Stevenson, *Weir of Hermiston*, 25–6.
[132] Stevenson, *Weir of Hermiston*, 34–5.
[133] Stevenson, *Letters* VII, 25.
[134] Stevenson, *Weir of Hermiston*, 1.

and might have made the sunshine and the glory of a cloister'.[135] Of the four 'Black Brothers' of the younger Kirstie, Hob is a kirk elder and Gib, after youthful dabbling in revolutionary politics, turned to what some called 'heresy and schism'.[136] 'Sunday after Sunday' at the church, Archie 'sat down and stood up' and 'heard the voice of Mr. Torrance leaping like an ill-played clarionet from key to key'.[137] The younger Kirstie, pronounced 'fey' by her brother Dandie when she seems noticeably in 'high spirits' after her first church encounter with Archie, lies prone in bed and contemplates 'the suggested doom'.[138] She holds her 'psalm-book in her hands for hours' 'in a mere stupor of unconsenting pleasure and unreasoning fear':

> The fear was superstitious; there came up again and again in her memory Dandie's ill-omened words, and a hundred grisly and black tales out of the immediate neighbourhood read her a commentary on their force [. . .] the ominous words of Dandie – heard, not heeded, and still remembered – had lent to her thoughts, or rather to her mood, a cast of solemnity, and that idea of Fate – a pagan Fate, uncontrolled by a Christian deity, obscure, lawless, and august – moving indissuadably in the affairs of Christian men.[139]

This is an unexpected allusion to an unconverted presence – 'a pagan Fate' – moving not only in Kirstie Elliot's thoughts but in all 'Christian men'. As Julia Reid has demonstrated, Stevenson's writing is haunted by notions of the 'primitive' that lurked within seemingly civilised humankind.[140] Here, in what was to be his final work, we find a reason for the author's lifelong fascination with the idea as he inserts something fearfully uncontrollable in the struggle of a pious young woman to discipline her first romantic feelings and accommodate herself to the demands of her community. The attempt to subdue and tame wild impersonal forces from 'out of the immediate neighbourhood' is a familiar theme in the psychology of Christian conversion.[141] In Stevenson's time, the work that this involved was

---

[135] Stevenson, *Weir of Hermiston*, 10.
[136] Stevenson, *Weir of Hermiston*, 60, 61.
[137] Stevenson, *Weir of Hermiston*, 70.
[138] Stevenson, *Weir of Hermiston*, 81–2.
[139] Stevenson, *Weir of Hermiston*, 82, 83.
[140] Reid, *Stevenson, Science, and the Fin de Siècle*, 5.
[141] The Jesuit theologian Henri de Lubac wrote of 'the continual conversion of every Christian, in whom the pagan is never entirely dead'. Henri de Lubac, *Catholicism: A Study of Dogma in Relation to the Corporate Destiny of Mankind* (New York: Sheed and Ward, 1950), 101.

thought to be most pertinent to the neophyte Christian communities of Asia, Africa, and the Island Pacific.

The impact of Pacific Islands religion on the themes, settings, and characters of Stevenson's European fiction leads us to consider the question of influence. Unlike nineteenth-century European 'primitive' artists and writers, Stevenson did not leave the West behind in order to find community but rather to regain physical health. Nevertheless, in doing so he did discover a religious community, albeit in a form that was new to him. The connections between Samoa and his homeland, which he to some extent invented or exaggerated to suit his purposes, aided his accommodation to this new life. In his stories of 1890–4, we see him breaking through the buffered self of Western modernity to explore communal experiences of belief. It is notable that Wiltshire, the leading European character in Stevenson's Pacific novella 'The Beach of Falesá', is a lapsed Christian who seems unwilling to embrace the mixed Christian community of the island and finally moves on to another place. By contrast, religious life in Samoa was beginning to shape Stevenson's imagination of the European past and his reckoning of the place of community in questions of identity and value. The Samoan respect for ancestors may even have encouraged his turn to genealogy in his later years.[142] Whatever the degree of local influence, Stevenson's was also a peculiarly Scottish rediscovery of community in Samoa. The situation in which he found himself as an exile from an individualised Western spiritual existence somewhat resembled the younger Kirstie's dilemma in *Weir* as she becomes more vividly aware of the communal dimension of her identity. For Stevenson, the social world of the Samoan people, in its familiarity as well as in its otherness, was a way of becoming a 'person-in-community'.[143]

Pacific contextualisation helps us to better appreciate the richness of Stevenson's European fiction. Knowledge of Islander appropriations of Western thought and practice can do the same with his Pacific fiction. That is the subject of the following chapter.

---

[142] Robert Louis Stevenson, 'Records of a Family of Engineers', in *The Works of Robert Louis Stevenson, Volume 16* (London: Chatto and Windus, 1912), 3–152.

[143] Beveridge and Turnbull, *Eclipse of Scottish Culture*, 99.

Chapter 4

Inculturation

In a piece that was published in 1901, the London Missionary Society (LMS) historian Richard Lovett wrote in pointed terms about the difference in attitude towards missionaries between Stevenson and other writers. Lovett opined that Stevenson 'saw the missionaries and missionary work as they are, and not as the modern pagan *litterateur* often imagines them to be'.[1] The Scottish author

> did what no other man of his training and standing has done in this generation. He came to know missionary work not in the superficial and often supercilious manner of the globe-trotter and of some government officials. He learned its true nature through living among Samoans who had been trained under missionary influence; by watching their daily life; by the knowledge he gained of their language and modes of thought and aims in life.[2]

Lovett grasped what made Stevenson's experience truly unique and something that few others in his time understood: his recognition that Christianity's flourishing in the Pacific depended on the work of Pacific Islanders.[3] It was they, not missionaries, who were chiefly responsible

---

[1] Richard Lovett, 'R. L. Stevenson in Relation to Christian Life and Christian Missions', *The Sunday at Home* (1901–2), 229–32 (229).
[2] Lovett, 'R. L. Stevenson', 229.
[3] See Richard Lovett, *The History of the London Missionary Society 1795–1895, Volume 1* (of 2) (London: Henry Frowde, 1899), 117–474. Modern historical studies of this important subject began in the 1960s with Ron and Marjorie Crocombe's *The Works of Ta'unga: Records of a Polynesian Traveller in the South Seas, 1833–1896* (Canberra: Australian National University Press, 1968). The development of the field has been uneven since then but other significant milestones include John Garrett, *To Live among the Stars: Christian Origins in Oceania* (Geneva and Suva: World Council of Churches in Association with the Institute of Pacific Studies, 1982) and

for the spread of the religion and its adaptation into local religious beliefs and practices. Through study and interaction with them, Stevenson acquired from Pacific Islanders a depth of understanding that distinguished him among the non-religious authorities on Pacific culture. As we saw in the previous chapter, such was his level of engagement that it would be more accurate to describe Stevenson as a participant in, rather than an observer of, mission work. He supported the LMS's efforts and conducted evangelical work himself through teaching, providing personal and financial support, observing and reporting on missionary efforts, and by trying to live according to established religious norms and practices in Samoa. He talked with missionaries and learned about their different attitudes, ideas, and methods. In a way that even Lovett may not have fully appreciated, by living among Samoan Christians Stevenson also began to grow aware of what Christianity looked like from the Pacific Islanders' point of view. As a religiously literate and culturally sensitive layperson, he was in a position to observe transformations in Christianity that foreign missionaries were not easily able to recognise.[4]

We have already seen how, when Christianity was established in Samoa, it relied on the joint efforts of Europeans and Pacific Islanders. When he first met the Samoan leader Malietoa Vainu'upo in 1830, the LMS missionary John Williams described how Malietoa enthusiastically adopted the new religion.[5] Mass Samoan conversions followed. Political benefits also accrued to those associating with foreigners, who could supply materials and prestige. Even before Williams's arrival, Islander converts and visitors to Samoa had helped to introduce forms of Christianity that would remain distinctive in certain villages. Therefore, in spite of its apparently sudden arrival, the development of Christianity in nineteenth-century Samoa took place rather gradually. The Samoan religious historian Latu Latai explains that 'Samoans appropriated the new religion based on Samoa's existing belief system.'[6] For example, pre-Christian ideas of

---

The Covenant Makers: Islander Missionaries in the Pacific, ed. by Doug Munro and Andrew Thornley (Suva: Pacific Theological College and the Institute of Pacific Studies, University of the South Pacific, 1996).

[4] Ronald James Crawford, 'The Lotu and the Fa'asāmoa: Church and Society in Samoa, 1830–1880' (PhD thesis, University of Otago, 1977), 63.

[5] *The Samoan Journals of John Williams 1830 and 1832*, ed. by Richard M. Moyle (Canberra: Australian National University Press, 1984), 74.

[6] Latu Latai, 'Covenant Keepers: A History of Samoan (LMS) Missionary Wives in the Western Pacific from 1839 to 1979' (PhD thesis, Australian National University, 2016), 42.

atonement and a 'spiritual realm' suggesting life after death were elements of traditional Samoan religion that survived into the Christian era and continued to inform local ideas about the new faith. Latai states that 'When Malietoa received Williams [. . .] he expressed his wish that the missionaries and Samoa would be *aiga tasi*, one kin', in the sense of belonging to one group that transcended biological affinity.[7] Latai interprets the inclusion of missionaries within an expanded sense of belonging as part of an indigenous strategy wherein 'the new religion would be integrated into their own existing systems, social structures and long genealogical history'.[8] While this move could be said to demonstrate indigenous autonomy and self-awareness, however, it also risked the problem of a merely cultural transmission of the new faith rather than an authentic spiritual witness.[9] As we shall see, this describes a fundamental dilemma that has exercised religious thinkers down to the present day.[10]

When Stevenson arrived in Samoa he observed the results of more than half a century of accommodation between Western Christianity and Pacific Islands culture. A sense of his attentiveness to that encounter may be found in his South Seas Letters.[11] His interest in the relationship between Christian and non-Christian elements of indigenous cultures drew him to Islander converts, often royals with a turbulent past that had apparently been quelled. Thus Temoana, the high chief of the Marquesas Islands, 'was at first a convert of the Protestant mission' but later 'fell under the strong and benign influence of the late bishop [René Ildefonse Dordillon], extended his influence in the group, was for a while joint ruler with the prelate, and died at last the chief supporter of Catholicism and the French'.[12] The home of Temoana's widow, Vaekehu, was built

---

[7] Latai, 'Covenant Keepers', 43.

[8] Latai, 'Covenant Keepers', 43. Referring to the cross-denominational power of Samoan cultural ideas, Raeburn Lange observes that the term *feagaiga*, discussed in the context of covenant in Chapter 3, was applied to Catholic as well as Protestant catechists. Raeburn Lange, *Island Ministers: Indigenous Leadership in Nineteenth Century Pacific Islands Christianity* (Christchurch: Macmillan Brown Centre for Pacific Studies, University of Canterbury, and Canberra: Pandanus Books, Research School of Pacific and Asian Studies, the Australian National University, 2005), 98.

[9] This is the situation that appears to be realised in Albert Wendt's novel *Leaves of the Banyan Tree* (London: Penguin, 1980).

[10] For example, see Lange, *Island Ministers*, 328.

[11] See Chapter 2 for a discussion of the South Seas Letters.

[12] Robert Louis Stevenson, *In the South Seas*, ed. by Neil Rennie (London: Penguin, 1998), 55.

'on the European plan' and contained 'religious pictures on the wall'.[13] Stanislao Moanatini, her son, put to an end Stevenson's speculations about the queen's cannibalistic past: 'she is content; she is religious, she passes all her days with the [Catholic religious] sisters'.[14] In Butaritari in the Gilbert Islands, Stevenson found King Tebureimoa, once a feared hitman, now 'a convert, a reader of the Bible, perhaps a penitent'.[15] These exalted figures struck a curiously Westernised image of Christian piety, which perhaps contributed to the drollery with which Stevenson described their lives as converts.

Things were somewhat different in Samoa, however. While his expressions still sometimes convey mild amusement at the novelty of his subject, Stevenson was touched by the authenticity of religious witness that he found there. In a letter to Sidney Colvin of 2 November 1892 he described a scene in which he conducted 'proceedings' to determine whether one of his household retinue had stolen a pig. Respectful irony about his servants' credulity finally gives way to a serious impression of their conviction:

> The proceedings opened by my delivering a Samoan prayer, which may be translated thus – 'Our God, look down upon us and shine into our hearts. Help us to be far from falsehood so that each one of us may stand before thy face in his integrity.' Then [. . .] everyone came up to the table, laid his hand on the Bible, and repeated clause by clause after me the following oath – I fear it may sound even comic in English, but it is a very pretty piece in Samoan and struck direct at the most lively superstitions of the race. 'This is the Holy Bible here I am touching. Behold me, O God. If I know who it was that took away the pig, or the place to which it was taken, or have heard anything relating to it, and shall not declare the same – be made an end of by God this life of mine!' They all took it with so much seriousness and firmness [. . .] I was so far impressed by their bearing that I went no further, and the funny and yet strangely solemn scene came to an end.[16]

Stevenson's deepest and most extensive reflections about the local appropriation of Christianity are to be found in his Pacific fiction, which he completed in Samoa. In this chapter, I analyse this body

---

[13] Stevenson, *In the South Seas*, 56.
[14] Stevenson, *In the South Seas*, 58.
[15] Stevenson, *In the South Seas*, 164.
[16] *The Letters of Robert Louis Stevenson*, ed. by Bradford A. Booth and Ernest Mehew (New Haven, CT: Yale University Press, 1994–5), VII, 410.

of writing through the anthropo-theological concept of *inculturation* to demonstrate how far he was engaged with the relationship between Christianity and Pacific Islands culture. Besides being among his greatest literary products, these works also stand as highly personal meditations on the author's religious anthropology. Although entirely overlooked by modern scholarship, Islander Christianity was a critical context for Stevenson's fiction. Almost all of the main indigenous characters in his Pacific prose works – Uma, Namu, Keawe, Kokua, Keola, and Lehua – are Christians. By contrast, most of the white characters cannot be classed as religious, with the outstanding exceptions of the missionary Tarleton and the would-be missionary Attwater.[17]

Manfred Malzahn describes Stevenson's South Seas fiction as 'ambiguous and ironic', and says that it 'defies attempts to brand his work as either pro- or anticolonial'.[18] To this we could add that, in order to better understand his seemingly paradoxical position, we should try to locate Stevenson's ideas in history: in this respect, commentators have tended to miss the originality of the author's vision of the relationship between Pacific culture and the West. One general line of interpretation has been to emphasise Stevenson's criticism of Western missionaries, for example by portraying Islanders' rejection of Christianity.[19] While one can certainly find passages in his writing that are critical of missionary impositions on indigenous populations, such an interpretation tends to rest on the assumption that the Christianity Stevenson encountered in the Pacific was an imported faith that was indistinguishable from, or at least closely connected to, Western colonialism. A second line of interpretation of Stevenson's Pacific fiction presents the author as a pioneer: a postcolonial novelist and cultural

---

[17] Stevenson's only other prose fiction with a partially Pacific setting, *The Wrecker*, consists of a white cast of characters, not one of whom is a Christian in any substantial sense.

[18] Manfred Malzahn, 'Voices of the Scottish Empire', in *Robert Louis Stevenson: Writer of Boundaries*, ed. by Richard Dury and Richard Ambrosini (Madison: University of Wisconsin Press, 2006), 160.

[19] See, for example, Barry Menikoff, *Robert Louis Stevenson and 'The Beach of Falesá': A Study in Victorian Publishing with the Original Text* (Stanford, CA: Stanford University Press, 1984); Robert I. Hillier, *The South Seas Fiction of Robert Louis Stevenson* (New York: Peter Lang, 1989), 6; Mandy Treagus, 'Crossing "the beach": Samoa, Stevenson, and "The Beach at Falesá"', *Literature Compass* 11, 5 (2014), 312–20. Ann C. Colley, *Robert Louis Stevenson and the Colonial Imagination* (New York: Routledge, 2017 [2004]) takes a more nuanced position on Stevenson's relationship with missionaries. See pp. 23–46.

innovator, a theorist of 'the primitive' in humankind and a harbinger of psychological theories of anthropology.[20] Although it is important to situate Stevenson's work within the culturally relativising milieu of late-nineteenth-century industrial globalisation, as I suggested earlier, this approach can lose sight of the Christian roots of Stevenson's anthropology and remove him from his intellectual context.[21]

The two established patterns of interpretation are grounded in the study of Stevenson's writing and in relevant cultural contexts, yet they could be pressed further. In the first instance, this is done by acknowledging the scholarly consensus that the growth of Christianity in the Pacific was inseparable from indigenous agency. Any representation of the relationship between Christianity and colonialism is complicated by this historical fact. Missionaries could not hope to achieve a foothold without the active support of Pacific Islanders, many of whom were political and social authorities in their societies. In their turn, Pacific Islands Christians were adapters and transmitters, not merely recipients and least of all victims of the agents of a foreign religion.[22] The identity of Pacific Christianity was not straightforwardly Western, and opinions of various shades coloured the debate.[23] The meaningful local appropriation of Christianity was a contested subject in Samoa as elsewhere and it forms an essential context towards understanding Stevenson's fiction.[24]

A key argument of this book is that a richer intellectual appraisal of Stevenson's oeuvre should take seriously the Christian formation

---

[20] Sylvie Largeaud-Ortega, 'A Scotsman's Pacific: Shifting Identities in R. L. Stevenson's Postcolonial Fiction', *International Journal of Scottish Literature* 9 (2013), 85–98; Roslyn Jolly, 'Introduction', in Robert Louis Stevenson, *South Sea Tales*, ed. by Roslyn Jolly (Oxford: Oxford University Press, 1996), ix–xxxiii; Julia Reid, *Robert Louis Stevenson, Science, and the Fin de Siècle* (Basingstoke: Palgrave Macmillan, 2006).

[21] See Chapter 2. Charlot connects Polynesian religion with a de-Christianised Scottishness in Stevenson's writing. John Charlot, 'The Influence of Polynesian Literature and Thought on Robert Louis Stevenson', *The Journal of Intercultural Studies* 14 (1987), 82–106.

[22] Peggy Brock, 'Introduction', in *Indigenous Peoples and Religious Change*, ed. by Peggy Brock (Leiden: Brill, 2005), 1–11; Peter C. Phan, 'World Christianity: Its Implications for History, Religious Studies, and Theology', *Horizons* 39, 2 (2012), 171–88; Brian Stanley, 'Editorial: Appropriations of Christianity', *Studies in World Christianity* 23, 1 (2017), 1–3.

[23] For an excellent example of the emerging indigenous Pacific Christian historiography, see Kealani Cook, *Return to Kahiki: Native Hawaiians in Oceania* (Cambridge: Cambridge University Press, 2018).

[24] Latai, 'Covenant Keepers', 67–9.

of his mind. In trying to analyse his writing, it makes little sense to set aside or reduce the influence of religious language, ideas, and images. Rather, as with other modern authors such as Charles Darwin, it can be helpful to draw on the theological foundations of Stevenson's thought in order to better understand how his anthropology developed from it in a distinctive way.[25] In Stevenson's writing, the notion of 'the primitive' refers not only to something that is intrinsically disordered or violent but to that which transgresses the boundaries of civility and common decency – it implies a social dimension. It can describe the human being before he or she has learned the virtues associated with certain expectations of social life, such as the illiterate and 'savage' John Breck Maccoll in *Kidnapped*. From a Christian perspective, the idea of the primitive also gestures towards the idea of humankind in a state of original sin, which is a spiritual reality that is separate from the sociocultural question of how 'civilised' a person is.[26] Since original sin cannot be ministered to except through supernatural grace, people of all cultures are perpetually in need of conversion. To Stevenson, raised as a Presbyterian in the Reformed Church of Scotland, this would have been self-evident.[27]

This chapter therefore focuses on the ways in which Pacific Islanders in Stevenson's fiction appropriate ideas and materials in order to lead Christian lives. As Stevenson explored issues that can best be understood using the term 'inculturation', the object of his analysis shifted

---

[25] See Neal C. Gillespie, *Charles Darwin and the Problem of Creation* (Chicago: University of Chicago Press, 1979).

[26] Romans 5: 12–19.

[27] The term 'Reformed' is difficult to define precisely. Paul Nimmo and David Fergusson explain how, during the Reformation, 'it came to refer to the theology and practice held broadly in common by a particular series of churches which claimed to be "reformed according to the Word of God"' and 'came in time to be distinguished ever more clearly not only from the Roman Catholic Church but also from both the Lutheran churches and the more radical movements of the Reformation' (2). However, defining Reformed theology according to documentary bases (2–3), 'confessional uniformity' (3), or 'intellectual habits' (4) is unsatisfactory. In the end, they claim that if there is not 'univocity across all its expressions', then at least there are 'material and thematic resonances across its diverse texts at a most profound level' (4). Paul T. Nimmo and David A. S. Fergusson, 'Introduction', in *The Cambridge Companion to Reformed Theology*, ed. by Paul T. Nimmo and David A. S. Fergusson (Cambridge: Cambridge University Press, 2016). On the origins and outlines of Presbyterianism, see Gary Scott Smith and P. C. Kemeny, 'Introduction', in *The Oxford Handbook of Presbyterianism*, ed. by Gary Scott Smith and P. C. Kemeny (Oxford: Oxford University Press, 2019), 1–6.

towards indigenous people. He wrote about the novel ways in which Pacific Islanders took up, thought about, and reordered the Christianity that they had been taught by missionaries. He approached this sensitive subject from the point of view of a mid-nineteenth-century native of Edinburgh who was intellectually formed in the Scottish Presbyterian tradition. In portraying Islander religious thought and practice, he was also extending the limits of his own assumptions about denominational Christianity, what it meant and how it should be observed. Stevenson's literary preoccupation with themes of religious materiality, Scriptural literacy, and political community reflected concerns that ultimately sprang from the historical and theological foundations of Reformed Protestantism.

Explaining Inculturation

In using the word *inculturation*, I am primarily describing a process by which Christianity comes to be expressed through a culture's deepest collective beliefs and assumptions.[28] It does not describe a final outcome but rather an approach or attitude towards cultural change that embraces social, moral, aesthetic, and other transformations. Inculturation goes hand in hand with the methods and principles of World Christianity, which stress 'Christianity's inherently plural character'.[29] As such, it supports the effort 'to study particular Christian communities, beliefs, or practices in the light of and in relation to Christianity's wider (hi)story'.[30] An important goal of the process of inculturation is to bring about authentic religious witness in the culture. For example, the appearance of figures and institutions in a new Christian community that are associated with traditional expressions of Christianity (e.g. pastors, priests, churches) does not mean that inculturation is taking place or has happened. These may be signs of indigenisation; whereas, achieved through dialogue, inculturation depends on continuous and effective interaction

---

[28] For a profound analysis, see Joseph Cardinal Ratzinger, 'Christ, Faith and the Challenge of Cultures', Meeting with the Doctrinal Commissions in Asia (1993), accessed at: https://www.vatican.va/roman_curia/congregations/cfaith/incontri/rc_con_cfaith_19930303_hong-kong-ratzinger_en.html on 23 July 2021.

[29] Martha Frederiks and Dorottya Nagy, 'Introduction', in *World Christianity: Methodological Considerations*, ed. by Martha Frederiks and Dorottya Nagy (Leiden and Boston: Brill, 2021), 1–9 (3).

[30] Frederiks and Nagy, 'Introduction', 3.

between lay Christians, theologians, and religious authorities. To engender its object of a culturally meaningful Christianity is neither to reproduce the pre-Christian culture in a new guise nor to smuggle through an external culture in the outward religious form.[31] The significant challenges associated with this process mean that it can take time, perhaps several generations, in order to show signs of coming to fruition.

Inculturation is one of several terms ('contextualisation' and 'interculturation' are often applied in similar ways) that first began to be used around the middle of the twentieth century, during an era of decolonisation, to try to capture theologically what seemed to be happening as Christians in Africa, Asia, and the Pacific, many from newly independent countries, attempted to advance a version of the faith that better reflected their own situations and conditions.[32] The call for a non-Western Christianity was made in a mood of political optimism as part of the pursuit of total freedom. Inculturation should therefore be distinguished from acculturation, which implies the adoption of Western forms of Christianity by non-Western peoples. This would be contrary to the wider political project of decolonisation although the matter is complicated by arguments made by some theologians that Christianity may be infused with Western culture at its very roots in the forms of Greek philosophy and the Latin language.[33] Inculturation is

---

[31] See Matt Tomlinson, *God is Samoan: Dialogues between Culture and Theology in the Pacific* (Honolulu: University of Hawai'i Press, 2020), 9–14. See also Philip Gibbs, 'Encountering Difference: Interculturality and Contextual Theology', *Verbum SVD* 54, 1 (2013), 75–89 (82, 83–4). There are similarities between my presentation and the first two typologies presented by Stephen B. Bevans and Roger P. Schroeder in *Constants in Context: A Theology of Mission for Today* (New York: Orbis, 2004), 35. For a critique of theology that has become overly accommodating to local Pacific culture, see the work of the Tongan theologian Ma'afu Palu, e.g. Ma'afu 'o Tu'itonga Palu, 'Pacific Theology: A Reconsideration of its Methodology', *The Pacific Journal of Theology*, Series 2, 29 (2003), 30–58. The approach to Pacific theology that Palu criticises is represented by another Tongan theologian, Sione 'Amanaki Havea, and his 'quest for a Pacific theology' (30).

[32] Robert Schreiter does not situate the origins of what he terms 'local theology' quite as explicitly within the history of twentieth-century decolonisation, but the shift is parallel: 'The churches in Latin America, Africa, Asia, and Oceania are not satisfied to repeat the tradition as it has come to them, in rote fashion'. Robert J. Schreiter, *Constructing Local Theologies* (New York: Orbis, 1985), xi. See also Aylward Shorter, *Toward a Theology of Inculturation* (Eugene, OR: Wipf and Stock, 2006 [1988]), xi.

[33] Gavin D'Costa, 'Inculturation', in *The Cambridge Dictionary of Christian Theology*, ed. by Ian McFarland, David A. S. Fergusson, Karen Kilby, and Iain R. Torrance (Cambridge: Cambridge University Press, 2011), 238–9; Joseph Ratzinger (as Pope

also not indigenisation, a term which, as I explained above, commonly refers to the substitution of Western figures, objects, and words by indigenous equivalents, and typically focuses on church leadership.[34] While in the middle years of the twentieth century indigenisation was more politically acceptable to those seeking institutional decolonisation, such as by ordaining indigenous clergy and by producing vernacular translations of the liturgy, it left unanswered the more difficult question of how such actions would promote a true Christian witness.

The use of the concept of inculturation to analyse Stevenson's Pacific fiction could conceivably draw two kinds of criticism and these must now be addressed. In the first place, it could be argued that thinking about the relationship between faith and culture has always been an important part of Christianity from its very origins in the communities of the Near East. The deliberate use of a technical theological term such as 'inculturation' to analyse a perennial phenomenon would therefore be unnecessary and could even distort the proper context of study. One response to this is that scholarship in Scottish literature has begun to use cognate terms in ways similar to my own use of the word inculturation. For example, Linden Bicket explains how the Scottish poet George Mackay Brown (1921–96) '"encultures"' the Virgin Mary 'as the Catholic Church has (traditionally by missionaries and priests), so that is she is subtly woven into the very fabric of culture and takes on the attributes and features of her new locality'.[35] The localisation of religious figures and practices is precisely the theme that I explore and develop in Stevenson's Pacific fiction through the use of the term 'inculturation'.

Benedict XVI), 'Faith, Reason and the University: Memories and Reflections', University of Regensburg (12 September 2006), accessed at: https://www.vatican.va/content/benedict-xvi/en/speeches/2006/september/documents/hf_ben-xvi_spe_20060912_university-regensburg.html on 14 May 2021.

[34] Andrew Walls contrasts a particularist 'indigenizing' principle and a universalist 'pilgrim' principle in Christian history. Andrew F. Walls, *The Missionary Movement in Christian History: Studies in the Transmission of Faith* (New York: Orbis, 1996), 7, 9. See also Allan A. Basas, 'Inculturation: An Ongoing Drama of Faith–Culture Dialogue', *Scientia* 9, 1 (2020), 92–108 (98–9).

[35] Linden Bicket, 'George Mackay Brown's Marian Apocrypha: Iconography and Enculturation in *Time in a Red Coat*', *Scottish Literature Review* 5, 2 (2013), 81–96 (86–7). A somewhat similar approach is found in Leith Davis and Kristen Mahlis, 'A Conceptual Alliance: "Interculturation" in Robert Burns and Kamau Brathwaite', in *Scottish Literature and Postcolonial Literature: Comparative Texts and Critical Perspectives*, ed. by Niall O'Gallagher, Graeme Macdonald, and Michael Gardiner (Edinburgh: Edinburgh University Press, 2011), 15–29.

Another criticism of the use of the term 'inculturation' in the present context might be that it is anachronistic. Stevenson died over half a century before the decolonising movements and postcolonial theories that are associated with inculturation had begun to appear.[36] The use of the term to study Stevenson's fiction therefore lacks justification in an era when formal colonialism was not even yet under way in Samoa.[37] A response to this objection is to point to how the origins of colonialism and anticolonial activity have been pushed back in time in Samoan historiography. No less a figure than the Samoan novelist Albert Wendt looked for the origins of the early-twentieth-century Mau independence movement in 'the growth of discontent' during the nineteenth century.[38] As Stevenson made clear in *A Footnote to History* (1892) and his other writings, he was openly supportive of movements for Samoan self-rule. While it is not the aim of this chapter to enter into debates about Samoan historiography, it is reasonable to assert that in the Pacific Islands of Stevenson's time Christianity was beginning to be seen as a religion of political as well as spiritual liberation. The Samoan civil war, in which fighting was mixed with prayer and people in exile were often venerated, intensified the sense of a natural connection.[39] Therefore inculturation, if it must be considered within the context of anticolonialism, can legitimately be applied to the Samoan situation at the end of the nineteenth century.

Inculturation in Stevenson's Pacific Fiction

The purpose of this chapter is to analyse what the literary scholar Sylvie Largeaud-Ortega has described as Stevenson's 'anthropologically sensitive works', namely the short stories 'The Isle of Voices'

---

[36] The limited nature of nineteenth-century Catholic efforts to adapt to Pacific culture might be characterised, for example, by a request to Rome to ask whether whale oil could be used for lamps in place of beeswax. Philip Gibbs, personal communication, 2021.

[37] The Samoan Islands were divided between German and American interests in 1899.

[38] Albert Wendt, '"Guardians and Wards": A Study of the Origins, Causes, and the First Two Years of the Mau in Western Samoa' (MA thesis, Victoria University Wellington, 1965), accessed at: https://nzetc.victoria.ac.nz/tm/scholarly/tei-WenGua.html on 10 December 2021.

[39] Stevenson described how the first victim of the Samoan war was carried from the fighting on a pole with his rosary. Robert Louis Stevenson, *A Footnote to History: Eight Years of Trouble in Samoa* (London: Cassell and Co., 1892), 114; Latu Latai, personal communication, 2021.

and 'The Bottle Imp', the novella 'The Beach of Falesá', and the novel *The Ebb-Tide*.[40] Written and published during the period 1889–94, these stories are set entirely in and around the Pacific. Their major theme is the encounter between Pacific Islanders and Western culture including Western people. Stevenson's knowledge of the Hawaiian and Samoan languages, and Pacific history and customs meant that these texts are filled with local knowledge and references. Moreover, the texts share a broad concern with perennial metaphysical questions: how did Islanders understand the relationship between divinity and nature? What did they think constituted a good life? How did evil manifest according to their understanding? By placing such concerns at the centre of his stories, as we shall see, Stevenson connected Pacific environments and modes of representation with theological matters pertinent to the Reformed Protestant tradition.

An Enduring Christian Presence

Stevenson's fiction documents the enduring presence of Christianity in the Pacific. Christian names, items, and figures abound across the Islands, sometimes intermingled with non-Christian Pacific ideas and practices, in ways that demonstrate the author's alertness to the materiality and persistence of local forms of the religion. In the Reformed tradition, which historically sought to distinguish itself from what it held to be an idolatrous Catholicism, the Bible ('the Word of God') is the central artefact of the faith and holds an unshakeable authority. Relics of the old religion, such as crucifixes and other images, were destroyed by iconoclasts, following the example of Calvin, while new kinds of worshipping communities, disciplinary organisations, and religious authorities came into existence.[41] The tension in Stevenson's religious representations can be found in the ways in which he portrays the relationship between materiality and divinity, whether in

---

[40] Sylvie Largeaud-Ortega, 'Stevenson's "little tale" is "a library": An Anthropological Approach to "The Beach of Falesá"', *Journal of Stevenson Studies* 6 (2009), 117–34 (117). For a reflection on the relationship between anthropology and fiction in Stevenson's writing, see Richard Ambrosini, 'The Four Boundary-Crossings of R. L. Stevenson, Novelist and Anthropologist', in Dury and Ambrosini, *Writer of Boundaries*, 23–35.

[41] Gijsbert van den Brink and Harro Höpfl, 'Calvin, the Reformed Tradition and Modern Culture', in *Calvinism and the Making of the European Mind*, ed. by Gijsbert van den Brink and Harro Höpfl (Leiden: Brill, 2014), 3–24 (11).

the form of practices in aid of moral discipline or in items that conferred spiritual power. As was highlighted in Chapter 2, Stevenson was alert to the sacramentality of objects, their plenitude with the life of the Christian God, and he explored the Eucharistic sacrifice from a distinctly Pacific (and Protestant) perspective in 'Something in It'. Stevenson's other Pacific prose fictions also feature sacramentals, whether in the form of figures, such as priests, or in the form of items, such as Bibles and religious medals.

The bedrock moral assumptions of local characters in stories such as 'The Beach of Falesá' and 'The Bottle Imp' are Christian. In Falesá, no local person asks why a certificate should be produced for the 'sham marriage' between the English trader Wiltshire and the Pacific Islander Uma that constitutes the novella's defining moment.[42] Instead, everyone assumes that marriage done properly and legally requires a material record. Rather than being regarded as a suspicious foreign innovation, the formal act of marriage was simply accepted as the way things should be done on the island. Wiltshire, the narrator and a newcomer to Falesá, even laments that the production of a marriage contract 'was the practice in these parts' and the work of 'missionaries', whose injunction had prevented traders from cheating native women 'with a clear conscience' (11).[43] Christian morality has thus permeated a key social practice on the island and presents an obstacle to the wanton foreign exploitation of women. The extent of the Christian impact on Falesá can be measured in the attitude of the scurrilous Case, Wiltshire's local business rival, who knows that he must work within the prescribed limits in order to trick Wiltshire into securing a marriage to the tabooed Uma through a paper contract.

The moral world of 'The Bottle Imp' is likewise framed by Christian assumptions.[44] Almost no character and certainly no indigenous person in the story believes that there is a worse human fate than to

---

[42] See Paul Shankman, 'Interethnic Unions and the Regulation of Sex in Colonial Samoa, 1830–1945', *Journal of the Polynesian Society* 110, 2 (2001), 119–47 (especially 122–5).

[43] All quotations from Stevenson's Pacific prose fiction discussed in this chapter are taken from Stevenson, *South Sea Tales*, ed. by Jolly.

[44] 'The Bottle Imp' was initially published in the Samoan missionary journal *O le Sulu Samoa*. A. E. Claxton, 'Stevenson as I Knew Him', *Chronicle of the London Missionary Society* (May 1908), 89–90 (90). The historian of missions and World Christianity Lamin Sanneh quotes Stevenson to demonstrate the great cultural value of 'missionary translations of both the Bible and indigenous literature'. Lamin Sanneh, *Encountering the West: Christianity and the Global Cultural Process: The African Dimension* (New York: Orbis, 1993), 20.

go to hell. Yet, the Islanders' knowledge that (1) hell exists and (2) that it is a bad place comes from, or was adapted from, a religion that was imported into the region. The bottle of the story is itself a kind of inverse sacramental object, doomed to curse rather than to bless whoever possesses it. Even as the story's Hawaiian hero Keawe contemplates repurchasing it in order to cure himself of leprosy so that he can marry Kokua, his betrothed, he considers that 'it is a dreadful thing to risk the flames of hell' (86). It is only love, as he explains to his seller, which gives him the courage to risk such an action (89). Stevenson also points out that, as soon as Keawe returns home to find he is cured of the disease, then he loses all interest in earthly things and 'had but the one thought, that here he was bound to the bottle imp for time and for eternity, and had no better hope but to be a cinder for ever in the flames of hell' (89–90). He sees a vision of his spiritual future and 'his soul shrank' (90). Keawe and Kokua later decide to try and sell the bottle at a cheaper price in Tahiti, but locals there are either incredulous about their story or 'drew away' from the pair 'as from persons who had dealings with the devil' (93). Indeed, 'all persons began with one accord to disengage themselves from their advances' (93). These words could only be written in the knowledge that the story's audience, which included Samoans reading it in their native language, would be able to grasp the theological significance of being taken to hell and to imagine its horror.[45]

The stories commonly depict not only conventional Christian morality and theology in a Pacific setting but also common Christian practices and devotions. In Falesá, on the first Sunday morning after his marriage to Uma, Wiltshire reports as a matter of fact that 'there was no business to be looked for' (20). All trading has ceased on the Sabbath. Uma asks him whether he is 'going to pray' (20). The habits of traditional Sabbath observance are so embedded in Falesan life that even this non-native couple (Wiltshire is English; Uma is from another, unnamed island) regard it as customary. As Stevenson's mother's Pacific travel diary attests, Sunday was normally a day when she, along with many Islanders, went to church,

---

[45] Crawford explains that 'the doctrine of sin and of an eternal punishment, was placed in the context of the Samoan concept of sala, or a punishment inflicted as a result of the committing of some unpropitious act. The standards of behaviour laid down by the missionaries were, it was argued, regarded as codes whereby those who had entered into particular relationships with the deity, could avoid such unpropitious acts.' Crawford, 'The Lotu and the Fa'asāmoa', 391–2.

often accompanied by her son.⁴⁶ Another common Christian practice described by Stevenson is the making of the sign of the cross, which Catholics do in Tahiti as they pass by the cursed Keawe and his wife Kokua (93) in 'The Bottle Imp'. The recording of such details in his stories highlights Stevenson's attention to adopted local religious practices, as well as to the natural way in which they have been accepted in the Pacific.

The material presence of Christianity is demonstrated in 'The Beach of Falesá' when Wiltshire meets the island's chiefs for the first time and notices that two of the younger ones 'wore Catholic medals' (23). These protective sacramental items around the necks of emerging island leaders gives him 'matter of reflection' (23). In a modern study of Catholic evangelisation in French Polynesia the author highlights the importance of 'material practices (rituals, exchanges, construction of churches and secular buildings, etc.) and imported objects (rosaries, calico, medals, etc.)'.⁴⁷ A more familiar religious item for Protestants, the Bible, is frequently mentioned in Stevenson's stories, but this too is often presented, as it is in the contemporary Pacific, as an object of intrinsic power rather than simply as the repository of God's word.⁴⁸ In Falesá, Wiltshire carries a Bible with him on his dangerous journey into the bush to destroy Case's hideout in order to assure his wife that he has spiritual protection. A more conventional use of the book is made by the indigenous crew of the *Farallone* in *The Ebb-Tide* as they gather every Sunday to worship and pray aboard the vessel. When we compare these two examples, it might seem that Stevenson considered Pacific Islanders to have appropriated the Bible for spiritually healthy and constructive purposes whereas Westerners, such as Wiltshire, sought to use it to deceive and manipulate others. But Islanders also do not doubt the book's intrinsic power. In 'The Isle of Voices', the Hawaiian 'warlock' Kalamake carefully places his Bible out of sight 'under the cushion of the sofa' (105) before conducting the magical ritual that will transport him and his son-in-law Keola to the island of the story's title. Kalamake, who boasted to Keola about the 'marvels' he will perform 'under the plain eye of day', does not do so while the Christian holy book is within sight. Perhaps he believes that it is an

---

⁴⁶ Margaret Isabella Stevenson, 'Diaries [1874–1889 {1888}]', GEN MSS 664, Box 54, Folder 1177, Beinecke Library, Yale University.
⁴⁷ Émilie Nolet, 'Coconuts and Rosaries: Materiality in the Catholic Christianisation of the Tuamotu Archipelago (French Polynesia)', *The Journal of the Polynesian Society* 129, 3 (2020): 275–302 (275).
⁴⁸ Tomlinson, *God is Samoan*, 32, 33.

object saturated with spiritual power, *mana*, and must therefore be treated carefully.[49]

In Stevenson's Pacific fiction, the identity of people, their practices, the objects they carry, the assumptions they make, and the conventions they follow all reveal Christianity's permanence and rootedness in the Island world. Far from being regarded as an unstable foreign imposition, the presence of the religion in Pacific culture is taken for granted, and indigenous people organise their lives around its doctrines and conventions. Stevenson's plots unfold and his characters develop within this Christian moral and material environment. Kalamake's hiding of the household Bible in preparation of his magical invocation shows that the Christian presence was by no means universally accepted, however. While Islanders acknowledged its power and influence, they sometimes tried to find ways to circumvent it. As Stevenson often observed in his South Seas Letters, the Pacific was the living theatre of a dramatic struggle for souls and cultures. This, too, bore a resemblance to the conditions of the European Reformations.

Intellectual Integrity of Religion

Stevenson's fiction affirms the intellectual integrity of religious discourse in the Pacific. The indigenous Christians that are portrayed in his stories are neither passive recipients of an Enlightened knowledge that was bestowed on them by Westerners nor are they promulgators of an essentially foreign message. Rather, they are engaged participants in a public conversation about the meaning and practice of Christianity. They are as concerned about its future in the Pacific as any Western figure is – often more so, in fact. In his stories, Stevenson presents Christian ideas and controversies as objects of communication between people who are learning about each other. Contrasting views of belief and worship undergird intercultural conversations. Debating these views helps people to situate themselves in relation to each other in the complex world into which they have been drawn together, in which interlocutors from different cultural and linguistic backgrounds must learn to negotiate mutually acceptable rules and values.

Extended conversations about religion also highlight a Reformed Christian appreciation of the importance of literacy in the life of the adult believer, which followed from a conviction of the primacy

---

[49] Tomlinson, *God is Samoan*, 32.

of the written and communicated word as the 'foremost vehicle of grace'.[50] A movement that emphasised the centrality of Scripture over all other forms of religious authority esteemed education as key to the development of spiritual maturity. In Scotland, the Reformers built on pre-Reformation institutions and attitudes towards learning, and an important part of Scotland's identity after Union with England in 1707 rested on its continuing independent educational traditions. Early nineteenth-century Protestant missionaries to the Pacific, who themselves were often educated in institutions that derived from this academic lineage, emphasised teaching converts to read and write and were responsible for innovations such as the first local printing presses.[51] We receive a vivid impression of the impact of these historical developments in Stevenson's Pacific fiction. The writing is remarkable for his careful and attentive presentation of Pacific Islanders' religious literacy – a striking insight.[52] His stories are filled with informed and articulate talk about subjects such as God, the church, prayer, spirits, hell, and the devil.[53]

In 'The Beach of Falesá', the English Protestant missionary Tarleton narrates to Wiltshire his conversation with the island pastor Namu, his most prized convert, who had fallen under the wicked influence of the trader Case. Religious reasoning forms the basis of Namu's explanation for his wayward actions. For example, in making the sign of the cross, Namu explains that it was acceptable for Protestants like himself to perform this action normally associated with Catholics 'when it is used only to protect men from a devil', as when Wiltshire's predecessor Vigours was believed to have been afflicted with the Evil Eye (38). Namu's understanding is that Christianity was differently observed in Italy, 'where men were often struck dead by that kind of devil [the Evil Eye], and it appeared the sign of the cross was a charm against its power' (38). A 'Catholic devil, or, at least, [one] used to Catholic ways' (38), required a Catholic form of protection, 'which is a thing harmless in itself' (38). In conclusion, he states, making the sign of the cross 'is neither good nor bad' unless it is 'made in idolatry' (39). Tarleton does

---

[50] Hans J. Hillerbrand, *Historical Dictionary of the Reformation and Counter-Reformation* (Chicago: Fitzroy Dearborn, 2000), 176. See also Nimmo and Fergusson, 'Introduction', 5.

[51] See Chapter 3.

[52] On the attractiveness of Christian literacy in nineteenth-century Polynesia, see David Lindenfeld, *World Christianity and Indigenous Experience: A Global History, 1500–2000* (Cambridge: Cambridge University Press, 2021), 268.

[53] Compare this fecund religious discourse with Stevenson's self-censorship in his letters to metropolitan literary colleagues, as discussed in Chapter 1.

not explicitly respond to Namu's instrumental interpretation of this religious act, but he reveals how little he thinks of it by reporting that Namu then, 'very like a native pastor', 'had a text apposite about the casting out of devils' (39). This episode closely accords with what we know from the historical record. Samoan mission 'teachers' that were trained by the LMS, *faife'au*, were confident and assertive, not merely in articulating the ideas they had learned from Europeans but in commenting on them and preaching about them.[54]

Tarleton frames his response to the larger problem of Namu's downfall in pastoral theological terms. Learning that Case is the source of the spread of disorder and corruption in Falesá, he determines to set Namu back on the right path because he is unlikely to find a better native pastor and also because he wants to avoid scandalising his flock (41). Trying to achieve his aim through a method of denunciation and reasoning, he reproaches Namu for 'his ignorance and want of faith' (41). He responds to the social problem created by Case's influence by recalling and reaffirming the values he had taught Namu and other island converts. Case's subsequent public 'conjuring trick' (42), drawing a dollar note from behind Tarleton's head, is designed to make the missionary look foolish and hypocritical and exposes the inadequacy of Tarleton's strategy. The missionary had failed to grasp Namu's falling away from denominational orthodoxy as an opportunity for an intercultural dialogue about signs and their spiritual efficacy. A gentle and well-meaning effort at correction could only succeed when it began by acknowledging the gap between different perceptions of the issue. Therefore, if in Pastor Namu Stevenson presents us with a shining example of the indigenisation of the church in the Pacific, then in Namu's relationships with Tarleton and Case he also introduces us to some of the obstacles that stood in the way of Pacific inculturation.

The account of the exchange between the missionary and his convert occupies the central chapter of 'The Beach of Falesá'. Meanwhile, Wiltshire and his wife Uma's conversations extend across the novella. Because Wiltshire is the narrator, his interpretation of Christianity tends to frame their dialogue. We may assume that, as a nineteenth-century Englishman, he most likely comes from either a Protestant nonconformist or Anglican religious background, that he

---

[54] Lange, *Island Ministers*, 91. With the character of Namu, Stevenson also appears to have presented us with a relatively rare portrait, albeit fictional, of an LMS-trained native pastor/mission teacher. Lange, *Island Ministers*, 100.

has some understanding of Christian doctrine and ethics, and that he is familiar with at least parts of the Bible.[55] Although he repeatedly signals in the text that he is not a believer in any orthodox sense, he nevertheless takes monogamous marriage seriously (36), prays when he senses that he is in danger (53), and appreciates the Bible's power to move sincere Christians (60). Like Namu, Uma is combative and outspoken about her religious beliefs and practices. Her view of Christianity appears to be derived from three sources: her native understanding of the spiritual world; Tarleton, who seems to have been involved in her catechesis (37); and Wiltshire.

In a conversation with Wiltshire, Uma explains the difference between the native *aitu* or spirit and *tiapolo*, which she describes as like the 'Christian devil' in its omnipresence, with Case being likened to 'his son' (47–8). To her puzzled and bemused husband she tells Islanders' stories about Case, the powers he supposedly possesses, and whether they believed that the source of those powers was sacred or profane. When Wiltshire decides that he will visit Case's mysterious place in the forest, Uma tries to reason him out of it by asserting that Wiltshire will not have God's protection as he claims because God 'got too much work' (48) while tiapolo 'work very hard' (48) in Falesá. Uma also keeps a Bible in her home that was printed in London (60). Wiltshire tries to trick her into thinking that this would protect him against harm in the bush but Uma is not impressed. When he tells her that her Bible keeps devils away in Europe, she replies, 'White man, he tell me you no got [devils in Europe]' (60). Wiltshire then tries to reason analogically, pleading, 'Why would these islands be chock full of them and none in Europe?' But his wife has an immediate and effective answer: 'Well, you no got breadfruit.' Wiltshire thinks he is cleverer than this native woman but he cannot argue his way through and, as a result, he must carry the heavy Bible with him into the bush in spite of Uma's scepticism about its inherent power. In a way that resembles Namu's conversation with Tarleton, Uma tries to draw her husband's mind towards a local understanding of the spiritual world that they inhabited. Through their dialogue, Stevenson portrays how the Western man, Wiltshire, unlike the Pacific Islander Uma, is unable to grasp the deeper menace underlying Case's plots and activities.

---

[55] John Wolffe, 'Anglicanism, Presbyterianism and the Religious Identities of the United Kingdom', in *The Cambridge History of Christianity: Volume 8. World Christianities c. 1815 – c. 1914*, ed. by Sheridan Gilley and Brian Stanley (Cambridge: Cambridge University Press, 2014), 301–22.

The conversations between Pacific Islanders and white Westerners in 'The Beach of Falesá' are marked by the intellectual freedom of the religious discourse. The buffered self also finds a Pacific echo in Stevenson's novel *The Ebb-Tide*, where the author seems to suggest that, even when they are far from Europe, Western people have lost the ability to communicate in a reasonable way about religion. The vibrancy, even audacity, of Pacific Islanders' religious claims and reasoning is further emphasised when compared with the strained and desperate exchange between the Englishmen Attwater and Herrick. Here are two men of different generations and social tiers, who nevertheless share a common cultural background. Attwater, the older man, appears to be from an aristocratic background whereas Herrick is middle class. They have both enjoyed elite educations (at Cambridge and Oxford, respectively) and they draw on a shared cultural and aesthetic heritage that runs from *The Aeneid* to Shakespeare. Critically, however, these apparent advantages are not sufficient to allow them to penetrate into a genuine conversation about spiritual life.

Like Conrad's Kurz, Stevenson's Attwater represents the loftiest in European civilisation. He also claims 'an interest in missions' (203–4) and seems well equipped to achieve his goal of evangelising Herrick.[56] But Herrick (or Hay, as he presents himself during the conversation) cannot be persuaded to reconsider his agnostic views, though this is not because Attwater's arguments are insufficient. In fact, Attwater's evangelical strategy barely rests on reason at all but rather on his personal charisma and dramatic power. 'There is nothing here . . . nothing there . . . and nothing there . . . nothing but God's Grace!', he exclaims mightily to the younger man (203). Herrick is ready to acknowledge his own weakness and inability to accept the fact of God's existence through dogmatic formulas: 'I do not believe there is any form of words under heaven, by which I can lift the burthen from my shoulders' (207). But, in a way that is reminiscent of Thomas Stevenson's quarrel with his son, Attwater dismisses Herrick's agnostic struggle as atheism (203). The sudden coldness of Attwater's response to the young man's revelation of his spiritual vulnerability is genuinely shocking: 'The rapture was all gone from Attwater's countenance; the dark apostle had disappeared; and in his place there stood an easy, sneering gentleman, who took off his hat and bowed' (207). Attwater's closure

---

[56] Herrick is in fact the subject of three evangelical overtures. First, through the kind acts of the indigenous crew of the *Farallone* (168), then by Attwater's cynical show of force, and finally, at the very end of the novel, by Davis's impotent enthusiasm (252).

and withdrawal makes his earlier passionate entreaties seem grimly calculated. The pearl trader is disinterested in the person, only desirous of capturing another soul. Taken in sum, the encounter represents the failure of a certain approach to evangelisation, which is characterised by the emotional unavailability of the evangeliser and the impossibility of intellectual accommodation. Pacific Christianity may have been in need of inculturation, but Stevenson appears to be warning that Europeans were in a far more precarious situation, unable even to communicate with each other across the chasm between dead certainty and agonised doubt.[57]

Religious Empowerment and Solidarity

A third theme in Stevenson's Pacific fiction that might benefit from the interpretive lens of inculturation is the centrality of Christianity in Pacific Islander empowerment and solidarity.[58] Stevenson's fiction evokes the social and political consequences of Christian evangelisation in these societies. Over and again in his stories, religious belief and practice provide an important vehicle of expression for indigenous people living under various kinds of colonial rule counteracting the impression that Christianity was merely the religion of the colonisers.[59] Indigenous peoples' readiness to apply to their own circumstances what was of lasting value in the Christian faith contributed to their survival at a time of disruption and uncertainty. Such episodes also help us to see how attentive Stevenson was to social change and to new movements in the Pacific. Careful observation of these processes shifted his writing towards a more activist stance.

As discussed in the previous chapter, the Protestant Reformation was accompanied by debates about how Christianity should relate to the political community.[60] Nimmo and Fergusson claim that 'the

---

[57] Note that, in comparison with the would-be evangelist Attwater, the missionary Tarleton never seeks to directly evangelise Wiltshire but only encourages him in his desire to keep his word to properly marry Uma. Tarleton further insists only that Wiltshire respect conventions and practices, such as the formal rites for Case's funeral and the injunction not to cheat indigenous people through his trade.

[58] For a wider discussion of this subject, see Michelle Keown, *Pacific Islands Writing: The Postcolonial Literatures of Aotearoa/New Zealand and Oceania* (Oxford: Oxford University Press, 2007).

[59] See R. S. Sugirtharajah, *The Bible and Empire: Postcolonial Explorations* (Cambridge: Cambridge University Press, 2005).

[60] It even arguably originated much earlier in Western Christianity, e.g. St Augustine's *The City of God against the Pagans*.

strong emphasis placed on social transformation in the Reformed churches generated a context in which ethics and politics were often dominant concerns'.[61] As his essays on figures such as John Knox demonstrate, Stevenson was well enough read in early modern European history to compare it with the dynamics of church–state tension in the Pacific. In fictional locales such as Falesá he portrayed a religiously ordered society that indicated a degree of cooperation between the spiritual and political powers. But his romantic instincts also led him to sympathise with outcasts and rebels like the Covenanters and the Jacobites. Communities were also open to malign influences that could simultaneously take spiritual and colonial forms, as with Case in Falesá, Attwater in Zacynthos, the economic wizardry on the Isle of Voices, and the bottle imp across the Pacific expanse. In many of these situations, the countermeasure that restores health and plenitude is collective action inspired by an educated Christian polity. The message seems to be that, when widespread moral and religious education is lacking or ineffective, then the dark forces of the age will likely prevail.

Christian education provides Pacific Islanders with mental resources during times of exceptional personal trial. Uma, the wife of Wiltshire, and Kokua, the wife of Keawe, are strong, mission-educated heroines who play critical supportive roles when their husbands face great danger. Tarleton proudly explains to Wiltshire that Uma combines natural courage with a solid missionary formation (37).[62] Although terrified of spirits, she runs across the darkening island to warn Wiltshire that Case has discovered the plot to blow up his secret hideaway. In 'The Bottle Imp', when her husband tells her about his curse, Kokua defiantly responds, 'I was educated in a school in Honolulu; I am no common girl. And I tell you, I shall save my lover' (92).[63] This mission-trained woman teaches her husband about how to persevere through trial. Sharing in his fear and suffering, we are told that the couple 'Sometimes [. . .] pray[ed] together' (93–4). Kokua's fidelity and intelligence ultimately helps Keawe to get rid of the bottle. His liberation is a shared achievement borne of unity in faith. As with other forms

---

[61] Nimmo and Fergusson, 'Introduction', 5.

[62] The first missionary school for girls in Samoa may have been established by a Scottish missionary, Lillias Mills, in the 1840s. Maureen Sier and Ruta Fiti-Sinclair, 'Nineteenth-Century Scottish Missionary Women and Sāmoan Morality', *Measina a Samoa* 3 (2005), 159–66 (161).

[63] Hawaiian mission education for girls began with Wailuku Female Seminary in 1837. Patricia Grimshaw, *Paths of Duty: American Missionary Wives in Nineteenth-Century Hawaii* (Honolulu: University of Hawai'i Press, 1989), 186.

of Christianity associated with the global South, here Stevenson concretely expresses how freedom from the colonising bottle is 'inseparable from deliverance from supernatural evil'.[64]

'The Beach of Falesá' contains several scenes in which we are shown how Pacific Islands Christians take the initiative in public religious life. In the second chapter, Stevenson provides us with a description of a native church service. Through the eyes of the trader Wiltshire we are given a precise description of the building: a coral structure with a large roof, open windows, and an open doorway (21). The native congregation is dressed in its Sunday finery, singing hymns in the vernacular, while an indigenous pastor preaches. The unassuming nature of this scene of indigenised Christianity presents a shock to the white trader, 'for things went quite different in the islands I was acquainted with' (21). Other examples of public religious expression include the Catholic medals worn by two of the younger chiefs, mentioned earlier, and the missionary boat that brings Tarleton to the island, which is rowed by indigenous men and has an indigenous pastor as steersman. On their first meeting, when Wiltshire impedes Tarleton from moving past him, we are told that the men on the boat begin to 'growl' (35).

The most striking of Stevenson's scenes of survival and endurance takes place in *The Ebb-Tide* when Herrick learns something about Christian worship and camaraderie through the example of the three indigenous crew members on the *Farallone*. The educational legacy of Christian evangelisation has provided these crewmen with the tools to persist and cohere on the margins of a corrupt and debilitated Western colonial enterprise, which is represented by the *Farallone*'s white crew. The three Islanders, who come from opposite ends of the Pacific and speak mutually incomprehensible languages, bring out their Bibles to read 'or made believe to read' on a Sunday and joined together 'in the singing of missionary hymns' (168). Meanwhile, Herrick's white colleagues, Davis and Huish, are almost constantly drunk on the Champagne they were meant to transport and Herrick is wracked with guilt for consenting to their criminal enterprise.

The story's narrator, commenting on the scene of Sunday worship, observes of the Islanders' piety that it was 'a cutting reproof to compare the islanders and the whites aboard the *Farallone*' (168). The Islanders' situation as hands aboard the vessel is akin to

---

[64] Philip Jenkins, *The Next Christendom: The Coming of Global Christianity* (3rd edn, Oxford: Oxford University Press, 2011), 7–8.

indigenous people's diminished political status in the era of Western political supremacy. One of them, 'Uncle Ned', tells Herrick that his real name is in fact 'Taveeta, all-e-same Taveeta King of Islael' (168), and he shares 'his simple and hard story of exile, suffering, and injustice among cruel whites' (167).[65] By continuing to work diligently and keeping their heads while the white men around them lose theirs, these Islanders display a resilience that is undergirded by shared belief and worship. Christian prayer has become the basis of their unity and solidarity, while the Melanesian crew mate 'Sally Day' adapts that other pillar of Western civilisation in the Pacific, the English language, to communicate with his Polynesian colleagues. Herrick is deeply moved by their humility and perseverance, 'so faithful to what they knew of good' (168). Stevenson presents inculturation, in the form of improvised Christian worship amid desperate circumstances, as a collective endeavour. The example accords with the theologian Robert Schreiter's description of the liberation model of inculturation, whose concern is with 'salvation' and people's 'lived experience' against 'the forces of oppression, struggle, violence, and power'.[66]

Inculturation and the Globalisation of Christianity

Sylvie Largeaud-Ortega has made a compelling case for Stevenson's Pacific cultural literacy. Through his telling use of Polynesian stories, ideas, and expressions, she claims, Stevenson adds depth and layers of meaning to his Pacific fiction that renders it 'postcolonial'. By this she means that in works such as 'The Bottle Imp' and 'The Isle of Voices' Stevenson tries 'to present things from Pacific Islanders' perspectives'.[67] She presses the argument further by suggesting that Stevenson's Pacific Islander heroes seek to rediscover or revive their traditional cultural roots in an attempt to recover what Western colonialism has destroyed. 'When Paradise is regained in the Pacific', she intimates, 'it may be Biblical no longer, but it may reflect indigenous cosmogony

---

[65] Audrey Murfin has shown how Stevenson gives a name and substance to the character of 'Uncle Ned', whom Stevenson's collaborator, Lloyd Osbourne, had left unidentified in his earlier draft of the novel. Audrey Murfin, *Robert Louis Stevenson and the Art of Collaboration* (Edinburgh: Edinburgh University Press, 2019), 170.
[66] Schreiter, *Constructing Local Theologies*, 15.
[67] Largeaud-Ortega, 'A Scotsman's Pacific', 86. Stevenson's writing may also be distinguished from colonial literature by his presentation of the wilful destructiveness of Western people. Largeaud-Ortega, 'A Scotsman's Pacific', 88.

instead.'⁶⁸ She takes one of her most vivid examples from 'The Isle of Voices', when the Hawaiian Keola lights a fire on the island:

> In the wake of Maui/Tane [divine figures through whose coupling and decoupling there came to be light], Keola sparks off a light by rubbing two sticks together – one supine and tender like Mother Earth, the other erect and hard like Father Sky. He does so in awe, for starting a fire in this ritualistic way could only be performed by consecrated priests. This explains why, although 'he made a lamp of cocoa-shell, and drew the oil of the ripe nuts, and made a wick of fibre; and [. . .] lit his lamp', every night he 'lay and trembled till morning' (p. 114). Keola's concern is not only, like Crusoe's, to engineer a way to make light; it is also to try and learn how to live with the terror of transgressing one of his own culture's fundamental and most fatal *tabu*. Yet at the same time he is reviving Polynesian awareness of this culture; he resuscitates the sacred rituals that have been left dormant by failing forefathers and wayward priests. Hence his name, *ke ola*, 'life' in Hawaiian: he resuscitates and carves out an identity for his own people. In a way, Keola is reaching for Paradise regained on the atoll – but this time, the Paradise is indigenous.⁶⁹

This is a rich and wonderfully fascinating reading of Stevenson's text set against the background of a Polynesian cosmogony, which demonstrates the author's knowledge of indigenous traditions and highlights the skilful way in which he incorporates them into his fiction. The interpretation proposes a new context for analysing Stevenson's Pacific writing while strengthening the existing arguments for considering him as a postcolonial author. But it seems an unnecessary step to separate the indigenous from the Christian contexts in which Stevenson interpreted so much of Pacific culture. Largeaud-Ortega's claim that he desired to have his indigenous characters in 'The Bottle Imp' and 'The Isle of Voices' (1) rediscover their traditional roots and (2) connect these roots with modern Pacific culture rather establishes Stevenson as an exponent of contextual theology, in which ideas about priestly ministry, taboo, and recovered rituals are explored in the light of the advent of Christianity.⁷⁰

---

⁶⁸ Largeaud-Ortega, 'A Scotsman's Pacific', 96.
⁶⁹ Largeaud-Ortega, 'A Scotsman's Pacific', 92–3.
⁷⁰ Tomlinson, *God is Samoan*, 48–9, 74–6. We may also wonder whether Stevenson would have thought it possible to completely sever Pacific modernity from Christianity and then fuse the former with a reconfigured indigeneity. On the problems with such an approach, see Ratzinger, 'Christ, Faith and the Challenge of Cultures'.

Stevenson's Pacific fiction documents important features of indigenous Christianity and complements the missionary record by offering a sympathetic portrayal of believers' attempts to live a Christian life during a colonising era. Stevenson perceived visible and material signs of Christian presence, affirmed Christian literacy as a conduit of cultural interaction, and was sensitive to the role of Christian faith in the formation of new communities. All of these themes would grow in importance as they were taken up by Pacific theologians in the following century.[71] As the anthropologist John Barker has explained,

> Christianity has a political presence due to its claims to spiritual and moral authority. The vast majority of Pacific Islanders today are at least nominally Christian. Most have grown up in church-centered communities, recited Christian Scriptures and prayers in school, sat through numerable homilies, and hummed along to ubiquitous gospel songs playing on the radio. The moral verities along with Scriptural references are deeply familiar and comforting in contrast to the complexities, compromises, and corruptions great and small of politics.[72]

While they do not exhaust the subjects through which Stevenson engaged local religion, the examples from his stories that have been highlighted in this chapter should amply demonstrate the value of his fiction for studying the cultural history of the Pacific.

It is also interesting to note that, as the memory of formal colonisation recedes across parts of the region, the appeal of the theological project of inculturation appears to be declining.[73] The religious emphasis, at least in some parts of the Pacific, seems to be turning towards a model of acculturation, with a foreign missionary focus on ritual that is somewhat complemented by an indigenous desire to enjoy the benefits of Western education and material culture.[74]

---

[71] Charles W. Forman, 'Finding Our Own Voice: The Reinterpreting of Christianity by Oceanic Theologians', *International Bulletin of Missionary Research* 29, 3 (2005), 115–22.

[72] John Barker, 'Comments to Part 1: Christian Transcendence and the Politics of Renewal', in *Christianity, Conflict, and Renewal in Australia and the Pacific*, ed. by Fiona Magowan and Carolyn Schwarz (Boston: Brill, 2016), 23–33 (24).

[73] Historical studies of Pacific inculturation emphasise the relationship between Christianity and decolonisation. See Helen Gardner, 'Culture and Christian Missions in Oceania', in *The Cambridge History of the Pacific Ocean, 2 Volumes*, ed. by Anne Perez Hattori, Jane Samson, Ryan Tucker Jones, and Matt K. Matsuda (forthcoming).

[74] Philip Gibbs, personal communication, 2021.

Assuming that this trend continues, Stevenson's writing could be said to demonstrate an acute historical interest in the relationship between religion and Pacific Islands societies. As Richard Lovett noted, only an observer with Stevenson's informed perspective could have written in such an insightful way about the religious life of the people of the Pacific Islands at that point in time.

Another important context for interpreting Stevenson's Pacific fiction is the global expansion of Christianity.[75] As this chapter has shown, local forms of this world religion are abundantly portrayed in works such as 'The Bottle Imp' and 'The Beach of Falesá'. These texts permit scholars to ask such questions about the ethnography of Islander religion as: which elements of historical Christian doctrine, belief, and practice have local populations retained and which have they adapted for their own purposes? To what extent are traditional elements of Pacific Islands cultures compatible with Christian orthodoxy? We can also turn from the exploration of these 'glocal' issues to consider how Stevenson's writing contributes to our understanding of global Protestantism.[76] Reformed theology was by no means a unified endeavour in the nineteenth century, and the term 'Protestantism' itself reflects a changing and diverse set of ideas and practices.[77] But the recurrence of themes of sacramentality, literacy, and polity in Stevenson's Pacific fiction indicates a set of religious priorities that is distinctively Presbyterian. Furthermore, it begs the question of how far Stevenson really moved intellectually from his religious roots. In the next chapter, this question is explored through a study of his changing view of the church.

---

[75] Brian Stanley, *Christianity in the Twentieth Century: A World History* (Princeton, NJ: Princeton University Press, 2018); Jenkins, *Next Christendom*.

[76] Carla Sassi, 'Glocalising Scottish Literature: A Call for New Strategies of Reading', *The Bottle Imp – Supplement 1* (March 2014), 1–4.

[77] On the varieties of opinion that have been held by Protestants, see Alec Ryrie, *Protestants: The Faith that Made the Modern World* (New York: Penguin Books, 2017).

Chapter 5

The Church in the Mind of Stevenson

A Kantian image of Stevenson as a writer who was more interested in moral and ethical questions than in religion per se has been the scholarly consensus of the late-twentieth and early-twenty-first centuries. In his influential biography, J. C. Furnas explains that 'What [Stevenson] meant by "God" was at most a metaphysical possibility necessarily implied by certain hypotheses that were probably as tenable as any others. His basic moral axiom has no backing from so tenuous a support.'[1] The idea that Stevenson was a believing Christian was not unknown around the turn of the twentieth century: the Free Church clergyman John Kelman asserted in 1903 that Stevenson's 'faith is to be taken seriously' but, even then, admitted, 'I have felt myself advocating this against a considerable body of common opinion.'[2] Revisionist accounts of the Victorian era ensured that other aspects of Stevenson's life and work would be prioritised while mainstream scholarship continued to neglect religion as a serious subject of study. The attack on the apparently damaging effects of Calvinism on Scottish culture was another prong of the general assault. Furnas offers a fair illustration of how religion has tended to be portrayed as a negative yet creative force, which caught Stevenson in its doctrinal and emotional shackles: all his life the Metrical Versions of Job's despair, the close inquiries and bleak replies of the Shorter Catechism, the arbitrary, legally unimpeachable pessimism of the Westminster Confession, put phrases in his mouth and shaped his thinking.[3] According to the established

---

[1] J. C. Furnas, *Voyage to Windward: The Life of Robert Louis Stevenson* (London: Faber and Faber, 1952), 208.
[2] John Kelman, *The Faith of Robert Louis Stevenson* (Edinburgh: Oliphant, Anderson and Ferrier, 1903), xi.
[3] Furnas, *Voyage to Windward*, 32.

interpretation, one should look to sources other than religion to find the key to what Stevenson truly believed and admired.

As the preceding chapters have demonstrated, in the Pacific Stevenson found sufficient reason to think carefully again about the relationship between religion and culture. But to move beyond the established analytical framework requires us to pay attention to the importance of institutional religion in Stevenson's mental world. Ideas about the form and the functions of the church were just as important to him as were morality and ethics. The 1891 letter to his friend Adelaide Boodle, discussed in Chapter 1, testifies to how much he continued to think about the church into his later years.[4] The letter's main thrust, in response to Boodle's concerns about not being able to receive Anglican communion in Samoa, is to articulate a rugged, almost Covenanter view of Christian ecclesiology. As Stevenson admonished his friend, 'many of the best Christians sit in [no church]' and the ones who come 'nearest' to 'divinity' in this 'great and rough' world are those that 'can accept that greatness and that roughness'. He added sharply that

> all my ancestors, for as far back as I can trace them, or with a very few exceptions, were denied, and somehow managed to breast through this life without the privilege of that communion on which you [. . .] would set so high a value.

As we saw in Chapter 1, the critic Ernest Mehew used this letter to demonstrate how the defining tension in Stevenson's mature thought was between belief and unbelief. Yet Stevenson seemed to be expressing a quite different problem, namely, while God is everywhere, 'a church is not the universe'. What, then, did Stevenson think were the church's proper limits? And what constituted true worship of the Christian God? In this chapter I explore Stevenson's view of the institutional church and show how he remained interested in the subject even after he stopped regularly attending services. When he went to the Pacific, his interest developed into a deeper appreciation of the church's impact on the community. By connecting European with Pacific influences in his thought, the chapter emphasises the globalisation of Christianity as an important context for his ideas.

---

[4] The quotations in this paragraph are from *The Letters of Robert Louis Stevenson*, ed. by Bradford A. Booth and Ernest Mehew (New Haven, CT: Yale University Press, 1994–5), VII, 72–5.

The literary scholar Pamela Dalziel's study of what she describes as Thomas Hardy's 'churchiness' offers a useful model for approaching this multifarious subject in the life and work of another late Victorian author. Like Stevenson, Hardy also 'had views' about the church as understood theologically, socially, and aesthetically. Dalziel demonstrates how 'many of his views evolved during the course of his life'.[5] In the sense that Hardy continued to remain a part of the Church of England without accepting many of the things for which it stood, Dalziel's account of his churchiness could be said to invert the sociologist Grace Davie's formula of believing without belonging.[6] Hardy wrote:

> We enter church, and we have to say, 'We have erred and strayed from thy ways like lost sheep', when what we want to say is, 'Why are we made to err and stray like lost sheep?' [. . .] Still, being present, we say the established words full of the historic sentiment only, mentally adding, 'How happy our ancestors were in repeating in all sincerity these articles of faith!' But we perceive that none of the congregation recognizes that we repeat the words from an antiquarian interest in them, and in a historic sense, and solely in order to keep a church of some sort afoot – a thing indispensable; so that we are pretending what is not true; that we are believers.[7]

In this respect, Hardy offers a strong contrast with Stevenson, who was an irregular churchgoer in Scotland after breaking his formal allegiance to the established church in the early 1870s.[8]

Stevenson's own attitude rather resembles that of another contemporary, the Lutheran theologian Adolf von Harnack (1851–1930). Von Harnack, like many in his time, sought through historical analysis to pare Christianity down and separate the 'kernel of truth about Jesus from the husk of contingent and irrelevant beliefs'.[9] In doing

---

[5] Pamela Dalziel, '"The Hard Case of the Would-Be-Religious": Hardy and the Church from Early Life to Later Years', in *A Companion to Thomas Hardy*, ed. by Keith Wilson (Oxford: Blackwell, 2009), 71–85 (71).

[6] Grace Davie, *Religion in Britain since 1945: Believing without Belonging* (Oxford: Blackwell, 1994). On desacralisation and religious modernism as a target of both orthodox Christians and freethinkers, see Ernestine van der Wall, 'Between Faith and Doubt: The Role of Fiction', *T. F. Blad van de Theologische Faculteit Universiteit, Leiden* 35 (December 2005), 56–75 (66).

[7] Thomas Hardy, quoted in Dalziel, 'The Hard Case', 80.

[8] See Chapter 1 for the biographical details.

[9] Nicholas M. Healy, 'The Church in Modern Theology', in *The Routledge Companion to the Christian Church*, ed. by Gerard Mannion and Lewis S. Mudge (New York and London: Routledge, 2008), 106–206 (113).

so, Harnack, like Stevenson, came to reject the Gospel of John for its unreal depiction of Christ.[10] While Stevenson would have accepted von Harnack's simpler Gospel, he also possessed a rich admiration of beauty that allowed him to tolerate ecclesiological practices and accoutrements at which the German may have looked askance. For these reasons Stevenson would likely have opposed the austerely Protestant ecclesiological view of the post-war neo-Reformation movement, for which the church was to be thought of as 'a pure communion of persons entirely without institutional character'.[11]

Set against these literary and theological contexts, the aim of this chapter is to demonstrate Stevenson's influences, development, and contribution as a thinker of religion by situating his writing within the history of later-nineteenth-century ecclesiology. I excavate something that later scholars have missed because of the post-Christian, secular culture of the modern West, in which religion has been rendered as largely an abstract and private matter. Stevenson and many of his contemporaries, whatever their personal religious views, thought deeply about the role that the institutional church should play in society. Stevenson grew up steeped in ecclesiology and in Scottish religious culture and he continued to think about the church's identity and function even after his formal break with it. That this occupied his mind to the end of his life is exemplified by the important role he accorded to the church in Samoan nation-building.

Although Stevenson wrote about the church throughout his life, he did not put his thoughts forward in any systematic way, so that one finds ecclesiological ideas and opinions scattered across his fiction, letters, and other writings. Since there is no modern scholarly account of this subject, I mainly draw for context on the wider historical and theological literature. While he left the established church in his early twenties, Stevenson remained closely aligned with elements of reform within the Church of Scotland through people he knew and ideas that he expressed about church structure, worship, and

---

[10] 'In particular, the fourth Gospel, which does not emanate or profess to emanate from the Apostle John, cannot be taken as an historical authority in the ordinary meaning of the word'. Adolf von Harnack, *What is Christianity? Lectures Delivered in the University of Berlin during the Winter Term 1899–1900*, trans. by Thomas Bailey Saunders (New York: G. P. Putnam's Sons, 1901), 21. '[Stevenson] said that he was never able to tolerate the view of the person of Christ which it seemed to him was held by the Gospel attributed to the Apostle John.' J. E. Newell, 'R. L. Stevenson as I Knew Him', *Christchurch Press*, 2 March 1907. National Library of Australia, nla.obj-2739135234.

[11] Jerome Brunner, quoted in Healy, 'The Church in Modern Theology', 114.

service. In his assumption that that there was a direct relationship between church and mission, he could be described as an 'Evangelical' rather than a 'Moderate' Scottish Presbyterian, and for most of his life he assumed that missionary work proceeded with the growth of regular and formal church structures in new settings rather than on the looser, voluntary basis advocated by other mission thinkers and organisations of the time.[12] His experience of the novel political, economic, and pastoral conditions in the Pacific led him to a more radical and prophetic view of mission that highlighted indigenous agency and the productive preservation of land.[13] In explicitly connecting evangelisation with issues of justice and cultural survival, he was in advance of the formal position of the Church of Scotland of his time and closer to the views of twentieth-century missionaries and theologians.[14]

A National Church

In religious historical terms, Stevenson's upbringing took place under the shadow of the Disruption of 1843, a split within the Church of Scotland that reflected members' deep differences over the relationship between church and state.[15] On one side of the conflict were 'Evangelicals', who were sometimes characterised in the 1840s as the 'missionary' group. Led by Thomas Chalmers (1780–1847), this

---

[12] Brian Stanley, 'The Theology of the Scottish Protestant Missionary Movement', in *The History of Scottish Theology, Volume III: The Long Twentieth Century*, ed. by David Fergusson and Mark W. Elliott (Oxford: Oxford University Press, 2019), 51–63; see also Andrew F. Walls, 'Three Hundred Years of Scottish Missions', in *Roots and Fruits: Retrieving Scotland's Missionary Story*, ed. by Kenneth R. Ross (Padstow: Regnum, 2014), 4–37.

[13] On the 'environmental sensitivity' that Stevenson brought to Samoa, see Jennifer Fuller, 'The Price of Paradise: Robert Louis Stevenson, Joseph Conrad and British Expansion in the Pacific', in *Dark Paradise: Pacific Islands in the British Nineteenth-Century British Imagination* (Edinburgh: Edinburgh University Press, 2016), 111–53 (112).

[14] Darrell L. Guder, 'Reformed Theology, Mission, and Ecumenism', in *The Cambridge Companion to Reformed Theology*, ed. by Paul T. Nimmo and David A. S. Fergusson (Cambridge: Cambridge University Press, 2016), 319–34.

[15] Michael Shaw has emphasised the value to Scottish cultural history of 'A focused assessment on the state of Presbyterianism across Victorian and Edwardian Scotland and its impact on literature'. Michael Shaw, 'Transculturation and Historicisation: New Directions for the Study of Scottish Literature c. 1840–1914', *Literature Compass* 13, 8 (2016), 501–10 (505).

group believed in active parishes and called for local control over religious appointments. On the other side were the 'Moderates', who had been in control of the established church since the previous century. They held that it was possible and indeed important to retain the historic connections between the Kirk and the Scottish state. The underlying Erastian tones of this conflict would shape Stevenson's thinking about the relationship between politics and institutional religion.[16] Attention to the Disruption and the wider impact of industrialisation should not obscure important continuities in Scottish religious life, however. As the author of a recent historical survey summarises, for the remainder of the nineteenth century 'Scotland remained overwhelmingly Presbyterian, and theologically Reformed'.[17]

Stevenson often seemed light-hearted in his denunciation of the ecclesiastical squabbling of his countrymen, as he was in *Edinburgh: Picturesque Notes* (1879) when he declared that the disagreements of his time were akin to those found among 'a large family of sisters', quibbling over trifles.[18] Nevertheless, through a turbulent period of church politics at mid-century, his family remained staunch members of the Church of Scotland and did not opt for either of the major breakaway denominations, the Free Church and the United Presbyterian Church. From 1869 the family attended St Stephen's, which was founded in 1828 with the completion of Edinburgh's New Town.[19] The church's construction was part of a wave of ecclesiastical responses to urban expansion and the fragmentation of older parish communities. Reflecting a spirit of amity in the local congregation, St Stephen's had the latitude to offer 'a place of worship for members of the Free Church'.[20]

To be a member of the Church of Scotland around the beginning of the nineteenth century meant to receive the sacraments of baptism and communion, to listen to correct preaching of Reformed doctrine, and to have some experience of the discipline of Kirk sessions.[21] Stevenson's

---

[16] Writing from Samoa to the LMS's Foreign Secretary in 1892, for example, Stevenson expressed 'my opinion, and my prayer, that the Mission should return to its old, traditional policy and maintain a strict neutrality in politics'. Stevenson, *Letters* VII, 255.

[17] R. Scott Spurlock, 'Scottish Presbyterianism', *Victorian Review* 46, 2 (2020), 162–6 (164).

[18] Robert Louis Stevenson, *Edinburgh: Picturesque Notes* (London: Seeley, Jackson and Halliday, 1879), 16.

[19] Stevenson, *Letters* I, 41.

[20] Samuel Lewis, *A Topographical Dictionary of Scotland* (London: S. Lewis & Co., 1846), 384.

[21] Spurlock, 'Scottish Presbyterianism', 162.

childhood was organised around his parents' close relationship with the established church and their eagerness to see that he followed family religious tradition. For the young Stevenson, attendance at church went hand in hand with an introduction to Scripture. An account such as the following is common in his mother's record of his childhood. The two-year-old Stevenson is visiting the church at Colinton to hear the preaching of his grandfather, the Reverend Lewis Balfour: 'Smout [Stevenson's pet name] sat in the front Gallery as grave as a judge the whole time. When asked who preached, he said "Gatty (Grandfather) and a man" (the precentor).'[22] It mattered greatly to his devout parents that their son quickly grew comfortable in church settings. In April 1853, Margaret Stevenson recorded how 'Smout [was] at Church and behaved very well.'[23] Beside its socialising environment, the church was also one of Stevenson's earliest sources of imaginative play. Soon his 'favourite occupation' at home was 'making a church': 'a pulpit with a chair and stool and [he] reads sitting and then stands up and sings by turns'.[24] Not only church aesthetics and liturgy but also homiletics was within the boy's purview, as a sermon he preached at home on 6 May 1855 attests:

> Whoever entereth into a field on the Sunday and reapeth or picketh sticks is not of God and shall not go to Heaven, but if he does anything more on the Sunday he must go to Hell. Everyone must do nothing that's wrong.[25]

As we know, these prodigious beginnings did not ultimately lead to a life of active churchgoing, but he did continue to attend services from time to time and he maintained an ambivalent attitude towards the formal institution through the 1870s and 1880s. The belligerent 'Sunday Thoughts', a poem from 1875, captures his youthful experiences of guilt and frustration:

> A plague o' these Sundays! How the church bells ring up the sleeping past! I cannot go into sermon; memories ache too hard; and so I bide out under the blue heaven, beside the small kirk whelmed in leaves.[26]

---

[22] Margaret Isabella Stevenson, *Stevenson's Baby Book; Being the Record of the Sayings and Doings of Robert Louis Balfour Stevenson, Son of Thomas Stevenson, C.E. and Margaret Isabella Balfour or Stevenson* (San Francisco: J. H. Nash, 1922), 42.
[23] Stevenson, *Stevenson's Baby Book*, 44.
[24] Stevenson, *Stevenson's Baby Book*, 45.
[25] Stevenson, *Stevenson's Baby Book*, 52.
[26] Stevenson, *Letters* II, 336.

He later reports in the same poem, 'I have both been to church and stayed away from church in my time.' A decade later, in one of his best short stories, 'Markheim' (1885), the church takes on the status of an important memory. The title character enters a pawnshop and kills its owner with a plan to steal his money. The story, which is steeped in predestinarian theology, progresses with the changing mental state of the murderer, who is eventually brought to repentance and confession through a dialogue with a mysterious visitor. The moment of the visitor's entry is fittingly ambivalent. As Markheim searches for a key to the pawnbroker's cabinet, he hears children singing outside and experiences reverie:

> his mind was thronged with answerable ideas and images; church-going children and the pealing of the high organ [. . .] and then, at another cadence of the hymn, back again to church, and the somnolence of summer Sundays, and the high genteel voice of the parson (which he smiled a little to recall) and the painted Jacobean tombs, and the dim lettering of the Ten Commandments in the chancel.[27]

At that moment, unknown to Markheim, these remembrances of the church will herald the arrival of the angelic presence of the visitor into his life.

In these middle years of his life, when Stevenson often wrote about irreligion and the experience of being outside the church, he did so in naturalistic terms that were familiar for the time. In his writing he expressed a new enjoyment of the sense of space and of bodily habitation. In perhaps the most famous of all his stories, the title character experiences a 'leap of welcome' upon his scientific conversion, a change that 'seemed natural and human'.[28] Compare this transformation of the spry Edward Hyde from out of the beleaguered Henry Jekyll with another 'loss of faith' novel, one which is centred more explicitly around the severing of ties to the established church. Robert Elsmere's moment of awakening from religious orthodoxy is also solitary and portrayed in terms of a magnification of space:

> The lane darkened round him. Not a soul was in sight. The only sounds were the sounds of a gently breathing nature, sounds of birds

---

[27] Robert Louis Stevenson, 'Markheim', in *The Merry Men and Other Tales and Fables* (London: Chatto and Windus, 1905), 118.

[28] Robert Louis Stevenson, *Strange Case of Dr. Jekyll and Mr. Hyde* (London: Longmans, Green, and Co., 1886), 114.

and swaying branches and intermittent gusts of air rustling through the gorse and the drifts of last year's leaves in the wood beside him. He moved mechanically onward, and presently, after the first flutter of desolate terror had passed away, with a new inrushing sense which seemed to him a sense of liberty – of infinite expansion.[29]

A feeling of boundlessness links the transformations of the two characters. An echo of the same boundlessness may be found in Stevenson's 1891 letter to Adelaide Boodle when he wrote that 'a church is not the universe'. Yet it must be emphasised that this determined embrace of the natural describes only one aspect of Stevenson's life outside the bounds of established religion. Just as important, he remained in touch with people, such as the clergyman and writer James Cameron Lees (1835–1913) and the theologian John Tulloch (1823–86), who were closely associated with reform in the Church of Scotland.[30] Stevenson's relationship with these figures offers a context for how he understood the changing role of religion in Scottish society.

The ecclesiastical historian Stewart J. Brown has claimed that, in the three decades after the Disruption, the Church of Scotland adapted to the fragmentation of Scottish Presbyterianism and to broader social and political changes in later-nineteenth-century Scotland by fashioning a new identity that allowed it to grow and remain relevant to the wider culture.[31] In highlighting the Kirk's 'remarkable recovery' during this period, Brown emphasises efforts by Tulloch and others 'to provide greater theological freedom and openness to social and cultural progress, including a willingness to question the Reformed doctrinal standards of the Westminster Confession of Faith'.[32] A concrete example of the latter may be found in the national debate which broke out in 1865 over sabbatarianism, which the clergyman Norman Macleod (1812–72) linked to 'the question of whether theological

---

[29] Mrs Humphry [Mary Augusta] Ward, *Robert Elsmere* (London: Macmillan and Co., 1888), 343.
[30] Stevenson, *Letters* III, 197, 243n, 334n.
[31] On broader developments in the nineteenth-century Church of Scotland, see A. C. Cheyne, *The Transforming of the Kirk: Victorian Scotland's Religious Revolution* (Edinburgh: The Saint Andrew Press, 1983). John MacKenzie has argued that the Disruption 'undoubtedly served to inject a new energy to Scottish missionary endeavour since the evangelical Free Church immediately became a significant provider of missions'. John M. MacKenzie, 'Presbyterianism and Scottish Identity in Global Context', *Britain and the World* 10, 1 (2017), 88–112 (99).
[32] Stewart J. Brown, 'After the Disruption: The Recovery of the National Church of Scotland, 1843–1874', *Scottish Church History* 48, 2 (2019), 103–25 (103).

understanding was progressive'.[33] John Tulloch defended Macleod's views with a manifesto address at the Edinburgh University Theological Society. He lamented 'the "very sad and painful" history of religious controversy in Scotland since the Reformation', insisting that it 'was the result of the passions, ignorance and insensitivity to human diversity', and he portrayed the Westminster Confession 'as a human product of a violent period in history'.[34]

Stevenson was personally close to some of these 'prominent public intellectuals' who 'believed that the national church had a special responsibility for guiding developments in the nation's cultural life'.[35] He was present in June 1882 when his family dined at home with Rev. James Cameron Lees, who was then in the midst of overseeing a large-scale restoration of St Giles' Cathedral, Edinburgh.[36] Lees and Tulloch were among those (others included the Free Church minister Alexander Whyte) who wrote testimonials for Stevenson's application for the position of Chair of History and Constitutional Law at the University of Edinburgh in 1881.[37] Tulloch had encouraged Stevenson to work on a book about the history of the Anglo-Scottish Union of 1707.[38] Stevenson had consulted him because of Tulloch's expertise in eighteenth-century Scottish history.[39] Stevenson's admiration of Tulloch as a theologian went back to the early 1870s when he praised one of his lectures at St Mary's College, University of St Andrews. Tulloch's subject was 'the present tendency to extremes in religion'.[40] For Stevenson, the recovery of national history went together with the discovery of a reforming clerisy.

Stevenson's own interventions in Scottish religious politics were closely connected with the work of these reforming figures. The provision of 'religious instruction and pastoral care' to the Scottish population, 'and especially to the urban poor', has been recognised

---

[33] Brown, 'After the Disruption', 116.
[34] Brown, 'After the Disruption', 117.
[35] Brown, 'After the Disruption', 119.
[36] Stevenson, *Letters* III, 334n; Bryan D. Spinks, *Scottish Presbyterian Worship: Proposals for Organic Change, 1843 to the Present Day* (Edinburgh: The Saint Andrew Press, 2020), 140–3.
[37] Stevenson, *Letters* III, 243n.
[38] Stevenson, *Letters* III, 98n.
[39] Stevenson, *Letters* III, 196.
[40] Stevenson, *Letters* I, 383n. According to N. R. Needham, 'Theologically, [Tulloch] pioneered a new school of thought, which aimed to transcend the traditional Scottish Presbyterian quarrel between Moderate and Evangelical.' N. R. Needham, 'Tulloch, John (1823–86)', in *Dictionary of Scottish Church History and Theology*, ed. by Nigel M. de S. Cameron (Edinburgh: T&T Clark, 1993), 830–1.

as perhaps the key aspect of the national church reformers' activities, and Stevenson also promoted this goal.[41] In May 1871, he wrote anonymously to the editor of *The Church of Scotland Home and Foreign Missionary Record* that the Kirk should be more actively engaged in the service of 'the poor and suffering'.[42] He proposed that this would happen if church authorities permitted lay members of every parish to do physical works of charity and to leave ministers, elders, and others with formal qualifications to focus on the spiritual works that were attendant upon parochial visitations. A church that was flexible in sharing its ministry was less likely to be open to the charges of 'inefficiency' that had been levelled at its 'sister body', the Church of Ireland.[43] Like Tulloch, Stevenson thought that the shadow of disestablishment hung threateningly over the Kirk.[44] To counter this, he expressed a widespread conviction, forcefully articulated earlier in the century by Thomas Chalmers, that in this age of rapid and unstable urban growth the church had a central responsibility to attend to the overall welfare of the poor.[45] The work of mission, at home as well as abroad, should be intrinsic to the Kirk and was becoming essential to its survival. Stevenson was therefore one of a number that encouraged institutional reform towards this end. Insofar as he pointed to the pressures on established religion by secular agencies and the prevalent 'doctrine of humanity', his justification for reform could be characterised as coming from outside of the church's purview. But in another way it should be interpreted internally, since Stevenson discerned an injunction of Christ at the root of modern criticism of the Kirk, which he quoted from his favourite Gospel: 'Inasmuch as ye did it unto the least of these'.[46] These words bound all believers, he asserted, 'not as individuals only, but as Churches'. The work of justice was both historically contingent and religiously corporate. These communitarian instincts kept him apart from the more individualistic strands of later-nineteenth-century Protestantism and continuously engaged with ecclesiology.

---

[41] Brown, 'After the Disruption', 109.

[42] All quotations from this letter are from Stevenson, *Letters* I, 212–13.

[43] See 'Irish Church Act, 1869': 'An Act to put an end to the Establishment of the Church of Ireland, and to make provision in respect of the Temporalities thereof [. . .]', accessed at: http://www.irishstatutebook.ie/eli/1869/act/42/enacted/en/print.html on 4 August 2021.

[44] Needham, 'Tulloch', 831.

[45] See Stewart J. Brown, *Thomas Chalmers and the Godly Commonwealth in Scotland* (Oxford: Oxford University Press, 1982).

[46] Matthew 25: 40.

A few years later, in August 1874, the British Parliament's accession to the request of the Church of Scotland to abolish patronage offered an opportunity for the dissenters of 1843 to reunite with the Kirk.[47] Stevenson's letter to his friend Frances Sitwell on 27 August 1874 records his thoughts about wading into 'Scotch ecclesiastical politics', a subject which had been occupying him 'for some time back'.[48] Ernest Mehew reports that the pamphlet concerning this issue that Stevenson published anonymously, *An Appeal to the Clergy of the Church of Scotland*, reached every member of the General Assembly in 1875. Not much else is known about the pamphlet's production and dissemination but the fact that Stevenson decided to write it, and then some six months later to publish it, demonstrates that the author continued to be seriously engaged in church affairs beyond the quarrel with his family over his religious beliefs.

'Had I a strong voice, as it is the weakest alive, yea, could I lift it up as a trumpet, I would sound a retreat from our unnatural contentions, and irreligious strivings for religion' – the pamphlet's frontispiece quotation, from the seventeenth-century Scottish divine Robert Leighton (1611–84), was Stevenson's acknowledgement of both the perennial nature of conflict within the church polity as well as the tradition of those who sought the middle ground.[49] In a manner reminiscent of Tulloch in Stevenson's day, Leighton unsuccessfully attempted to reconcile Episcopalians with Presbyterians during the reign of Charles II.[50] His personal holiness and gentle manner were also attributes that Stevenson wanted to remind his readers of as Scottish churchmen conflicted over patronage and the wide implications of its abolition.

Stevenson's pamphlet is an exhortation to the clergy of the General Assembly to generously offer support to dissenting brethren from the

---

[47] Finlay MacDonald connects this episode to the long-standing movement to disestablish the Church of Scotland. Finlay A. J. Macdonald, 'Liberal, Broad Church, and Reforming Influences in the Late Nineteenth Century', in *The History of Scottish Theology, Volume II: The Early Enlightenment to the Late Victorian Era*, ed. by David Fergusson and Mark W. Elliott (Oxford: Oxford University Press, 2019), 419–32 (420–1).

[48] Stevenson, *Letters* II, 41.

[49] Anon., *An Appeal to the Clergy of the Church of Scotland* (William Blackwood and Sons, 1875). Parenthetical references in the next two paragraphs are taken from this text.

[50] J. D. Douglas, 'Leighton, Robert (1611–84)', in Cameron, *Dictionary of Scottish Church History*, 478–9. Under the leadership of its Principal John Tulloch, the University of St Andrews was involved in bringing Presbyterians and Anglicans more closely together. Stewart J. Brown, personal communication.

Free Church that sought to reunite themselves with the Kirk. He opens by portraying the present situation: with the change in the patronage law comes the opportunity for reconciliation. He acknowledges obstacles that could come in the way of the latter, and his framing of the issue is political in the manner of the reformers: 'not only the credit of the Church, not only the credit of Christianity, but to some extent also that of the national character, is at stake' (3) in the clergy's decision. Now that it has achieved this victory, the Kirk must demonstrate responsible leadership. He urges the clergy to 'show yourselves worthy of a great opportunity, and do more for the public minds by the example of one act of generosity and humility than you could do by an infinite series of sermons' (5). Besides welcoming separated brethren back into the fold, Stevenson points out that the Kirk should provide material recompense for those who had dissented and now sought to return 'with a clear conscience' (6). Here is the crux of his appeal: first, Christian charity is the basis of a justice that is beyond those of 'courts of law or equity' (7). Secondly, the clergy acting with an uncalculating generosity would be more meaningful to this 'weary' generation than any 'visions, miracles, or prophecies' (8). The Kirk should seek to lead and not follow public opinion on this matter. Stevenson closes by asking his readers to accept his words, written with the 'freedom of an anonymous writer' (10), in a spirit of friendly advice from one who is 'apart from the battle' (10).

In the appended 'Note for the Laity' he explains that the previous pages 'have been in type since the beginning of last September' and that he has 'been advised to give them to the public' (11). He reminds his readers that 'the solution must come from the Church members' (11), not the leadership. It seems as if he has realised during the intervening time that speaking only to the clergy about this matter might not be effective. For, as he writes, it was the laity that could offer 'a new endowment scheme', whose substance is 'to do for (say) ten years, what the laymen of the Free Church have done cheerfully since 1843' (11). While Stevenson's plea is emotive and he appeals to shared Scottish sentiment, he also is shrewdly aware that such an act of generosity would gain the attention of those growing numbers that were outside the Church. These were the views of a man for whom the Church of Scotland's integrity and status were meaningfully linked. The Kirk was a national institution and Stevenson believed that it could play a guiding moral role in a country where scepticism was widely believed to be on the rise.

Perhaps the dominant figure in nineteenth-century Scottish religious life, certainly in the years immediately following the Disruption, was the clergyman and reformer Thomas Chalmers.[51] Chalmers had led the Free Church through the Disruption and its aftermath but he was not instinctively drawn to the politics of secession. He hoped that Dissent would strengthen the Kirk, if the Kirk were to survive this era of industrial change and urbanisation. Before the Disruption, he wrote in private correspondence:

> I have no veneration for the Church of Scotland merely *quasi* an Establishment, but I have the utmost veneration for it *quasi* an instrument of Christian good; and I do think, that with the means and resources of an Establishment, she can do more, and does more, for the religious interests of Scotland than is done by the activity of all the Dissenters put together. I think it a high object to uphold the Church of Scotland, but only because of its subserviency to the still higher object of upholding the Christianity of our land [. . .].[52]

In describing the potential impact of his 1874–5 pamphlet, Stevenson was equally unconcerned for the survival of the Kirk apart from the good that it might do for the country:

> If the Church be virtuous enough to take my suggestion, it has the elements of life in it, and would live whether or no [. . .] If, on the other hand, it has too little virtue or too much policy, I shall have done good service to unveiling a sham and struck another death blow at the existence of superannuated religion.[53]

In leading the Disruption, it has been claimed that Chalmers marked 'his church's retreat from societal influence in Scotland as the price of ecclesial independence'.[54] Despite the similarity between their views of the Kirk, it is unlikely that Stevenson would ever have conceived of such a political trade-off: his focus was on the national role of Christianity, not the autonomy of a particular church.

Stevenson shared other Kirk reformers' appreciation for the aesthetics of church building, decoration, and music. As places of worship,

---

[51] John Roxborogh, 'The Legacy of Thomas Chalmers', *International Bulletin of Missionary Research* (October 1999), 173–6.
[52] William Hanna, *Memoirs of the Life and Writings of Thomas Chalmers, Vol. III* (Edinburgh: Sutherland and Knox, 1851), 109.
[53] Stevenson, *Letters* II, 41.
[54] Mark W. Elliott, 'Natural and Revealed Rheology in Hill and Chalmers', in Fergusson and Elliott, *History of Scottish Theology, Volume II*, 170–85 (175).

churches came increasingly to be seen not just as buildings purposed for the dissemination and elaboration of Scripture but embodied artistic activity in service of God, which was meant to reflect and inspire holiness. In his sermon on the reopening of St Giles' on 23 May 1883, Lees spoke in starkly catholic and romantic terms about 'the ideal of infinite perfection – the good, the true, and the beautiful, and these three cannot be disjoined from the other'.[55] The Victorian outlines of this view can be discerned in the 'liturgical revival' that many Scottish Presbyterian churches underwent at the time.[56] Quoting a source from 1870, Bryan Spinks summarises the changes of the period: '"kneeling at prayer . . . carefully written prayers . . . the organ has been introduced . . . the music, instrumental and vocal, is generally well executed and carefully chosen" [. . .] Gothic revival architecture, stained glass'.[57] Rather than theology, Spinks explains, the main drivers of change in worship in nineteenth-century Scottish Presbyterianism were 'aesthetical', 'historical', and 'cultural', 'being an expression of Romanticism and the Victorian interest in respectability and things medieval'.[58]

As a self-conscious aesthete, the young Stevenson would have been familiar with the elements of this 'liturgical revival', which coincided with the mid-century revival of Roman Catholicism in England. During a visit to London in 1872, he spent a Sunday at The Church of Our Lady of Victories. It was not his first visit to a Catholic 'service' and he praised it for being 'very well done, the music good'. During the same period, on a visit to the Gustave Doré Gallery, he described to his mother how he was deeply moved by the artist's *Christ Leaving the Praetorium*: 'I like it perhaps better than any other single picture in the world.'[59] It is a striking claim, especially since he much preferred the human Christ of Matthew's Gospel to Doré's evidently Johannine depiction. Art seemed to cut through Stevenson's cooler ethical judgements to a deeper layer of religious romance.

---

[55] James Cameron Lees, quoted in Spinks, *Scottish Presbyterian Worship*, 142.
[56] Bryan D. Spinks, 'The Liturgical Revolution: Prayers, Hymns, and Stained Glass', in Fergusson and Elliott, *History of Scottish Theology, Volume II*, 329; Brown, 'After the Disruption', 115.
[57] Spinks, 'Liturgical Revolution', 329.
[58] Spinks, 'Liturgical Revolution', 338.
[59] Stevenson, *Letters* I, 230 and n.

Mission and the Church

Although he was personally conflicted about his involvement in the institution, Stevenson nevertheless believed that the established church had an important role to play in guiding the moral sense of the nation. The church, rightly ordered, could act as a beacon that brought together the faithful as well as those who had left the fray. In this he shared much in common with reformers within the Church of Scotland. His family also ingrained appreciation in him for the church's energetic virtue in seeding and sustaining missionaries.[60] Thomas Chalmers had forcefully propounded the missionary function of the church. Following the work of the Quaker minister Joseph John Gurney (1788–1847), Chalmers advanced a theory of 'the portable character of evidence for the truth of Christianity':

> The meaning of it is, that, unlike to the historical or literary evidence, which, as requiring a higher amount of scholarship and education than is found to obtain throughout the general mass of society, can only be addressed to a limited class of readers – the portable evidence, on the contrary, may be borne to every door, and find an opening for itself to the heart and the conscience even of the most unlettered of our species. Yet it is not by a reflex or philosophical exposition of this evidence [. . .] that it is made to obtain an entrance into the minds of the common people. It works a way for itself there, and there achieves its main triumphs through the direct preaching of the Gospel of Jesus Christ [. . .] It is thus that the subject matter of Christianity, instinct in itself with evidence, may, when simply told and explained, be left to vindicate its own authority; and does in fact carry its own proper weight, amounting to absolute and entire ascendancy, over the convictions of the most ignorant and unlearned hearers.[61]

To this notion of automatic understanding Chalmers attached a missionary significance that was to prove highly influential in the latter half of the century:

---

[60] On missions and the Scottish churches, see especially Andrew L. Drummond and James Bulloch, *The Church in Victorian Scotland* (Edinburgh: The Saint Andrew Press, 1975), 139–77; Esther Breitenbach, 'Scots Churches and Missions', in *Scotland and the British Empire*, ed. by John M. MacKenzie and T. M. Devine (Oxford: Oxford University Press, 2011), 196–226.

[61] Thomas Chalmers, *The Works of Thomas Chalmers, D.D. and LL.D., Volume Fourth: On the Miraculous and Internal Evidences of the Christian Revelation, and the Authority of its Records* (New York: Robert Carter, 1840), 170–1.

And this self-evidence which lies in the matter of revelation, and makes it so applicable to the unlearned within, makes it equally applicable to the rudest and most unlettered tribes without the limits of Christendom. In the power and effect of the internal evidence we behold the rationale of a missionary enterprise – the agents of which, with but the Bible in their hands and the spirit of prayer in their hearts, are in a state of full equipment for operating on the moral nature of man in every quarter of the globe.[62]

The formal simplicity of Chalmers's apostolic vision appealed to many in his time. When Stevenson wrote, late in life, about 'the vast reservoir of moral power' in Pacific Islander populations, he was drawing on a Scottish tradition of anthropology that took in Thomas Chalmers as well as the moral philosopher Francis Hutcheson (1694–1746).[63]

The historian Brian Stanley has written about the distinctiveness of the Scottish Presbyterian missionary movement in the nineteenth century. Both the Church of Scotland (1824) and the Free Church (1843) were unusual in deciding to '"do" foreign missions' rather than leaving them to 'specialist voluntary agencies'.[64] The idea of a church that was actively in mission, 'that foreign missions were properly an ecclesial activity, to be fully subject to the governing structures and confessional standards of a national church', was unusual among Protestant denominations in that period.[65] Having been raised within a Church of Scotland family, Stevenson was more familiar with the 'ecclesial' than with the 'voluntary' model of mission. A fundamental belief of the former was that mission work was intimately connected with the church and that it should consist of gaining converts and reproducing regular, formal ecclesial structures in new settings.[66] The rudiments of this belief appear to have been imbued in Stevenson at an extraordinarily young age. He was in his seventh year when he explained to his mother that 'The churches are much to blame for not sending missionaries to convert the Arabs.'[67] When she asked him whether he would go when he was big, he replied, 'If I'm spared.' Such were the roots that he would reflect on in Samoa, aged forty, to the Scottish missionary James Chalmers (1841–1901): 'O, Tamate

---

[62] Chalmers, *Works, Volume Fourth*, 171.
[63] Robert Louis Stevenson, 'Missions in the South Seas', in *Sophia Scarlet and Other Pacific Writings*, ed. by Robert Hoskins (Auckland: AUT Media, 2008), 107–9.
[64] Stanley, 'Theology of the Scottish Protestant Missionary Movement', 55.
[65] Stanley, 'Theology of the Scottish Protestant Missionary Movement', 55.
[66] Stanley, 'Theology of the Scottish Protestant Missionary Movement', 55.
[67] Stevenson, *Stevenson's Baby Book*, 58.

[the Rarotongan form of his surname], if I had met you when I was a boy and a bachelor, how different my life would have been.'[68] Notwithstanding his continuing interest in missions, the bedrock assumption of Stevenson's upbringing, that the work of conversion and the establishment of churches went hand in hand, would change when he began to directly encounter the conditions of mission work in the Pacific.

As his dialogue with the reform movement in the Church of Scotland has demonstrated, it would be misleading to suggest that Stevenson was again drawn to ecclesiology only after he settled in Samoa. The intellectual and emotional bond with the church remained throughout, and he appeared to gain new inspiration when he travelled away from Europe to discover just how much of a global institution it had become. In a piece first published anonymously in November 1879, Stevenson made some significant comments about a visit to an old Catholic mission in California that foreshadow his writing about mission and church in the Island Pacific. In the first place, he urges funds for repairs to a church which is 'of extreme interest' but 'is going the way of all roofless and neglected buildings'.[69] 'When I think how that bell first sounded from that Mission Church among the Indians of Carmello, and the echoes of Monterey first learned the unaccustomed note, I am moved, by sentiment, to pray for restitution or at least repair' (210–11). Stevenson joined his interest in the aesthetics of church decoration to an ethic of preservation. Such a connection made sound business sense in the United States since, unlike historic-minded England and France, here 'you cannot afford to lose what you have' (210). This preservationist view would develop into something approaching a theory of culture in Stevenson's later writing.[70]

Stevenson's second point in the 1879 article consists of a reflection on the Catholic Native Americans whom he witnessed singing mass in the church. He remarked that this was 'a new experience and one, I think, well worth hearing' (211). 'They sang by tradition, from the teaching of early missionaries long since turned to clay' (211). As so often in his Pacific writing, we find him in sympathy with the Europeans who

---

[68] Stevenson, *Letters* VII, 48; Patricia A. Prendergast, 'Chalmers, James (1841–1901)', in *Australian Dictionary of Biography*, National Centre of Biography, Australian National University, accessed at: https://adb.anu.edu.au/biography/chalmers-james-3187/text4781 on 5 August 2021.

[69] The Monterey Barbarian, 'San Carlos Day', *Scribner's Magazine* (August 1920), 209–11 (210). All bracketed references in this and the next paragraph are from this source.

[70] I would like to thank Brian Stanley for suggesting this connection.

founded the mission: 'I could not help thinking that if there had been more priests and fewer land sharks and Indian agents, there would have been happier days for a considerable number of human bipeds on your American continent' (211). He encouraged church repair as a way of supporting the Catholic Native American community, since 'both' had been 'brutally neglected' (211). According to Stevenson's preservationist ideal, the fate of indigenous people ran together with the fate of the church. The church would play an even larger role in the way he came to think about the survival of Pacific Islanders.

Raeburn Lange has written of how, at least since the early twentieth century, 'Church buildings are to be found wherever there is human habitation and Christianity is an important feature of Pacific life almost everywhere.'[71] When Stevenson first arrived in the Island Pacific, he noted and described churches in all the different places he visited. His eyes were accustomed to them, and the buildings helped to visually accommodate him to the region in a similar way to how the local use of the English and French languages across the Islands aided his aural reception. For example, in one Hawaiian village he identified a Catholic church, and his full description of another, Honaunau, consisted of the following: 'A scattered village, two white churches, one Catholic, one Protestant, a grove of tall and scraggy palms, and a long bulk of ruin, occupy the end.'[72] On the atoll of Penrhyn (Tongareva), he observed an 'ill-tended church' as a sign of 'a more sad calamity', which turned out to be 'plague'.[73] A church at Hatiheu, in the Marquesas, had better fortune. Stevenson described its sculpture, the work of its architect, Brother Michel Blanc, in witty and admiring detail:

> It is impossible to tell in words of the angels (although they are more like winged bishops) that stand guard upon the door, of the cherubs in the corners, of the scapegoat gargoyles, or the quaint and spirited relief, where St. Michael (the artist's patron) makes short work of a protesting Lucifer.[74]

---

[71] Raeburn Lange, *Island Ministers: Indigenous Leadership in Nineteenth Century Pacific Islands Christianity* (Christchurch: Macmillan Brown Centre for Pacific Studies, University of Canterbury, and Canberra: Pandanus Books, Research School of Pacific and Asian Studies, the Australian National University, 2005), 8.

[72] Robert Louis Stevenson, *The Works of Robert Louis Stevenson, Volume 18: In the South Seas*, ed. by Andrew Lang (London: Chatto and Windus, 1912), 204.

[73] Robert Louis Stevenson, 'A Pearl Island: Penrhyn' and 'Leprosy at Penrhyn', *The Sun* (New York), 24 May 1891, 23–30.

[74] Robert Louis Stevenson, *In the South Seas*, ed. by Neil Rennie (London: Penguin, 1998), 46–7. All bracketed in-text references in this chapter are to this edition of *In the South Seas*.

The European church in its Island Pacific setting was oddly revelatory: 'it was in looking on the church of Hatiheu that I seemed to perceive the secret charm of mediaeval sculpture' (47).

If Stevenson was surprised to indulge his fascination for European ecclesiastical art in these islands, he was equally captivated by the native churches and communities that had sprouted across the Pacific during the previous half century. At Butaritari in the Gilberts, 'the church stands like an island' in the midst of the main road (157). Stevenson provided a rich description of its architecture, dimensions, and interior decoration. 'The proportions of the place, in such surroundings, and built of such materials, appeared august; and we threaded the nave with a sentiment befitting visitors in a cathedral' (157). He gave a vivid account of a Sunday prayer service in the Catholic church at Fakarava atoll in the Paumotus, where in the absence of a priest, the native lay *katekita* (catechist), Taniera Mahinui, preached after singing a hymn and praying with the congregation in the traditional antiphonal style. Stevenson's mother, Margaret, recorded a rough sketch of the same service, most likely on the same day (16 September 1888), in her diary:

> The catechist gets on very well and looks quite ministerial. He has a black gown with small cardinal cape with lace put on. Hat round it. There are 8 men and 7 women present they all take part in the service indeed they do the most of it. A woman leads the singing.[75]

Stevenson noted a Tahitian Bible and, although he understood nothing of the sermon besides the word for God, he and his mother were both impressed with the catechist's delivery (122–4). Margaret Stevenson 'was reminded of the Italian sermon at Genoa', while 'The singing was like the Gaelic singing in Arran'; 'Louis and I were both greatly and deeply moved', she added.[76] Her comments suggest that Stevenson's ideas about inculturation and the global church developed at least in part out of conversations with his mother, in which the two shared their experiences of religious places and people.

Taniera Mahinui, the Paumotuan catechist who presided over the service, was a layperson in whom Stevenson sensed a desire for high

---

[75] Margaret Isabella Stevenson, 'Diaries [1874–1889 {1888}]', GEN MSS 664, Box 54, Folder 1177, Beinecke Library, Yale University.

[76] Margaret Isabella Stevenson, *From Saranac to the Marquesas and Beyond; Being Letters written by Mrs. M. I. Stevenson during 1887–88, to her Sister, Jane Whyte Balfour, with a Short Introduction by George W. Balfour, M. D., LL. D., FRSE* (London: Methuen, 1903), 160.

church office, perhaps even 'the cardinal's hat' (123). 'I never met a man of a mind more ecclesiastical', he remarked playfully, adding that 'he loved to dispute and to inform himself of doctrine and the history of sects' (122). He concluded his description of that Sunday morning:

> The plain service, the vernacular Bible, the hymn-tunes mostly on an English pattern [. . .] all, save some paper flowers upon the altar, seemed not merely but austerely Protestant. It is thus the Catholics have met their low island proselytes half-way. (124)[77]

The Catholic Paumotuan Islanders had responded to the absence of ordained clergy (the priest was away) with a stripped-down, low church service in place of the traditional Sunday high mass.[78] Stevenson grasped the ecclesiological significance of this improvisation and articulated the ways in which it represented a strikingly indigenised Catholic outlook towards Scripture, liturgy, and the role of the laity in worship.

Stevenson's literary imagination fed on the novel experience of Pacific Christian ecclesiology. In 'The Beach of Falesá', he describes an indigenous Islander Protestant Sunday service which includes a careful description of the church:

> It was a little long low place, coral built, rounded off at both ends like a whale-boat, a big native roof on the top of it, windows without sashes and doorways without doors [. . .] The congregation sat on the floor on mats, the women on one side, the men on the other, all rigged out to kill – the women with dresses and trade hats, the men in white jackets and shirts.[79]

In encountering the native church, the English trader Wiltshire experiences a surprise that was likely modelled on Stevenson's own initial experience of such an occasion. In the fable 'Something in It', discussed in Chapter 2, Stevenson renders his British missionary

---

[77] Cf. Raeburn Lange's comparison of the Catholic *katekita* and Protestant 'teachers' in nineteenth-century French Polynesia in his *Island Ministers*, 52–4.

[78] Stevenson, *From Saranac to the Marquesas*, 160; John Garrett, *To Live among the Stars: Christian Origins in Oceania* (Geneva and Suva: World Council of Churches in Association with the Institute of Pacific Studies, 1982), 138; Colin Newbury, *Tahiti Nui: Change and Survival in French Polynesia, 1767–1945* (Honolulu: University of Hawai'i Press, 1980), 147.

[79] Robert Louis Stevenson, 'The Beach of Falesá', in *South Sea Tales*, ed. by Roslyn Jolly (Oxford: Oxford University Press, 1996), 3–71 (20–1).

incapable of grasping the ecclesiastical significance of the house in the bay towards which he is pulled while swimming:

> he was aware of a house raised on piles above the sea; it was built of yellow reeds, one reed joined with another, and the whole bound with black sinnet; a ladder led to the door, and all about the house hung calabashes.[80]

We learn that the house is a gateway to another realm where the missionary is presented with an inculturated ritual in which, in a way similar to Wiltshire, he refuses to participate.

In Stevenson's writing, the sacramental richness of such images is balanced by an equally fertile re-evaluation of the relationship between church and mission. The readiness of Pacific Islands Christians to take on the task of serving their religious communities in new arrangements nudged him towards a conception of mission work that was less dependent on formal and established churches. Samoa provided perhaps the most advanced model of all. The London Missionary Society's (LMS) Samoan mission had early sought to educate and form native pastors who would lead the village parishes so that the foreign missionaries could focus on education and church administration.[81] The parish-level schooling provided by pastors was the primary Samoan educational institution until the 1950s. By empowering Samoans as pastors, preachers, and teachers, the LMS 'created the first independent church in the South Pacific with a fully indigenous ministry and administration'.[82] The LMS missionaries' Congregationalism appeared to have successfully mapped itself on to the traditional Samoan chiefly system while emphasising the looser and more decentralised principles of local religious practice. As we have seen, Pacific Islanders played a central role in the propagation of the Christian religion so that it quickly came to be accommodated within Samoan traditions.

By the end of the nineteenth century, however, several elements had contributed to make the period one of religious transition. From the perspective of the foreign mission organisations, declining enthusiasm in the West led to practical difficulties such as the reduction

---

[80] Stevenson, 'Something in It', in *South Sea Tales*, 255–7 (255).
[81] Malama Meleisea and Penelope Schoeffel Meleisea, *Lagaga: A Short History of Western Samoa* (Suva: University of the South Pacific, 1987), 59.
[82] Meleisea and Meleisea, *Lagaga*, 60.

of financial and other support.[83] The problem worsened in the latter half of the century and a range of remedies was proposed, from the Christian encouragement of commercial enterprise in mission fields to the promotion of a more stripped down, autonomous style of missionary living. The efflorescence of Samoan denominations presented a challenge to the older Christian communities and this was coupled with new spiritual movements that arose within the more established churches, as Stevenson also identified on his travels in the Paumotus Islands. Growing indigenous pastoral autonomy, which was crowned by the LMS's reluctant decision to grant rites of ordination to Samoans, accelerated local calls for a greater voice in the affairs of the mission.[84] As these intrareligious conflicts were taking shape war broke out in Samoa. Stevenson had no doubt that the colonial powers bore much responsibility for creating the conditions. Besides the political journalism that he undertook at this time, he also began to reimagine the role of the church through the prism of the conflict. His experience of the political and economic conditions of indigenous people in Samoa and across the Pacific led him to develop a more prophetic view of mission, which highlighted Islander agency and the productive conservation of land. In this he also drew on Scottish traditions of political economy.

In October 1894, he gave a speech urging a group of Samoan chiefs 'to occupy and use your country. If you do not others will.'[85] He explained that he knew what it was like, as a Scotsman, to be a member of a people that was dispossessed of their land.[86] These Samoans should know that he, Stevenson, had visited the Hawaiian island of Oahu, where

---

[83] See Andrew Porter, 'Missions and Empire, c. 1873–1914', in *The Cambridge History of Christianity: Volume 8. World Christianities c. 1815 – c. 1914*, ed. by Sheridan Gilley and Brian Stanley (Cambridge: Cambridge University Press, 2014).

[84] Latu Latai, 'Covenant Keepers: A History of Samoan (LMS) Missionary Wives in the Western Pacific from 1839 to 1979 (PhD thesis, Australian National University, 2016), 67.

[85] Stevenson, *Sophia Scarlet*, 122. I further develop this theme in L. M. Ratnapalan, '"Our Father's Footprints": Robert Louis Stevenson's Anthropology of Conversion, 1888–1894', *Journal of Irish and Scottish Studies* (forthcoming).

[86] There is no space here to discuss the communal focus of national identity and resistance in Stevenson's linking of Scotland and Samoa, but for suggestive Scottish literary comparisons, see Scott Lyall, '"Tenshillingland": Community and Commerce, Myth and Madness in the Modern Scottish Novel', in *Community in Modern Scottish Literature*, ed. by Scott Lyall (Leiden and Boston: Brill, 2016), 1–24.

> we saw, still standing, the churches that have been built by the Hawaiians of old. There must have been many hundreds, many thousands, dwelling there in old times, and worshipping God in these now empty churches. For today they were empty, the doors were closed, the villages had disappeared, the people were dead and gone; only the church stood on like a tombstone over a grave, in the midst of the white men's sugar field.[87]

Stevenson wanted the empty churches in Oahu to stand as a vivid warning for these Samoans. For churches to be out of use meant a people had been 'swept away', lost from God, since they had 'occupied [the land] for nothing' and these useless servants were sent to where there is 'weeping and gnashing of teeth'.[88] All that remained was the spiritually empty economic activity pursued by the 'white man' in Hawai'i.

The Biblical images Stevenson used to persuade his important Samoan listeners should not surprise us. He well understood that the Christian tradition offered a common moral language in the Pacific. The explicit linking of mission work with a people's survival also extends the thought of Chalmers and others on the importance of the church to the Scottish nation. These are marks of continuity, but from another perspective it could be said that Stevenson had moved substantially beyond his earlier views. As late as the 1950s, few Scots, in spite of their professed support for indigenous people, had believed in the decolonisation of African parts of the British Empire as opposed to a form of self-government within Empire.[89] This included those associated with the Church of Scotland. However, Scottish missionaries, because they worked closely with colonised peoples, saw much earlier than others that the writing was on the wall for imperial rule.[90] When Stevenson pushed for British protection of Samoans he wanted to keep the missionaries out of politics. But, while he came to realise the futility of his own efforts, he grasped the political potential of a religiously inspired conception of indigenous self-rule. Arguably, this combination represents the dominant conception of Samoan sovereignty today.[91]

---

[87] Stevenson, *Sophia Scarlet*, 123.
[88] Stevenson, *Sophia Scarlet*, 123.
[89] Bryan S. Glass, *The Scottish Nation at Empire's End* (Basingstoke: Palgrave Macmillan, 2014), 17–18, 48–9.
[90] Glass, *Scottish Nation*, 19.
[91] See Chapter 3 on the relationship between Christianity and modern Samoan identity.

According to an optimistic view, the modern Church of Scotland could learn much from its pioneering post-war experiences of

> God's mission being rooted in the life of the world and not the church building [...] and, centrally, of the residual potential of ordinary people in expressing the Gospel, whether within the institutional parish church or outwith in new worshipping communities arising from pioneer ministry and church plants [...].[92]

As this chapter has suggested, these words convey rather well the position of Robert Louis Stevenson in relation to the churches of the Pacific Islands. How was he able to arrive at a conclusion that took many of his countrymen more than half a century to understand? After all, they shared the same cultural and intellectual background in Scottish Presbyterianism, moral philosophy, and political economy. Yet an important difference was that the major contexts of twentieth-century theology of church and mission had imposed themselves on Stevenson much earlier. He had directly experienced the symptoms of the end of Christian society in Europe, when 'the Church's survival is at stake and membership loss needs to be stemmed'.[93] In the Pacific, he was able to recognise 'the need for "contextualization" and "cross-cultural translation" of the Gospel in mission'.[94] To a large degree, Stevenson's place in Scotland's intellectual history rests on the interfusion of the local and the global in his religious thought.[95]

---

[92] Alexander Forsyth, 'Theology and Practice of Mission in Mid-Twentieth-Century Scotland', in Fergusson and Elliott, *History of Scottish Theology, Volume III*, 256.
[93] Peter Bisset, quoted in Forsyth, 'Theology and Practice of Mission', 256.
[94] Forsyth, 'Theology and Practice of Mission', 256.
[95] John MacKenzie argues for the importance of Scottish Presbyterianism to global Scottish identity. MacKenzie, 'Presbyterianism and Scottish Identity'. Werner Ustorf proposes that we reimagine Western ideas of mission. Werner Ustorf, 'A Missiological Postscript', in *The Decline of Christendom in Western Europe, 1750–2000*, ed. by Werner Ustorf and Hugh McLeod (Cambridge: Cambridge University Press, 2003), 218–25.

Conclusion

In this book I have tried to offer a fresh interpretation of Robert Louis Stevenson's global significance by contextualising the religious themes in his Pacific writing. While Stevenson's enduring popularity transcends particular characterisations, we surely benefit from placing his Scottish Presbyterian identity within global contexts that are not normally associated with it. In a similar way, his distinctive perspectives become clearer when we engage his writing with changes in Western religious life. Identification with formal or established religion became a marker of social difference in nineteenth-century Britain. Because Stevenson was steeped in Scriptural knowledge and Presbyterian devotional practices, he exhibited a religious literacy that distinguished him from many contemporaries, especially those in the professional world of letters. He retained an interest in historical and contemporary manifestations of Christianity that went beyond the aesthetic to reflect on social and ethical questions. Shaped by the culture of the Kirk, even after he chose to separate himself from it, he remained concerned about its future and was convinced that it could exert a moral influence on Scottish society. His response to the impact of industrial modernity drew from personal religious knowledge and experiences that were significantly different to our own.

Pacific Islands societies in Stevenson's time were also undergoing dramatic changes. Traditional structures of island life and political organisation were often replaced by hybrid forms that developed through a process of gradual accommodation to foreign ideas and institutions. Stevenson knew that the foundations of much of this change lay in the arrival of Christianity earlier in the century. The work of Western missionaries, indigenous converts, and others had transformed Pacific societies while also retaining important elements of continuity with tradition in places like Samoa. Stevenson's analysis of the contemporary Pacific built on this historical analysis, while the core of his anthropology grew out of his denominational identity as a Protestant Christian. This meant that he was able to identify and engage with facets of the Christian Pacific cultures that the wider social changes had brought forth. He acknowledged missionaries' role in these changes and offered a balanced assessment of their influence, explored Christianity's impact on traditionally non-Christian societies, and amplified indigenous Christian responses to colonising pressures.

Recognition of the complexity of religious cultures was a pronounced feature of Stevenson's writing in the Pacific and reflected the influence of locality on his thought. But Stevenson's intellectual roots lay in Scottish Presbyterianism, and the ideas and history of this tradition provide us with the key to understanding his mind. Stevenson's thought can be described as religious to the extent that he was instinctively drawn towards religious subjects and terms in order to absorb and organise new information. Scripture and religious history provided a vocabulary with which he articulated, sometimes playfully, his sense of the originality and distinctiveness of Pacific culture. His conception of religion in places such as Samoa was also deeply influenced by Scottish Presbyterianism in the sense that it was grounded in the idea of communal relationships that were closely tied to the local setting. His mind was shaped by concepts associated with this religious tradition. Stevenson possessed a religious literacy that was situated within a specific place and time: it was neither universal nor abstract, and conversely, this gave it a portable and malleable quality.

Pacific appropriations of Christianity provided Stevenson with material that stimulated ethnographic reflexivity. His anthropology neither was straightforwardly Calvinist nor dispensed entirely with Christianity. Especially because he acquired much of his information about the Pacific and its people from missionaries and converts, his ethnography reflected the understanding that Islanders believed they were part of a cosmic struggle involving invisible forces. Stevenson's ethnography was therefore grounded in a Pacific Islands idea of the religiously transcendent, a space inaccessible to the senses but according to which people ordered their lives. The tension between an increasingly immanent view of reality in Western societies, ordered in a way that was set apart from the transcendent, and his experience of something like the contrary in the Pacific, encouraged Stevenson to experiment with his fiction. The fable 'Something in It' particularly suggests that Pacific culture may have been pushing Stevenson towards a more sacramental view of denominational Christianity.

The same transfigured vision of a familiar religion is perceptible in Stevenson's historical fiction, which built on his experience of living among a moral community of believers in Samoa. Awareness of Scottish and Samoan religious parallels encouraged cultural experimentation, while proximity to mission work led him to think in a more personal way about the meaning of conversion. The years in Samoa, I have suggested, transformed Stevenson's identity as a writer by embedding him in a novel Christian setting. In particular, he was impressed by the encounter with a transcultural religious community and its pious awe of the supernatural. Stevenson found that he had to work with and negotiate these social realities. His later Scottish and European fiction is unsurprisingly centred on the dilemmas of moral personhood within communal religious settings.

Living in the Samoan moral community represented an intensified experience of the religiosity that Stevenson had encountered during his Pacific travels. It left an indelible mark on him, just as similar experiences would impact later Western discoverers of Christianity in the global South. The strange familiarity of localised forms of the religion inspired Stevenson to write a series of meditations on inculturation in the form of his Pacific fiction. In these works, recurrent themes of sacramentality, literacy, and polity demonstrate the ways in which he connected Scottish Presbyterian theological sensitivities to the emergent forms of the 'half-Christian' Pacific. In its manifold oceanic crossings and cultural revitalisations, Stevenson's Pacific fiction points prophetically to twentieth-century global intermixtures of religion and literature.

Wherever he was, Stevenson's thoughts were never far from the cultural history of Scottish Presbyterianism. But as churches have become less a part of everyday life for most people in the West, it has also become more difficult to understand and appreciate Stevenson's interest in them. One of the most important discoveries that he made about Pacific Christianity was that it produced its own churches, which were often unique in style and quite autonomous. These facts fired his imagination. As he understood the significance of Pacific churches as social and political institutions, he also began to develop the ecclesiology that had engaged him in post-Disruption Scotland. His discovery cemented his view of the church as a global missionary endeavour shaped as much by local custom as by inherited tradition.

These key insights of the book connect to broader scholarly concerns. A religiously contextualised approach to analysing Stevenson's writing can stimulate research in a variety of fields. Perhaps first and foremost, it is useful to situate his work within the post-secular view that religion and art 'no longer bear an antagonism towards each other'.[1] Because the nineteenth century was often characterised as religious in comparison with the more secular twentieth century, the rebellion against Victorian values enacted by the likes of Lytton Strachey was driven by a belief in the weakening hold of religion in the modern age. But research highlighting secularism's social and intellectual vulnerability has stimulated thinking about desecularisation and the post-secular.[2] A revised view of the relationship between literature and theology has been one product of this renewal of interest in religion. The changing conditions and assumptions of academic scholarship encourages us to reconsider Stevenson's relationship to his own time as well to reassess his posthumous critical reputation.[3]

The destabilisation of spatial as well as temporal markers stimulates new approaches to the study of Stevenson's writing. Globalisation, understood as the modern worldwide acceleration in communications, has helped to dissolve some of the older signifiers of difference between nations and cultures.[4] For example, religious scholars no longer consider it satisfactory to narrate the history of modern Christianity as simply a one-way diffusion from the West to the rest of the world.[5] This reversal likewise impels us to consider how Stevenson's ideas about Christianity were influenced by the religious beliefs and practices of Pacific Islanders. As his literary identity was subject to change, so was his outlook on religion. As this book has demonstrated, we can begin to recognise such changes when we take the Christianity of the nineteenth-century Pacific seriously as an influence on Stevenson's writing.

However, it is important not to overstate the case. For example, we may readily acknowledge the ambiguity and irony of Stevenson's

---

[1] Andrew Hass, 'The Future of English Literature and Theology', in *The Oxford Handbook of English Literature and Theology*, ed. by Andrew Hass, David Jasper, and Elisabeth Jay (Oxford: Oxford University Press, 2009), 841–58 (842).
[2] For an influential collection, see *The Desecularization of the World: Resurgent Religion and World Politics*, ed. by Peter L. Berger (Grand Rapids, MI: William B. Eerdmans, 1999).
[3] For example, Michael Shaw offers a recontextualised literary history in *The Fin-de-Siècle Scottish Revival: Romance, Decadence and Celtic Identity* (Edinburgh: Edinburgh University Press, 2020).
[4] Hass, 'Future of English Literature', 845.
[5] Lamin Sanneh was a prominent exponent of the revised view. See, for example, his *Whose Religion is Christianity? The Gospel Beyond the West* (Grand Rapids, MI: William B. Eerdmans, 2003).

writing and its resistance to easy categorisation as either pro- or anti-colonial.[6] But the products of his imagination were always rooted in the conviction of humanity's fallen nature. Christian anthropology rendered a judgement on all peoples, which meant Samoans as well as Scots. The Calvinist accent on the doctrine of original sin never left him, as attested by the dark attraction of stories such as 'The Bottle Imp' and *The Ebb-Tide*. On the contrary, the doctrine gained in explanatory power the more clearly Stevenson was able to grasp the working and effects of colonialism in places such as Hawai'i and Samoa.

If we wish to gain a better understanding of where a writer as unique as Robert Louis Stevenson might be situated in the history of modern Christianity, then we also need to attend to the intellectual and social currents of nineteenth-century British religious culture. Although the adult Stevenson never acknowledged that he was Christian in any orthodox sense, Christian thinking and assumptions naturally shaped him just as they filtered into many important aspects of nineteenth-century British life. The historian Hugh McLeod has described how, even as church attendance declined, Britain was held together by 'a common Protestantism, a common investment in the empire, and loyalty to the monarchy'.[7] Stevenson was born into this mid-Victorian generation whose imperial heroes, including men whom he admired such as the Scottish missionary David Livingstone and General Charles Gordon, were 'devoutly evangelical Protestants, convinced that the British Empire was an instrument of Providence'.[8] However, by the time of Stevenson's death, the revelation of the British imperial world was led by agnostics such as Rudyard Kipling. Not faith but virtue now explained the nation's ascendency.[9] Stevenson's writing about religion, nation, and empire can be situated within this broader change in British culture.

While the substance of Christianity was becoming peripheral to the British national conversation, it was growing more important in other parts of the world including the Island Pacific. The emphasis

---

[6] Manfred Malzahn, 'Voices of the Scottish Empire', in *Robert Louis Stevenson: Writer of Boundaries*, ed. by Richard Dury and Richard Ambrosini (Madison: University of Wisconsin Press, 2006), 160.

[7] Hugh McLeod, 'Protestantism and British National Identity', in *Nation and Religion: Perspectives on Europe and Asia*, ed. by Peter van der Veer and Hartmut Lehmann (Princeton, NJ: Princeton University Press, 1999), 44–70 (45).

[8] McLeod, 'Protestantism and British National Identity', 59.

[9] McLeod, 'Protestantism and British National Identity', 56.

in Stevenson's later writing on inculturation and the emergence of an authentically Pacific Christian culture gives strong witness to this fact. The global religious balance was changing and Islander Christianity was becoming significant: it was not a mere fashion or an appendage to the 'real' culture of the Pacific. Stevenson sensed that it could have powerful political and social effects and he attempted to articulate this in his addresses to Samoans. From our distant standpoint, we may also interpret his stress on inculturation as expressing the view that Pacific Islanders had not yet made Christianity entirely their own, that for many of them it was a foreign gift for which they had found remarkable uses. Stevenson implicitly understood that Christianity and civilisation – meaning a modern, Western, property-holding civilisation – went together but he thought that Pacific Islanders had yet to properly realise this. Another way in which to historicise Stevenson's Pacific oeuvre might therefore be to analyse it as the product of an era of anticolonial consciousness that gave rise to idealised expectations of Pacific Islands sovereignty. The political dream of independence would have its religious equivalent in the attainment of an autonomous Christian culture. But, when the euphoria of independence began to diminish after the 1970s, so did the desire for inculturation. These postcolonial narratives offer possibilities for engaging Stevenson's writing with Pacific history.

There is a coda. At the end of the twentieth century, Stevenson's colonial-era portrayal of a mobile Islander world was given new significance by another religion-inspired vision. The Tongan anthropologist Epeli Hau'ofa claimed to experience a 'road to Damascus' moment when he saw the enormous volcanoes on a drive to an academic conference along the Kona coast of Hawai'i.[10] It was from this moment that he began to conceive of the Pacific not as small and dependent islands in an enormous sea but rather as a vast and connected 'Sea of Islands', a vision that captured the manifold tensions

---

[10] Epeli Hau'ofa, 'Our Sea of Islands', in *A New Oceania: Rediscovering Our Sea of Islands*, ed. by Epeli Hau'ofa, Vijay Naidu, and Eric Waddell (Suva: University of the South Pacific, 1993), 1–16. On Hau'ofa and Christianity, see Rob Wilson's evocative meditation in *Be Always Converting, Be Always Converted: An American Poetics* (Cambridge, MA: Harvard University Press, 2009), 119–42. For another discussion of the connection between Stevenson's writing and Hau'ofa's vision, see 'Power and Geography in Robert Louis Stevenson's South Sea Tales', accessed at: https://thefifthe.wordpress.com/2020/06/10/power-and-geography-in-robert-louis-stevensons-south-sea-tales/ on 11 December 2021.

of that post- yet neo-colonial moment. James Clifford has described how Hauʻofa and other Pacific writers built 'dynamic connections in both space and time' involving themselves in 'world-making, globalising projects [. . .] enmeshed in powerful, large-scale webs of transport, labour migration, missionization and education'.[11] The vitality of Stevenson's Pacific fiction is, arguably, a product of the same tensions. As with Hauʻofa, Stevenson's writing depicts a world of movement (think of all the travelling Islanders in his stories) that expands our imagination of the Pacific and makes us ask new questions about its peoples and their history.

Points of contact also may be found between the indigeneity of this vision and Stevenson's Scottishness. David Armitage has noted Scots' 'ameliorating effect' on the British Empire, for example with 'missionary Presbyterianism in softening the after effects of conquest and acculturation'.[12] Another historian, John MacKenzie, has written about how Presbyterianism 'contributed a good deal to a sense of Scottish global identity'.[13] MacKenzie and Tom Devine draw attention to the distinctiveness of the Scottish experience of empire which makes it 'possible to argue that Scots produced different responses from indigenous peoples throughout the empire'.[14] The experience of exile, so marked in Stevenson's writing, may also have provoked sympathy with other displaced peoples.[15] We need only observe how Stevenson's depiction of Pacific Islander language use and perspectives was smothered or rendered exotic by metropolitan editors to understand how contrasting were his and their

---

[11] James Clifford, 'Hauʻofa's Hope: Association for Social Anthropology in Oceania 2009 Distinguished Lecture', *Oceania* 79, 3 (2009), 238–49 (240–1).

[12] David Armitage, 'The Scottish Diaspora', in *Scotland: A History*, ed. by Jenny Wormald (Oxford: Oxford University Press, 2005), 272–303 (299).

[13] John M. MacKenzie, 'Presbyterianism and Scottish Identity in Global Context', *Britain and the World* 10, 1 (2017), 88–112 (111).

[14] John M. MacKenzie and T. M. Devine, 'Introduction', in *Scotland and the British Empire*, ed. by John M. MacKenzie and T. M. Devine (Oxford: Oxford University Press, 2011), 1–29 (15). See also *Irish and Scottish Encounters with Indigenous Peoples: Canada, the United States, New Zealand, and Australia*, ed. by Graeme Morton and David A. Wilson (Montreal: McGill-Queen's University Press, 2013).

[15] Christy Di Frances, '"Weary for the Heather and the Deer": R. L. Stevenson Depicts the Scottish Diasporic Experience', *International Review of Scottish Studies* 40 (2015), 61–93. See also Robert Louis Stevenson, *The Amateur Emigrant*, ed. by Julia Reid (Edinburgh: Edinburgh University Press, 2018).

perceptions of indigenous cultures.[16] The opportunities afforded by the British Empire may have strengthened the connection between Scottish identity and the Union, but Stevenson's peculiarly Scottish subversion of empire also highlights the potential for diverse interpretations.[17] Although he was less dependent on the British Empire for professional opportunities than were other diasporic Scots, the passions and juxtapositions that were generated by colonialism offered him abundant literary material.

One of the least understood aspects of Stevenson's Scottishness concerns his relationship to the legacy of the Enlightenment. In the context of this discussion about diaspora and identity, Cairns Craig has offered the remarkable thesis that in the aftermath of the 1707 Union with England, 'Scotland was a nation which existed only in and through its institutions' and that 'Scottish migrants sought to build their national values anew within the fabric of the communities to which they had migrated.'[18] We may find a ready example of this in Stevenson's community building at his Vailima estate – a project, as we have seen, which shaped its author as much as it did the community that he tried to build. Craig continues that the Scottish Enlightenment developed out of the migrant experience, which he characterises as 'the long, sustained interaction of Scotland and its cultural empire'.[19] Therefore, he concludes, 'far from being an intellectual wasteland, nineteenth-century Scotland was itself the effective breeder of new disciplines only foreshadowed by its "Enlightenment" predecessors'.[20] How far should we press for the inclusion of Stevenson's ethnographic art alongside the ranks of William Robertson Smith and James Frazer, to whom Craig draws our attention? It is in the nature of a movement that variations exist within the larger theme. Perhaps a place could be found for an anthropology of Pacific Islanders. According to the authors of another brilliant reimagining of the Scottish intellectual tradition,

---

[16] See Chapter 2.
[17] Bryan S. Glass, *The Scottish Nation at Empire's End* (Basingstoke: Palgrave Macmillan, 2014), 7; Malzahn, 'Voices of the Scottish Empire', 158.
[18] Cairns Craig, 'Empire of Intellect: The Scottish Enlightenment and Scotland's Intellectual Migrants', in MacKenzie and Devine, *Scotland and the British Empire*, 84–117 (92).
[19] Craig, 'Empire of Intellect', 115.
[20] Craig, 'Empire of Intellect', 116.

the central refrain of that tradition is religious, and more precisely Calvinist.[21] Stevenson's place in Scottish thought would then rest on rediscovering him as a religious writer, which is what this book has tried to do.

---

[21] Craig Beveridge and Ronald Turnbull, *Scotland after Enlightenment: Image and Tradition in Modern Scottish Culture* (Edinburgh: Polygon, 1997), 116. In this context, see also Crawford Gribben's introduction to *Literature and the Scottish Reformation*, in which he asserts that 'since the seventeenth century, the Scottish literary canon has been forged in a climate deliberately opposed to the theological ideas – especially the Calvinist ideas – that repeatedly appear at its heart' (1). Crawford Gribben, 'Introduction', in *Literature and the Scottish Reformation*, ed. by Crawford Gribben and David George Mullan (Farnham: Ashgate, 2009), 1–18 (1).

Bibliography

Manuscript Collections

(See chapter notes for specific items.)

American Board of Commissioners for Foreign Missions Archives, Houghton Library, Harvard University.
Edwin J. Beinecke Collection of Robert Louis Stevenson and Robert Louis Stevenson Collection, Beinecke Rare Book and Manuscript Library, Yale University.
Records of the London Missionary Society, National Library of Australia.
Robert Louis Stevenson Collection, Harry Ransom Center, University of Texas at Austin.
Robert Louis Stevenson papers, National Library of Scotland.

Published Works by Robert Louis Stevenson

Across the Plains (London: Chatto and Windus, 1892).
The Amateur Emigrant. Edited by Julia Reid (Edinburgh: University of Edinburgh Press, 2018).
An Appeal to the Clergy of the Church of Scotland (William Blackwood and Sons, 1875).
'Books Which Have Influenced Me: A Paper Contributed to "The British Weekly", May 13, 1887' (Greenwich, CT: The Literary Collector Press, 1905).
A Child's Garden of Verses (London: Longmans, Green, and Co., 1885).
David Balfour (New York: Charles Scribner's Sons, 1905).
Edinburgh: Picturesque Notes (London: Seeley, Jackson and Halliday, 1879).
Fables (New York: Charles Scribner's Sons, 1896).
Familiar Studies of Men and Books (London: Chatto and Windus, 1882).
Familiar Studies of Men and Books (New York: Charles Scribner's Sons, 1891).
Father Damien: An Open Letter to the Reverend Doctor Hyde of Honolulu (London: Chatto and Windus, 1890).

A Footnote to History: Eight Years of Trouble in Samoa (London: Cassell and Co., 1892).
In the South Seas. Edited by Neil Rennie (London: Penguin, 1998).
Kidnapped (New York: Charles Scribner's Sons, 1886).
Lay Morals and Other Papers (London: Chatto and Windus, 1911).
The Letters of Robert Louis Stevenson. In 8 volumes. Edited by Bradford A. Booth and Ernest Mehew (New Haven, CT: Yale University Press, 1994–5).
The Merry Men and Other Tales and Fables (London: Chatto and Windus, 1905).
'A Pearl Island: Penrhyn' and 'Leprosy at Penrhyn'. *The Sun* (New York), 24 May 1891.
Prayers Written at Vailima, with an Introduction by Mrs. Stevenson (New York: Charles Scribner's Sons, 1904).
'Records of a Family of Engineers'. In *The Works of Robert Louis Stevenson, Volume 16* (London: Chatto and Windus, 1912), 3–152.
St. Ives: Being the Adventures of a French Prisoner in England (New York: Charles Scribner's Sons, 1905).
'San Carlos Day'. *Scribner's Magazine* (August 1920), 209–11.
Songs of Travel and Other Verses (London: Chatto and Windus, 1896).
Sophia Scarlet and Other Pacific Writings. Edited by Robert Hoskins (Auckland: AUT Media, 2008).
South Sea Tales. Edited by Roslyn Jolly (Oxford: Oxford University Press, 1996).
Strange Case of Dr. Jekyll and Mr. Hyde (London: Longmans, Green, and Co., 1886).
Tales and Fantasies (London: Chatto and Windus, 1920).
Travels with a Donkey in the Cévennes (London: Kegan Paul, 1879).
Weir of Hermiston; Some Unfinished Stories (London: William Heinemann, 1924).
The Works of Robert Louis Stevenson; Miscellanies, Volume IV. Edited by Sidney Colvin (Edinburgh: Longmans, Green, and Co., 1896).
The Works of Robert Louis Stevenson, Volume 18: In the South Seas. Edited by Andrew Lang (London: Chatto and Windus, 1912).
The Works of Robert Louis Stevenson, Volume 29: Memories and Portraits; Memoirs of Himself; Selections from His Notebook (London: William Heinemann, 1924).

Secondary and Other Works

Abrahamson, Robert-Louis. 'Truth Out of Tusitala Spoke: Stevenson's Voice in Post-Darwinian Christianity'. In *Persona and Paradox: Issues of Identity for C. S. Lewis, His Friends and Associates*, edited by Suzanne Bray and William Gray (Newcastle upon Tyne: Cambridge Scholars Publishing, 2012), 237–54.

'Acts: 1793' ['The General Assembly's dutiful address to His Majesty on the subject of the present War']. In *Acts of the General Assembly of the Church of Scotland 1638–1842*. Edited by Church Law Society (Edinburgh: Edinburgh Printing & Publishing Co., 1843), 840–2. *British History Online*. Accessed at: http://www.british-history.ac.uk/church-scotland-records/acts/1638-1842/pp840-842 on 10 April 2021.

Ahdar, Rex Tauati. 'Samoa and the Christian State Ideal'. *International Journal for the Study of the Christian Church* 13, 1 (2013), 59–72.

Allan, David. *Virtue, Learning and the Scottish Enlightenment: Ideas of Scholarship in Early Modern History* (Edinburgh: Edinburgh University Press, 1993).

Annan, Noel. *Leslie Stephen: The Godless Victorian* (Chicago: University of Chicago Press, 1984).

Armitage, David. 'The Scottish Diaspora'. In *Scotland: A History*, edited by Jenny Wormald (Oxford: Oxford University Press, 2005), 272–303.

Balfour, Graham. *The Life of Robert Louis Stevenson* (London: Methuen, 1920).

Barker, John. 'Comments to Part 1: Christian Transcendence and the Politics of Renewal'. In *Christianity, Conflict, and Renewal in Australia and the Pacific*, edited by Fiona Magowan and Carolyn Schwarz (Boston: Brill, 2016), 23–33.

— 'Converts, Christians and Anthropologists: A Critique of Mark Mosko's Partible Penitent Thesis'. *The Australian Journal of Anthropology* 30, 3 (2019), 277–93.

Basas, Allan A. 'Inculturation: An Ongoing Drama of Faith–Culture Dialogue'. *Scientia* 9, 1 (2020), 92–108.

Beal, Edward. 'Stevenson's Ideal Missionary'. *International Review of Mission* 7, 3 (1918), 353–62.

Bebbington, David. *Evangelicalism in Modern Britain: A History from the 1730s to the 1980s* (London and New York: Routledge, 1993).

Berger, Peter L., ed. *The Desecularization of the World: Resurgent Religion and World Politics* (Grand Rapids, MI: William B. Eerdmans, 1999).

Bevans, Stephen B. *Models of Contextual Theology* (Maryknoll, NY: Orbis, 2002).

Bevans, Stephen B., and Roger P. Schroeder. *Constants in Context: A Theology of Mission for Today* (New York: Orbis, 2004).

Beveridge, Craig, and Ronald Turnbull. *The Eclipse of Scottish Culture* (Edinburgh: Polygon, 1989).

— *Scotland after Enlightenment: Image and Tradition in Modern Scottish Culture* (Edinburgh: Polygon, 1997).

Bickett, Linden. *George Mackay Brown and the Scottish Catholic Imagination* (Edinburgh: Edinburgh University Press, 2017).

— 'George Mackay Brown's Marian Apocrypha: Iconography and Enculturation in *Time in a Red Coat*'. *Scottish Literature Review* 5, 2 (2013), 81–96.

Bowie, Karin. 'Popular Resistance, Religion and the Union of 1707'. In *Scotland and the Union, 1707–2007*, edited by T. M. Devine (Edinburgh: Edinburgh University Press, 2008), 39–53.

Brague, Rémi. *Eccentric Culture: A Theory of Western Civilization*, translated by Samuel Lester (South Bend, IN: St. Augustine's Press, 2002).

Breitenbach, Esther. 'The Influence of the Missionary Movement in Scotland'. In *Roots and Fruits: Retrieving Scotland's Missionary Story*, edited by Kenneth R. Ross (Padstow: Regnum, 2014), 57–69.

Brock, Peggy. 'Introduction'. In *Indigenous Peoples and Religious Change*, edited by Peggy Brock (Leiden: Brill, 2005), 1–11.

Brooke, John Hedley. *Science and Religion: Some Historical Perspectives* (Cambridge: Cambridge University Press, 1991).

Brown, Callum G. *The Death of Christian Britain: Understanding Secularisation, 1800–2000* (London: Routledge, 2009).

— *The People in the Pews: Religion and Society in Scotland since 1780* (Glasgow: Economic and Social History Society of Scotland, 1993).

— *Religion and Society in Scotland since 1707* (Edinburgh: Edinburgh University Press, 1997).

Brown, Stewart J. 'After the Disruption: The Recovery of the National Church of Scotland, 1843–1874'. *Scottish Church History* 48, 2 (2019), 103–25.

— 'Beliefs and Religions'. In *A History of Everyday Life in Scotland*, edited by T. Griffiths and G. Morton (Edinburgh: Edinburgh University Press, 2010), 116–46.

— 'The Ten Years' Conflict and the Disruption of 1843'. In *Scotland in the Age of the Disruption*, edited by Stewart J. Brown and Michael Fry (Edinburgh: Edinburgh University Press, 1993), 1–27.

— *Thomas Chalmers and the Godly Commonwealth in Scotland* (Oxford: Oxford University Press, 1982).

Brown, Stewart J., and George Newlands, eds. *Scottish Christianity in the Modern World: In Honour of A. C. Cheyne* (Edinburgh: T&T Clark, 2000).

Buckton, Oliver S. *Cruising with Robert Louis Stevenson: Travel, Narrative, and the Colonial Body* (Athens, OH: Ohio University Press, 2007).

Bueltmann, Tanja, Andrew Hinson, and Graeme Morton, eds. *The Scottish Diaspora* (Edinburgh: Edinburgh University Press, 2013).

Calder, Jenni. *Stevenson and Victorian Scotland* (Edinburgh: Edinburgh University Press, 1981).

Cameron, Nigel M. de S. *Dictionary of Scottish Church History and Theology* (Edinburgh: T&T Clark, 1993).

Cannell, Fenella, ed. *The Anthropology of Christianity* (Durham, NC: Duke University Press, 2006).

Carruthers, Gerard, David Goldie, and Alastair Renfrew, eds. *Scotland and the 19th-Century World* (Amsterdam: Rodopi, 2012).

Chadwick, Owen. *The Secularization of the European Mind in the Nineteenth Century* (Cambridge: Cambridge University Press, 1975).
Chalmers, Thomas. *The Works of Thomas Chalmers, D.D. and LL.D., Volume Fourth: On the Miraculous and Internal Evidences of the Christian Revelation, and the Authority of its Records* (New York: Robert Carter, 1840).
Chapman, Alister, John Coffey, and Brad S. Gregory, eds. *Seeing Things Their Way: Intellectual History and the Return of Religion* (Notre Dame, IN: University of Notre Dame Press, 2009).
Charlot, John. 'The Influence of Polynesian Literature and Thought on Robert Louis Stevenson'. *The Journal of Intercultural Studies* 14 (1987), 82–106.
Chesterton, Gilbert Keith. *Robert Louis Stevenson* (London: Hodder and Stoughton, 1927).
Cheyne, A. C. *The Transforming of the Kirk: Victorian Scotland's Religious Revolution* (Edinburgh: The Saint Andrew Press, 1983).
Clark, J. C. D. 'Secularization and Modernization: The Failure of a Grand Narrative'. *The Historical Journal* 55, 1 (2012), 161–94.
Clarke, W. E. 'Personal Recollections of Robert Louis Stevenson'. *Chronicle of the London Missionary Society* (April 1908), 66–71.
— 'Robert Louis Stevenson in Samoa'. *Yale Review* 10 (1921), 275–96.
Claxton, A. E. 'Stevenson as I Knew Him'. *Chronicle of the London Missionary Society* (May 1908), 89–90.
Clifford, James. 'Hauʻofa's Hope: Association for Social Anthropology in Oceania 2009 Distinguished Lecture'. *Oceania* 79, 3 (2009), 238–49.
Coleman, James J., *Remembering the Past in Nineteenth-Century Scotland: Commemoration, Nationality and Memory* (Cambridge: Cambridge University Press, 2014).
Colley, Ann C. *Robert Louis Stevenson and the Colonial Imagination* (New York: Routledge, 2017 [2004]).
Colley, Linda. *Britons: Forging the Nation 1707–1837* (New Haven, CT: Yale University Press, 1992).
Cook, Kealani. *Return to Kahiki: Native Hawaiians in Oceania* (Cambridge: Cambridge University Press, 2018).
Cox, Jeffrey. 'Master Narratives of Long-Term Religious Change'. In *The Decline of Christendom in Western Europe, 1750–2000*, edited by Hugh McLeod and Werner Ustorf (Cambridge: Cambridge University Press, 2003), 201–17.
— 'Secularization and Other Master Narratives of Religion in Modern Europe'. *Kirkliche Zeitgeschichte* 14, 1 (2001), 24–35.
Craig, Cairns. *The Wealth of the Nation: Scotland, Culture and Independence* (Edinburgh: Edinburgh University Press, 2018).
Crawford, Ronald James. 'The Lotu and the Fa'asāmoa: Church and Society in Samoa, 1830–1880' (PhD thesis, University of Otago, 1977).

Crocombe, Ron and Marjorie Crocombe. *The Works of Ta'unga: Records of a Polynesian Traveller in the South Seas, 1833–1896* (Canberra: Australian National University Press, 1968).

Dalglish, Doris N. *Presbyterian Pirate: A Portrait of Stevenson* (London: Oxford University Press, 1937).

Dalziel, Pamela. '"The Hard Case of the Would-Be-Religious": Hardy and the Church from Early Life to Later Years'. In *A Companion to Thomas Hardy*, edited by Keith Wilson (Oxford: Blackwell, 2009), 71–85.

Daudin, Guillaume, Matthias Morys, and Kevin H. O'Rourke, 'Globalization, 1870–1914'. In *The Cambridge Economic History of Modern Europe*, edited by Stephen Broadberry and Kevin H. O'Rourke (Cambridge: Cambridge University Press, 2019), 5–29.

Davidson, Allan K. 'The Legacy of Robert Henry Codrington'. *International Bulletin of Missionary Research* 27, 4 (2003), 171–6.

Davie, Grace. *Religion in Britain since 1945: Believing without Belonging* (Oxford: Blackwell, 1994).

Davis, Leith, and Kristen Mahlis. 'A Conceptual Alliance: "Interculturation" in Robert Burns and Kamau Brathwaite'. In *Scottish Literature and Postcolonial Literature: Comparative Texts and Critical Perspectives*, edited by Niall O'Gallagher, Graeme Macdonald, and Michael Gardiner (Edinburgh: Edinburgh University Press, 2011), 15–29.

De Capitani, Lucio. 'World Literature and the Anthropological Imagination: Ethnographic Encounters in European and South Asian Writing, 1885–2016' (PhD thesis, Università Ca' Foscari Venezia, 2019).

de Lubac, Henri. *Catholicism: A Study of Dogma in Relation to the Corporate Destiny of Mankind* (New York: Sheed and Ward, 1950).

Di Frances, Christy. '"Weary for the Heather and the Deer": R. L. Stevenson Depicts the Scottish Diasporic Experience'. *International Review of Scottish Studies* 40 (2015), 61–93.

Dinham, Adam. 'Public Religion in an Age of Ambivalence: Recovering Religious Literacy after a Century of Secularism'. In *Issues in Religion and Education*, edited by Lori G. Beaman and Leo Van Arragon (Leiden: Brill, 2015), 19–33.

Dinham, Adam, and Matthew Francis, *Religious Literacy in Policy and Practice* (Bristol: Policy Press, 2015).

Drummond, Andrew L., and James Bulloch. *The Church in Victorian Scotland* (Edinburgh: The Saint Andrew Press, 1975).

Douglas, Bronwen. 'From Invisible Christians to Gothic Theatre: The Romance of the Millennial in Melanesian Anthropology'. *Current Anthropology* 42, 5 (2001), 615–50.

— *Science, Voyages, and Encounters in Oceania, 1511–1815* (New York: Palgrave Macmillan, 2014).

Dubois, Martin. 'Sermon and Story in George Macdonald'. *Victorian Literature and Culture* 43, 3 (2015), 577–87.

Dury, Richard, and Richard Ambrosini, eds. *Robert Louis Stevenson: Writer of Boundaries* (Madison: University of Wisconsin Press, 2006).

Elazar, Daniel J. *Covenant and Polity in Biblical Israel: Biblical Foundations and Jewish Expressions. The Covenant Tradition in Politics, Volume I* (Abingdon: Routledge, 2017 [1995]).

Ernst, Manfred, and Anna Anisi. 'The Historical Development of Christianity in Oceania'. In *The Wiley Blackwell Companion to World Christianity*, edited by Lamin Sanneh and Michael J. McClymond (Hoboken, NJ: Wiley Blackwell, 2016), 588–604.

Farrell, Joseph. *Robert Louis Stevenson in Samoa* (London: Quercus, 2017).

Fer, Yannick. 'Politics of Tradition: Charismatic Globalization, Morality, and Culture in Polynesian Protestantism'. In *The Anthropology of Global Pentecostalism and Evangelicalism*, edited by Simon Coleman and Rosalind I. J. Hackett (New York: New York University Press, 2015), 228–42.

Fergusson, David, and Mark W. Elliott, eds. *The History of Scottish Theology, Volume II: The Early Enlightenment to the Late Victorian Era* (Oxford: Oxford University Press, 2019).

— *The History of Scottish Theology, Volume III: The Long Twentieth Century* (Oxford: Oxford University Press, 2019).

Forman, Charles W. 'Finding Our Own Voice: The Reinterpreting of Christianity by Oceanic Theologians'. *International Bulletin of Missionary Research* 29, 3 (2005), 115–22.

Frederiks, Martha, and Dorottya Nagy. 'Introduction'. In *World Christianity: Methodological Considerations*, edited by Martha Frederiks and Dorottya Nagy (Leiden and Boston: Brill, 2021), 1–9.

Fuller, Jennifer. *Dark Paradise: Pacific Islands in the Nineteenth-Century British Imagination* (Edinburgh: Edinburgh University Press, 2016).

Furnas, J. C. *Voyage to Windward: The Life of Robert Louis Stevenson* (London: Faber and Faber, 1952).

Gardner, Helen Bethea. 'Culture and Christian Missions in Oceania'. In *Cambridge History of the Pacific Ocean, 2 Volumes*, edited by Anne Perez Hattori, Jane Samson, Ryan Tucker Jones, and Matt K. Matsuda (forthcoming).

— *Gathering for God: George Brown in Oceania* (Dunedin: Otago University Press, 2006).

Garrett, John. *To Live among the Stars: Christian Origins in Oceania* (Geneva and Suva: World Council of Churches in association with the Institute of Pacific Studies, 1982).

Gibbs, Philip. 'Encountering Difference: Interculturality and Contextual Theology'. *Verbum SVD* 54, 1 (2013), 75–89.

Gillespie, Neal C. *Charles Darwin and the Problem of Creation* (Chicago: University of Chicago Press, 1979).

Gilley, Sheridan, and Brian Stanley, eds. *The Cambridge History of Christianity: Volume 8. World Christianities c. 1815 – c. 1914* (Cambridge: Cambridge University Press, 2014).

Gilson, R. P. *Samoa 1830–1900: The Politics of a Multi-cultural Community* (Melbourne: Oxford University Press, 1970).

Gladstone, W. E. *'Robert Elsmere' and the Battle of Belief* (New York: Anson D. F. Randolph and Co., [1888]).

Gladwin, Michael. 'Mission and Colonialism'. In *The Oxford Handbook of Nineteenth-Century Christian Thought*, edited by Joel D. S. Rasmussen, Judith Wolfe, and Johannes Zachhuber (Oxford: Oxford University Press, 2017), 282–307.

Glass, Bryan S. *The Scottish Nation at Empire's End* (Basingstoke: Palgrave Macmillan, 2014).

Gosse, Edmund. *Father and Son* (Oxford: Oxford University Press, 2004 [1907]).

Graham, Lesley. 'From Scotland to Sāmoa: Margaret Isabella Balfour Stevenson in Polynesia'. *Studies in Travel Writing* 24, 1 (2020), 1–15.

Gray, William. *Fantasy, Art and Life: Essays on George MacDonald, Robert Louis Stevenson and Other Fantasy Writers* (Newcastle upon Tyne: Cambridge Scholars Publishing, 2011).

Graham, Gordon. *Scottish Philosophy in the Nineteenth and Twentieth Centuries* (Oxford: Oxford University Press, 2015).

Grenby, M. O. 'History in Fiction: Contextualization as Interpretation in Robert Louis Stevenson's *Kidnapped*'. In *The Oxford Handbook of Children's Literature*, edited by L. Vallone and J. Mickenberg (Oxford: Oxford University Press, 2011), 275–92.

Gribben, Crawford. 'Afterword: Finding Religion in Scottish Literary History'. *Studies in Scottish Literature* 45, 2 (2019), 75–80.

— 'Introduction'. In *Literature and the Scottish Reformation*, edited by Crawford Gribben and David George Mullan (Farnham: Ashgate, 2009), 1–18.

Grimshaw, Patricia. *Paths of Duty: American Missionary Wives in Nineteenth-Century Hawaii* (Honolulu: University of Hawai'i Press, 1989).

Gunson, Niel. *Messengers of Grace: Evangelical Missionaries in the South Seas, 1797–1860* (Melbourne: Oxford University Press, 1978).

Hamilton, Andrew. 'Nineteenth-Century French Missionaries and Fa'a Samoa'. *Journal of Pacific History* 33, 2 (1998), 163–77.

Hanciles, Jehu J. *Migration and the Making of Global Christianity* (Grand Rapids, MI: William B. Eerdmans, 2021).

Hanna, William. *Memoirs of the Life and Writings of Thomas Chalmers, Vol. III* (Edinburgh: Sutherland and Knox, 1851).

Harries, Patrick. 'Anthropology'. In *Missions and Empire*, edited by Norman Etherington (Oxford: Oxford University Press, 2008), 238–60.

Hass, Andrew. 'The Future of English Literature and Theology'. In *The Oxford Handbook of English Literature and Theology*, edited by

Andrew Hass, David Jasper, and Elisabeth Jay (Oxford: Oxford University Press, 2009), 841–58.

Hauʻofa, Epeli. 'Our Sea of Islands'. In *A New Oceania: Rediscovering Our Sea of Islands*, edited by Epeli Hauʻofa, Vijay Naidu, and Eric Waddell (Suva: University of the South Pacific, 1993), 1–16.

Healy, Nicholas M. 'The Church in Modern Theology'. In *The Routledge Companion to the Christian Church*, edited by Gerard Mannion and Lewis S. Mudge (New York and London: Routledge, 2008), 106–206.

Hempenstall, Peter J. *Pacific Islanders under German Rule: A Study in the Meaning of Colonial Resistance* (Acton: ANU Eview, 2016 [1978]).

Hetzler, Leo A. 'Chesterton and Robert Louis Stevenson'. *The Chesterton Review* 17, 2 (1991), 177–87.

Hill, Richard J. *Robert Louis Stevenson and the Great Affair: Movement, Memory, and Modernity* (London: Routledge, 2017).

Hillerbrand, Hans J. *Historical Dictionary of the Reformation and Counter-Reformation* (Chicago: Fitzroy Dearborn, 2000).

Hillier, Robert I. *The South Seas Fiction of Robert Louis Stevenson* (New York: Peter Lang, 1989).

Hilton, Boyd. *The Age of Atonement: The Influence of Evangelicalism on Social and Economic Thought, 1785–1865* (Oxford: Clarendon Press, 1988).

Hitchen, John M. 'Relations between Missiology and Anthropology Then and Now – Insights from the Contribution to Ethnography and Anthropology by Nineteenth-Century Missionaries in the South Pacific'. *Missiology: An International Review* 30, 4 (2002), 455–78.

Holland, Tom. *Dominion: The Making of the Western Mind* (London: Little, Brown, 2019).

Hoppen, K. Theodore. *The Mid-Victorian Generation 1846–1886* (Oxford: Oxford University Press, 1998).

Itzhak, Nofit. 'A Sacred Social: Christian Relationalism and the Re-enchantment of the World'. *Journal of the Royal Anthropological Institute* 27, 2 (2021), 265–84.

Jack, Alison. 'The Death of the Master: The Gospel of John and R. L. Stevenson's *The Master of Ballantrae*'. *Scottish Journal of Theology* 59, 3 (2006), 297–306.

Jenkins, Philip. *The Next Christendom: The Coming of Global Christianity* (3rd edn, Oxford: Oxford University Press, 2011).

Johnstone, J. Charteris. 'The Story of the Western College'. *Transactions of the Congregational History Society* 7, 2 (1916–18), 98–109.

Jolly, Roslyn. 'Essays on R.L.S.' *English Literature in Transition* 50, 4 (2007), 454–7.

— *Robert Louis Stevenson in the Pacific: Travel, Empire, and the Author's Profession* (Farnham: Ashgate, 2009).

Kama, Bal. 'Christianising Samoa's Constitution and Religious Freedom in the Pacific'. Devpolicy Blog (2017). Accessed at: https://devpolicy.org/

christianising-samoas-constitution-religious-freedom-pacific-20170427 on 10 December 2020.

Keane, Webb. 'Sincerity, "Modernity", and the Protestants'. *Cultural Anthropology* 17, 1 (2002), 65–92.

Kearney, Richard. 'Sacramental Imagination: Eucharists of the Ordinary Universe in the Works of Joyce, Proust, and Woolf'. In *Through a Glass Darkly: Suffering, the Sacred, and the Sublime in Literature and Theory*, edited by Holly Faith Nelson, Jens Zimmerman, and Lynn Szabo (Waterloo, ON: Wilfrid Laurier University Press, 2010), 183–222.

Kelman, John. *The Faith of Robert Louis Stevenson* (Edinburgh: Oliphant, Anderson and Ferrier, 1903).

Kennedy, Paul M. *The Samoan Tangle: A Study in Anglo-German–American Relations, 1878–1900* (St Lucia: University of Queensland Press, 1974).

Keown, Michelle. *Pacific Islands Writing: The Postcolonial Literatures of Aotearoa/New Zealand and Oceania* (Oxford: Oxford University Press, 2007).

Ker, Ian. *G. K. Chesterton: A Biography* (Oxford: Oxford University Press, 2011).

Knight, Alanna. *The Robert Louis Stevenson Treasury* (London: Shepheard-Walwyn, 1985).

Knight, Mark, and Emma Mason. *Nineteenth-Century Religion and Literature: An Introduction* (Oxford: Oxford University Press, 2006).

Lange, Raeburn. *Island Ministers: Indigenous Leadership in Nineteenth Century Pacific Islands Christianity* (Christchurch: Macmillan Brown Centre for Pacific Studies, University of Canterbury, and Canberra: Pandanus Books, Research School of Pacific and Asian Studies, the Australian National University, 2005).

Largeaud-Ortega, Sylvie. 'A Scotsman's Pacific: Shifting Identities in R. L. Stevenson's Postcolonial Fiction'. *International Journal of Scottish Literature* 9 (2013), 85–98.

— 'Stevenson's "little tale" is "a library": An Anthropological Approach to "The Beach of Falesá"'. *Journal of Stevenson Studies* 6 (2009), 117–34.

Larsen, Timothy. *Crisis of Doubt: Honest Faith in Nineteenth-Century England* (Oxford: Oxford University Press, 2006).

— *John Stuart Mill: A Secular Life* (Oxford: Oxford University Press, 2018).

— *The Slain God: Anthropologists and the Christian Faith* (Oxford: Oxford University Press, 2014).

Latai, Latu. 'Covenant Keepers: A History of Samoan (LMS) Missionary Wives in the Western Pacific from 1839 to 1979' (PhD thesis, Australian National University, 2016).

Lemons, Derrick J. 'An Introduction to Theologically Engaged Anthropology'. *Ethnos* 86, 3 (2021), 401–7.

Lewis, Samuel. *A Topographical Dictionary of Scotland* (London: S. Lewis & Co., 1846).

Lim, Jeremy. 'Calvinism and Forms of Storytelling: Mackellar's Parental Voice in *The Master of Ballantrae*'. *Journal of Stevenson Studies* 7 (2010), 83–105.

Lindenfeld, David. *World Christianity and Indigenous Experience: A Global History, 1500–2000* (Cambridge: Cambridge University Press, 2021).

Liua'ana, Featuna'i Ben. 'Samoa Tula'i: Ecclesiastical and Political Face of Samoa's Independence, 1900–1962' (PhD thesis, Australian National University, 2001).

Lovett, Richard. *The History of the London Missionary Society 1795–1895, Volume 1* (of 2) (London: Henry Frowde, 1899).

— 'R. L. Stevenson in Relation to Christian Life and Christian Missions'. *The Sunday at Home* (1901–2), 229–32.

Lyall, Scott. '"Tenshillingland": Community and Commerce, Myth and Madness in the Modern Scottish Novel'. In *Community in Modern Scottish Literature*, edited by Scott Lyall (Leiden and Boston: Brill, 2016), 1–24.

MacColl, Allan W. *Land, Faith and the Crofting Community: Christianity and Social Criticism in the Highlands of Scotland, 1843–1893* (Edinburgh: Edinburgh University Press, 2006).

Macdonald, Catriona M. M. 'Imagining the Scottish Diaspora: Emigration and Transnational Literature in the Late Modern Period'. *Britain and the World* 5, 1 (2012), 12–42.

Macdonald, Fraser, and Christiane Falck. 'Positioning Culture within Pacific Christianities'. *The Australian Journal of Anthropology* 31, 2 (2020), 123–38.

McFarland, Ian, David A. S. Fergusson, Karen Kilby, and Iain R. Torrance, eds. *The Cambridge Dictionary of Christian Theology* (Cambridge: Cambridge University Press, 2011).

MacIntyre, Alasdair. *After Virtue: A Study in Moral Theory* (Notre Dame, IN: University of Notre Dame Press, 2007).

McIntyre, W. David. *Winding Up the British Empire in the Pacific Islands* (Oxford: Oxford University Press, 2014).

MacKenzie, John M. 'Presbyterianism and Scottish Identity in Global Context'. *Britain and the World* 10, 1 (2017), 88–112.

MacKenzie, John M., and T. M. Devine, eds. *Scotland and the British Empire* (Oxford: Oxford University Press, 2011).

Mackenzie, Kenneth Starr. 'The Last Opportunity: Robert Louis Stevenson and Samoa, 1889–1894'. In *More Pacific Islands Portraits*, edited by Deryck Scarr (Canberra: Australian National University Press, 1978), 155–72.

— 'Robert Louis Stevenson and Samoa 1889–1894' (PhD thesis, Dalhousie University, 1974).

McLeod, Hugh. 'Protestantism and British National Identity, 1815–1945'. In *Nation and Religion: Perspectives on Europe and Asia*, edited by Peter Van der Veer and Hartmut Lehmann (Princeton, NJ: Princeton University Press, 1999), 44–70.

— *Secularisation in Western Europe, 1848–1914* (Basingstoke: Macmillan, 2000).
Manfredi, Carla. *Robert Louis Stevenson's Pacific Impressions: Photography and Travel Writing, 1888–1894* (Cham: Palgrave Macmillan, 2018).
Mehew, Ernest. 'God and the Novelists: 12. Robert Louis Stevenson'. *Expository Times* 110, 10 (1999), 312–16.
— 'Robert Louis Stevenson'. In *Oxford Dictionary of National Biography* (Oxford: Oxford University Press, 2004). Accessed at: https://doi.org/10.1093/ref:odnb/26438 on 5 August 2021.
Meleisea, Malama. 'Introduction'. In Robert Louis Stevenson, *A Footnote to History: Eight Years of Trouble in Samoa* (Honolulu: University of Hawai'i Press, 1996), vii–xvi.
Meleisea, Malama, and Penelope Schoeffel Meleisea. *Lagaga: A Short History of Western Samoa* (Suva: University of the South Pacific, 1987).
Menikoff, Barry. *Narrating Scotland: The Imagination of Robert Louis Stevenson* (Columbia: University of South Carolina Press, 2005).
— *Robert Louis Stevenson and 'The Beach of Falesá': A Study in Victorian Publishing with the Original Text* (Stanford, CA: Stanford University Press, 1984).
Mills, Kevin. 'The Stain on the Mirror: Pauline Reflections in *The Strange Case of Dr. Jekyll and Mr. Hyde*'. *Christianity and Literature* 53, 3 (2004), 337–48.
Moore, Diane L. 'Overcoming Religious Illiteracy: A Cultural Studies Approach'. *World History Connected* 4, 1 (2006).
Morton, Graeme, and David A. Wilson, eds. *Irish and Scottish Encounters with Indigenous Peoples: Canada, the United States, New Zealand, and Australia* (Montreal: McGill-Queen's University Press, 2013).
Moyle, Richard M., ed. *The Samoan Journals of John Williams 1830 and 1832* (Canberra: Australian National University Press, 1984).
Muaiava, Sadat. 'The Samoan Parsonage Family: The Concepts of Feagaiga and Tagata'ese'. *Journal of New Zealand & Pacific Studies* 3, 1 (2015), 73–83.
Munro, Doug, and Andrew Thornley, eds. *The Covenant Makers: Islander Missionaries in the Pacific* (Suva: Pacific Theological College and the Institute of Pacific Studies at the University of the South Pacific, 1996).
Munro, Doug, and Andrew Thornley. 'Pacific Islander Pastors and Missionaries: Some Historiographical and Analytical Issues'. *Pacific Studies* 23, 3–4 (2000), 1–31.
Murfin, Audrey. *Robert Louis Stevenson and the Art of Collaboration* (Edinburgh: Edinburgh University Press, 2019).
Newbury, Colin. *Tahiti Nui: Change and Survival in French Polynesia, 1767–1945* (Honolulu: University of Hawai'i Press, 1980).
Newell, J. E. 'R. L. Stevenson as I Knew Him'. *Christchurch Press*, 2 March 1907. National Library of Australia, nla.obj-2739135234.

Newman, John Henry Cardinal. *Certain Difficulties Felt by Anglicans in Catholic Teaching Considered, Vol. II* (London: Longmans, Green, and Co., 1900 [1874]).

Nimmo, Paul T., and David A. S. Fergusson, eds. *Cambridge Companion to Reformed Theology* (Cambridge: Cambridge University Press, 2016).

Nolet, Émilie. 'Coconuts and Rosaries: Materiality in the Catholic Christianisation of the Tuamotu Archipelago (French Polynesia)'. *The Journal of the Polynesian Society* 129, 3 (2020), 275–302.

Noll, Mark A. *The Scandal of the Evangelical Mind* (Grand Rapids, MI, and Cambridge: William B. Eerdmans, 1994).

Norquay, Glenda. *Robert Louis Stevenson and Theories of Reading: The Reader as Vagabond* (Manchester: Manchester University Press, 2007).

— *Robert Louis Stevenson, Literary Networks and Transatlantic Publishing in the 1890s: The Author Incorporated* (London: Anthem Press, 2020).

O'Loughlin, Thomas. 'Inculturation: The Eucharistic Dimension'. *Japan Mission Journal* 74, 3 (2020), 146–53.

Orel, Harold. 'The Letters of Robert Louis Stevenson: A Review Essay'. *English Literature in Transition* 40, 1 (1997), 60–8.

Palu, Ma'afu 'o Tu'itonga. 'Pacific Theology: A Reconsideration of its Methodology'. *The Pacific Journal of Theology*, Series 2, 29 (2003), 30–58.

Parr, Patrick. 'Robert Louis Stevenson Says No to Religion'. *The Humanist* (September/October 2015), 20–2.

Phan, Peter C. 'World Christianity: Its Implications for History, Religious Studies, and Theology'. *Horizons* 39, 2 (2012), 171–88.

Polatti, Alessia. 'The "Myth of Tusitala" in Samoa: R. L. Stevenson's Presence in Albert Wendt's Fiction'. *Loxias* 48 (2016). Accessed at: http://revel.unice.fr/loxias/index.html?id=8233 on 2 November 2021.

Pratt, George. *A Grammar and Dictionary of the Samoan Language* (The Religious Tract Society, 1893).

Prendergast, Patricia A. 'Chalmers, James (1841–1901)'. In *Australian Dictionary of Biography*, National Centre of Biography, Australian National University. Accessed at: https://adb.anu.edu.au/biography/chalmers-james-3187/text4781 on 5 August 2021.

Prothero, Stephen, *Religious Literacy: What Every American Needs to Know – and Doesn't* (New York: HarperOne, 2007).

Ratnapalan, Laavanyan. 'E. B. Tylor and the Problem of Primitive Culture'. *History and Anthropology* 19, 2 (2008), 131–42.

— 'Robert Louis Stevenson's South Seas Writing: Its Production and Context within the Victorian Study of Culture' (PhD thesis, University of London, 2007).

— 'Stevenson and Cultural Survivals in the South Seas'. *Journal of Stevenson Studies* 3 (2006), 69–85.

Ratnapalan, Laavanyan M. 'Sereno Bishop, Robert Louis Stevenson and "Americanism" in Hawai'i'. *The Journal of Imperial and Commonwealth History* 40, 3 (2012), 439–57.

Ratnapalan, L. M. '"This Greater Issue of Light against Darkness": Sereno Edwards Bishop, Missionary Religion, and the Hawaiian Islands, 1827–1909'. *Journal of Religious History* 43, 1 (2019), 3–24.

— 'Missionary Christianity and Culture in Robert Louis Stevenson's "The Beach of Falesá"'. *Religion & Literature* 53, 3 (2021), 47–62.

— '"Our Father's Footprints": Robert Louis Stevenson's Anthropology of Conversion, 1888–1894'. *Journal of Irish and Scottish Studies* (forthcoming).

Ratzinger, Joseph Cardinal. 'Christ, Faith and the Challenge of Cultures'. Meeting with the Doctrinal Commissions in Asia (1993). Accessed at: https://www.vatican.va/roman_curia/congregations/cfaith/incontri/rc_con_cfaith_19930303_hong-kong-ratzinger_en.html on 23 July 2021.

— *Many Religions, One Covenant: Israel, the Church, and the World* (San Francisco: Ignatius Press, 1999).

— (as Pope Benedict XVI), 'Faith, Reason and the University: Memories and Reflections'. University of Regensburg (12 September 2006). Accessed at: https://www.vatican.va/content/benedict-xvi/en/speeches/2006/september/documents/hf_ben-xvi_spe_20060912_university-regensburg.html on 14 May 2021.

Reid, Julia. *Robert Louis Stevenson, Science, and the Fin de Siècle* (Basingstoke: Palgrave Macmillan, 2006).

Robbins, Joel. 'Anthropology and Theology: An Awkward Relationship?' *Anthropological Quarterly* 79, 2 (2006), 285–94.

— 'The Anthropology of Christianity: Unity, Diversity, New Directions'. *Current Anthropology* 55, Supplement 10 (2014), S157–71.

— 'Continuity Thinking and the Problem of Christian Culture: Belief, Time, and the Anthropology of Christianity'. *Current Anthropology* 48, 1 (2007), 5–38.

— *Theology and the Anthropology of Christian Life* (Oxford: Oxford University Press, 2020).

— 'Transcendence and the Anthropology of Christianity: Language, Change, and Individualism'. *Suomen Antropologi: Journal of the Finnish Anthropological Society* 37, 2 (2012), 5–23.

Robert, Dana L. 'Locating *Relocating World Christianity*: Interdisciplinary Studies in Universal and Local Expressions of the Christian Faith'. *International Bulletin of Missionary Research* 43, 2 (2019), 126–33.

Robertson Smith, William. *Lectures and Essays of William Robertson Smith* (London: A. & C. Black, 1912).

Robson, Andrew E. 'Malietoa, Williams and Samoa's Embrace of Christianity'. *Journal of Pacific History* 44, 1 (2009), 21–39.

Ross, Kenneth R., Katalina Tahaafe-Williams, and Todd M. Johnson, eds. *Christianity in Oceania* (Edinburgh: Edinburgh University Press, 2021).

Rowland, Tracey. 'Oceania'. In *The Blackwell Companion to Catholicism*, edited by James J. Buckley, Frederick Christian Bauerschmidt, and Trent Pomplun (Malden, MA: Blackwell, 2008), 221–34.

Roy, G. Ross. 'The Bible in Burns and Scott'. In *The Bible in Scottish Life and Literature*, edited by David F. Wright, Ian Campbell, and John Gibson (Edinburgh: The Saint Andrew Press, 1988), 79–93.

Roxborogh, John. 'The Legacy of Thomas Chalmers'. *International Bulletin of Missionary Research* (October 1999), 173–6.

Ryrie, Alec. *Protestants: The Faith that Made the Modern World* (New York: Penguin Books, 2017).

Saada, Angelica. 'Samoa: A Truly Religious Place? Views toward Religion in Samoa' (SIT Samoa, 2008).

Sacks, Benjamin. *Cricket, Kirikiti and Imperialism in Samoa, 1879–1939* (Cham: Palgrave Macmillan, 2019).

Samoa: Population and Housing Census Report 2006 (Apia: Samoa Bureau of Statistics, 2008).

Sanneh, Lamin. *Encountering the West: Christianity and the Global Cultural Process: The African Dimension* (New York: Orbis, 1993).

— *Whose Religion is Christianity? The Gospel Beyond the West* (Grand Rapids, MI: William B. Eerdmans, 2003).

Sassi, Carla. 'Glocalising Scottish Literature: A Call for New Strategies of Reading'. *The Bottle Imp – Supplement 1* (March 2014), 1–4.

Schaefer, Richard. 'Intellectual History and the Return of Religion'. *Historically Speaking* 12, 2 (2011), 30–1.

Schreiter, Robert J. *Constructing Local Theologies* (New York: Orbis, 1985).

Scott, Patrick. 'Introduction: The Ghost at the Feast: Religion in Scottish Literary Criticism'. *Studies in Scottish Literature* 45, 2 (2019), 3–6.

Seiple, Chris, and Dennis R. Hoover. 'A Case for Cross-Cultural Religious Literacy'. *The Review of Faith and International Affairs* 19, 1 (2021), 1–13.

Shankman, Paul. 'Interethnic Unions and the Regulation of Sex in Colonial Samoa, 1830–1945'. *Journal of the Polynesian Society* 110, 2 (2001), 119–47.

Shaw, Michael. *The Fin-de-Siècle Scottish Revival: Romance, Decadence and Celtic Identity* (Edinburgh: Edinburgh University Press, 2020).

— 'Transculturation and Historicisation: New Directions for the Study of Scottish Literature c. 1840–1914'. *Literature Compass* 13, 8 (2016), 501–10.

Shorter, Aylward. *Toward a Theology of Inculturation* (Eugene, OR: Wipf and Stock, 2006 [1988]).

Sibree, James. *A Register of Missionaries, Deputations, etc. from 1796 to 1923* (London: London Missionary Society, 1923).

Sier, Maureen, and Ruta Fiti-Sinclair. 'Nineteenth-Century Scottish Missionary Women and Sāmoan Morality'. *Measina a Samoa* 3 (2005), 159–66.

Smith, Gary Scott, and P. C. Kemeny. 'Introduction'. In *The Oxford Handbook of Presbyterianism*, edited by Gary Scott Smith and P. C. Kemeny (Oxford: Oxford University Press, 2019), 1–6.

Spinks, Bryan D. *Scottish Presbyterian Worship: Proposals for Organic Change, 1843 to the Present Day* (Edinburgh: The Saint Andrew Press, 2020).

Spurlock, R. Scott. 'Scottish Presbyterianism'. *Victorian Review* 46, 2 (2020), 162–6.

Stafford, Tim. 'Andrew Walls: Historian Ahead of His Time'. *Christianity Today*, 13 August 2021.

Stanley, Brian. *Christianity in the Twentieth Century: A World History* (Princeton, NJ: Princeton University Press, 2018).

— 'Editorial: Appropriations of Christianity'. *Studies in World Christianity* 23, 1 (2017), 1–3.

Steinfels, Peter. 'Modernity and Belief: Charles Taylor's *A Secular Age*'. *Commonweal*, 5 May 2008.

Stevenson, Margaret Isabella. *From Saranac to the Marquesas and Beyond; Being Letters written by Mrs. M. I. Stevenson during 1887–88, to her Sister, Jane Whyte Balfour, with a Short Introduction by George W. Balfour, M. D., LL. D., FRSE* (London: Methuen, 1903).

— *Letters from Samoa 1891–1895*. Edited by Marie Clothilde Balfour (London: Methuen, 1906).

— *Stevenson's Baby Book; Being the Record of the Sayings and Doings of Robert Louis Balfour Stevenson, Son of Thomas Stevenson, C.E. and Margaret Isabella Balfour or Stevenson* (San Francisco: J. H. Nash, 1922).

Stevenson, Thomas. *Christianity Confirmed by Jewish and Heathen Testimony and the Deductions from Physical Science, etc.* (Edinburgh: David Douglas, 1879).

Sugirtharajah, R. S. *The Bible and Empire: Postcolonial Explorations* (Cambridge: Cambridge University Press, 2005).

Swain, Tony, and G. W. Trompf. *The Religions of Oceania* (London: Routledge, 1995).

Swearingen, Roger. 'Ernest Mehew in Memoriam'. Accessed at: http://rogers99.users.sonic.net/ernest_mehew_in_memoriam.pdf on 1 May 2020.

— 'New Light on the South Seas'. *EDRLS* Blog. Accessed at: https://edrls.wordpress.com/2014/04/04/new-light-on-the-south-seas/ on 17 September 2021.

Taylor, Charles. *A Secular Age* (Cambridge, MA: Belknap Press, 2007).

Thomas, Nicholas. 'Further Notes on Marquesan Dictionaries'. *Journal of the Polynesian Society* 95, 1 (1986), 127–30.

Thomson, Alex. 'Stevenson's Afterlives'. In *The Edinburgh Companion to Robert Louis Stevenson*, edited by Penny Fielding (Edinburgh: Edinburgh University Press, 2010), 147–59.

Tiffany, Sharon W. 'The Politics of Denominational Organization in Samoa'. In *Mission, Church, and Sect in Oceania*, edited by James A. Boutilier, Daniel T. Hughes, and Sharon W. Tiffany (Ann Arbor: University of Michigan Press, 1978), 423–56.

Tomlinson, Matt. *God is Samoan: Dialogues between Culture and Theology in the Pacific* (Honolulu: University of Hawai'i Press, 2020).
Tonks, Paul. 'Shaping Scotland's Identity: The Historical Impact of Covenanting Presbyterianism'. *Korean Journal of British Studies* 18, 12 (2007), 321–40.
Treagus, Mandy. 'Crossing "the beach": Samoa, Stevenson, and "The Beach at Falesá"'. *Literature Compass* 11, 5 (2014), 312–20.
Tulloch, Graham. '*A Footnote to History*: Stevenson, the Past and the Samoan Present'. In *Robert Louis Stevenson and the Great Affair: Movement, Memory, and Modernity*, edited by Richard J. Hill (London: Routledge, 2017), 148–61.
Turner, Frank. *Contesting Cultural Authority: Essays in Victorian Intellectual Life* (Cambridge: Cambridge University Press, 1993).
Ustorf, Werner. 'Global Christianity, New Empire, and Old Europe'. In *Global Christianity: Contested Claims*, edited by Frans Wijsen and Robert Schreiter (Amsterdam and New York: Rodopi, 2007), 35–49.
— 'A Missiological Postscript'. In *The Decline of Christendom in Western Europe, 1750–2000*, edited by Werner Ustorf and Hugh McLeod (Cambridge: Cambridge University Press, 2003), 218–25.
van den Brink, Gijsbert, and Harro Höpfl, eds. *Calvinism and the Making of the European Mind* (Leiden: Brill, 2014).
van der Wall, Ernestine. 'Between Faith and Doubt: The Role of Fiction'. *T. F. Blad van de Theologische Faculteit Universiteit, Leiden* 35 (December 2005), 56–75.
von Harnack, Adolf. *What is Christianity? Lectures Delivered in the University of Berlin during the Winter Term 1899–1900*, translated by Thomas Bailey Saunders (New York: G. P. Putnam's Sons, 1901).
Wallace, Valerie, and Colin Kidd. 'Between Nationhood and Nonconformity: The Scottish Whig-Presbyterian Novel and the Denominational Press'. In *Literature and Union: Scottish Texts, British Contexts*, edited by Gerard Carruthers and Colin Kidd (Oxford: Oxford University Press, 2018), 193–220.
Walls, Andrew F. *The Missionary Movement in Christian History: Studies in the Transmission of Faith* (New York: Orbis, 1996).
— 'Three Hundred Years of Scottish Missions'. In *Roots and Fruits: Retrieving Scotland's Missionary Story*, edited by Kenneth R. Ross (Padstow: Regnum, 2014), 4–37.
Wandel, Lee Palmer. *The Eucharist in the Reformation: Incarnation and Liturgy* (Cambridge: Cambridge University Press, 2006).
Ward, Mrs Humphry [Mary Augusta]. *Robert Elsmere* (London: Macmillan and Co., 1888).
Weis, Earl August. 'Stevenson and the Catholic Church; A Background for the Damien Letter' (MA thesis, Loyola University of Chicago, 1948).
Wendt, Albert. '"Guardians and Wards": A Study of the Origins, Causes, and the First Two Years of the Mau in Western Samoa' (MA thesis, Victoria

University Wellington, 1965). Accessed at: https://nzetc.victoria.ac.nz/tm/scholarly/tei-WenGua.html on 10 December 2021.
— *Leaves of the Banyan Tree* (London: Penguin, 1980).
Wild-Wood, Emma. 'The Interpretations, Problems and Possibilities of Missionary Sources in the History of Christianity in Africa'. In *World Christianity: Methodological Considerations*, edited by Martha Frederiks and Dorottya Nagy (Leiden and Boston: Brill, 2021), 92–112.
Wilson, Rob. *Be Always Converting, Be Always Converted: An American Poetics* (Cambridge, MA: Harvard University Press, 2009).
Wolfart, Johannes C. '"Religious Literacy": Some Considerations and Reservations'. *Method and Theory in the Study of Religion* (2022), 1–28.
Wormald, Jenny. *Court, Kirk, and Community: Scotland 1470–1625* (Edinburgh: Edinburgh University Press, 1991).
Zinkina, Julia, David Christian, Leonid Grinin, Ilya Ilyin, Alexey Andreev, Ivan Aleshkovski, Sergey Shulgin, and Andrey Korotayev. *A Big History of Globalization: The Emergence of a Global World System* (Cham: Springer, 2019).

Index

anthropology of Christianity, 11, 45–72
　continuity and rupture, 64
　denominational consciousness, 11, 53, 54–60, 66, 68
　transcendence, 11, 53, 61–6, 68, 157
Apemama *see* Kiribati, Abemama
Australia, 45

Balfour, Graham, 88
Balfour, Lewis, 137
Baxter, Charles, 37, 45
Bible, 7, 16, 20, 21, 25n, 32, 30, 33, 36, 37, 39, 40, 41, 43, 56, 69, 78n, 81, 84, 87, 96, 97, 107, 111, 115, 116, 118, 119, 120, 122, 126, 127, 129, 137, 145, 147, 150, 151, 154, 156, 157
Bishop, Sereno Edwards, 52
Blanc, Michel, 55
Boodle, Adelaide, 24, 25, 43, 132, 139
Brague, Rémi, 47
British Empire, 31n, 47, 65n, 73, 154, 160, 162–3
Burns, Robert, 20n, 34, 34n, 56

Calvin, John, 84, 115
Calvinism *see* Presbyterianism, Reformed Christianity
Cameronians, 55–6
Cannell, Fenella, 49–50, 54, 61, 71n
Cannibalism, 51, 58, 67

Chalmers, James 147–8
Chalmers, Thomas, 135, 144, 146–7, 154
Chesterton, Gilbert Keith, 26–8
Church of Scotland, 5, 8, 12–13, 15n, 30–2, 33, 38, 39, 84, 85, 134–7, 139–45, 146, 147, 154–5, 156; *see also* ecclesiology
Clarke, William, 88, 89, 90, 91, 92, 93, 94
Claxton, Arthur, 90
Codrington, Robert Henry, 52
Colvin, Sidney, 27, 40, 67, 94, 101, 107
community *see* religious community
Congregational Christian Church of Samoa (CCC), 80
contextualisation *see* inculturation
Cook Islands
　Penrhyn, 45, 56, 149
　Mangaia, 67
covenant, 83–7, 99
Covenanters, 33, 84–6, 97, 99, 100, 125, 132
Cunningham, Alison, 30, 33–4

Darwin, Charles, 46
Davie, Grace, 9–10, 25, 39n, 133
Delmas, Father Siméon, 51
de Lubac, Henri, 102n
de Veuster, Father Damien ('Damien of Molokai'), 54

Disruption of 1843, 5, 8, 28, 31, 135–6, 144, 158; *see also* Church of Scotland
Donat-Rimarau, François, 53
Dordillon, René Ildefonse, 52, 55, 106
Doré, Gustave, 145

ecclesiology, 8, 13, 30n, 43, 70, 87n, 126, 131–55, 158
Evangelicalism, 32, 33, 38, 40, 54, 135

fa'asāmoa, 79
feagaiga, 86–7
Father Damien *see* Damien de Veuster
Frazer, James, 163
Fréchou, Father Orens, 51, 55
Free Church (Scottish), 8, 15n, 31, 37n, 65, 136, 139n, 140, 142–4, 147
Furnas, J. C., 131

Gilbert Islands *see* Kiribati
Gordon, Charles, 160

Hau'ofa, Epeli, 161–2
Hawai'i, 45, 52, 58, 70, 81, 117, 149, 153–4, 161
Hegel, George Wilhelm Friedrich, 35n, 37
Hogg, James, 16
Hume, David, 33, 34
Hyde, Charles McEwan

inculturation, 2, 8, 12, 30, 70, 93–4, 104–30, 150, 152, 155, 158, 161
Iosefo, Mata'afa, 74–5, 94, 95n

Jacobites, 21, 41–2, 125
Jenkins, Philip, 6, 12n
Job, Book of, 37, 39

Ka'ahumanu, 56
kailyard, 77
Kalakaua, David, 53, 81
kava, 67, 69, 71
Kelman, John, 131
Kipling, Rudyard, 160
Kiribati, 45
   Abemama, 58, 65
   Abaiang, 64, 100
   Butaritari 56, 107, 150
Kirk *see* Church of Scotland
Knox, John, 20, 34n, 84, 99, 125

Laupepa, Susuga Mālietoa, 74–5
Lees, James Cameron, 139, 140, 145
Leighton, Robert, 142
leprosy, 62, 117
Livingstone, David, 160
London Missionary Society (LMS), 52, 63, 75n, 80, 82, 86, 88–92, 104–5, 121, 136n, 152–3
Lovett, Richard, 104, 105, 130

MacDonald, George, 41
MacIntyre, Alasdair, 92n
Mahinui, Taniera, 150, 151
Malo, David, 56
Malua (Samoan school and seminary), 81, 89
mana, 83
Marists, 82
Marquesas Islands, 45, 51–2, 55, 58, 67, 81, 106, 149–50
Marshall Islands, 45
Mary I, Queen, 56
Mehew, Ernest, 24–5, 27, 43, 132
Methodist Church, 80n, 82
mission, 31, 33, 68, 135, 141, 146–55, 158

missionaries, 48, 50–2, 55, 67–71, 80–2, 86–7, 88–94, 104–6, 108–9, 111, 116, 116n, 120, 125, 129, 146, 152, 154, 157, 158, 160, 162
  Pacific Islander, 51, 81, 82, 121, 152
Moanatini, Stanislao, 53
Mormon Church, 80n, 82
Mormons, 63, 59n
Moore, Diane L., 19–21

Nahinu, D. H., 53
New Caledonia, 45
New Hebrides *see* Vanuatu
Newell, James, 89, 94
Newman, John Henry, 41n
New Zealand, 45

Osbourne, Lloyd, 93, 127n

Paumotus *see* Tuamotus
Penrhyn *see* Cook Islands
Poepoe, Joseph, 53
Pratt, George, 86
Presbyterianism, 2, 7, 8, 9, 13, 15, 16, 17, 18–19, 21, 24, 25, 27, 28, 30–3, 38, 48, 50, 54, 55, 56, 60, 81n, 90n, 110, 111, 130, 135, 136, 139, 140n, 142, 145, 147, 155, 156, 157, 158, 162, 164; *see also* Reformed Christianity

Ratzinger, Joseph, 84n, 111n, 112n
Reformation, 47–8, 54, 69, 77–8, 83, 84, 120, 124
Reformed Christianity, 2, 8, 18–19, 21n, 22, 26n, 39, 40, 84, 99, 101, 115, 119, 131, 157, 160, 164; *see also* Presbyterianism
religion in Victorian society, 22–4

religious community, 34, 39, 41–2, 43, 76–9, 83–7, 91, 92, 94–103, 153–4, 158
religious literacy, 7–8, 9, 10, 11, 14–44, 53, 55, 56, 66, 120, 156, 157
Robbins, Joel, 4, 60, 61
Robertson Smith, William, 37n, 78n, 163
Roman Catholicism, 9, 14, 15, 21, 32, 54, 56–9, 69–70, 75, 78n, 80, 82, 94, 106–7, 114n, 115, 118, 120, 145, 148–9, 150, 151
Roman Empire, 47–8, 55

sabbath, 92, 98, 99, 117
sacrament/sacramentality, 32, 58, 67, 70, 71, 116, 117, 118, 130, 136, 157, 158
Samoa, 11–12, 45, 73–95, 100, 103, 104–6, 107, 114, 117, 121, 125n, 132, 134, 147, 148, 152–4, 157, 158, 161
  religious demography, 79, 80, 80n
St Matthew, Gospel of, 36–7, 39, 97, 145
Scott, Sir Walter, 16, 20n, 34, 34n
Scottish Presbyterianism *see* Presbyterianism
Scripture *see* Bible
secularisation, 5, 9, 17, 23, 25, 29, 43, 44, 155, 159
Shorter Catechism, 30
Smith, Adam, 34
Society Islands, 80–1
Spencer, Herbert, 35–6, 46
Stephen, Leslie, 40
Stevenson, Frances Van de Grift, 40
Stevenson, Margaret Isabella Balfour, 33, 88, 89, 91, 117–18, 137, 150

Stevenson, Robert Louis, works
- *An Appeal to the Clergy of the Church of Scotland*, 142
- 'Beach of Falesá', 5, 12, 21, 90, 103, 114–18, 120–3, 125, 126, 151
- 'Body Snatcher', 39, 95
- 'Books which have influenced me', 35–7
- 'Bottle Imp', 90, 114–18, 125–6, 128, 160
- *Catriona (David Balfour)*, 76, 95–9
- *Child's Garden of Verses*, 33
- *Ebb-Tide*, 76, 114, 118, 123–4, 125, 126, 160
- 'Edinburgh: Picturesque Notes', 31, 60n, 136
- 'Father Damien', 54
- *Footnote to History*, 74–5, 76, 114, 114n
- *Heathercat*, 76, 78, 95, 96, 99–101
- *In the South Seas*, 45–72, 106, 149
- 'Isle of Voices', 65n, 114, 118–19, 125, 128
- 'John Knox and His Relations to Women', 20
- *Kidnapped*, 14–15, 21, 42, 96, 110
- 'Lay Morals', 41
- 'Markheim', 138
- *Master of Ballantrae*, 20
- *Misadventures of John Nicholson*, 31–2, 39
- 'Pearl Island', 56n
- 'Pentland Rising', 20
- 'Pulvis et Umbra', 40
- *St. Ives*, 76, 98–9
- 'San Carlos Day', 148–9
- 'Something in It', 11, 54, 66–72, 116, 151–2, 157
- *Strange Case of Dr. Jekyll and Mr. Hyde*, 21, 101, 138
- 'Sunday Thoughts', 137–8
- 'Thrawn Janet', 95
- 'To S. R. Crockett', 85
- *Travels with a Donkey in the Cévennes*
- *Treasure Island*, 20
- *Weir of Hermiston*, 76, 95, 96, 99, 101–3
- *Wrecker*, 76
- *Young Chevalier*, 76, 99

Stevenson, Thomas, 33, 37, 41, 123
Strong, Isobel, 86n, 93

Tahiti, 45, 58, 59, 63, 80, 117, 118, 150
Taylor, Charles, 9, 19n, 29, 40n, 42, 92
buffered self, 29, 40, 41, 42, 92, 95, 103, 123
Tebureimoa, 56
Tembinok' (Tem Binoka), 58
Tonga, 82, 161
Tuamotus, 45, 46n, 55–6, 63, 64, 65, 66, 150, 153
Tulloch, John, 139–42
Turner, George, 52
Tylor, Edward Burnett, 57

Vailima, 76, 88, 91, 163
Vainu'upo, Malietoa, 81–2, 105, 106
Vanuatu, 81
von Harnack, Adolf, 133–4

Wallis Island, 82, 94
Walls, Andrew, 6–7
Ward, Mrs Humphrey (Mary Augusta), *Robert Elsmere*, 42, 138–9
Westminster Confession, 30–1, 139
Whitman, Walt, 36, 36n
Whitmee, Samuel James, 82n, 88
Williams, John, 81–2, 105, 106
World Christianity, 6, 10, 111

EU representative:
Easy Access System Europe
Mustamäe tee 50, 10621 Tallinn, Estonia
Gpsr.requests@easproject.com

www.ingramcontent.com/pod-product-compliance
Lightning Source LLC
Chambersburg PA
CBHW070358240426
43671CB00013BA/2549